FICTION EDITING TOOLS

Fiction Editing Tools

Two Bestselling Guidebooks on Deeper POV Combined Into One Amazing Volume

S. A. Soule

FWT

No part of this publication may be reproduced, stored in a retrieval system, or transmitted, in any form or by any means, without the prior permission in writing of the publisher, nor be otherwise circulated in any form of binding or cover other than that in which it is published and without a similar condition including this condition being imposed on the subsequent purchaser.

FBI Anti-Piracy Warning: The unauthorized reproduction or distribution of a copyrighted work is illegal. Criminal copyright infringement, including infringement without monetary gain, is investigated by the FBI and is punishable by up to five years in federal prison and a fine of $250,000.

All rights reserved. Your support of the author's rights is appreciated.

FICTION EDITING TOOLS
The Writer's Guide to Character Emotion (Book 1)
The Writer's Guide to Deep POV (Book 2)
ISBN:978-1530760824
ASIN: B01DIAT5CW

Copyright © 2014 S.A. Soule

Cover art by SwoonWorthy Book Covers

FWT appreciates its readers, and every effort has been made to properly edit this guidebook. However, typos do get overlooked. If you find an error in the text, please send us an email so the issue can be corrected. Thank you!

Typesetting services by BOOKOW.COM

For fiction writers who yearn to take their writing skills to the next level!

Contents

INTRODUCTION	1
DEEP POINT-OF-VIEW	3
SHALLOW WRITING	8
SHOWING	12
TELLING	17
INFO-DUMPS	26
FILTER WORDS	30
DEEPER POV	35
SHOW DON'T TELL	39
SENSORY DETAILS	43
DIALOGUE SCENES	46
ENHANCE CONVERSATIONS	49
DESCRIPTIVE EXCHANGES	57
TALKING HEADS	60
INTERNAL EXPOSITION	64
REALISTIC SETTINGS	68
VIVID DESCRIPTIONS	73
DRAMATIC SCENES	77
CHARACTERIZATION	84
CHARACTER VOICE	90

Contents

FIRST-PERSON POV	97
CHARACTER DESCRIPTIONS	105
FACIAL EXPRESSIONS	114
REDUNDANT PHRASES	118
RHETORICAL QUESTIONS	128
SHALLOW: FELT	133
SHALLOW: SEE	137
SHALLOW: HEARD	143
SHALLOW: LOOKED	148
SHALLOW: SOUND	152
SHALLOW: SMELL	157
SHALLOW: KNEW	161
SHALLOW: THOUGHT	166
SHALLOW: CAUSED	170
SHALLOW: DECIDED	173
SHALLOW: WONDERED	176
SHALLOW: NOTICED	180
SHALLOW: WISHED	184
SHALLOW: REALIZED	188
SHALLOW: CONFUSION	193
SHALLOW: ANTAGONISM	199
SHALLOW: INDIFFERENCE	202
SHALLOW: COLDNESS	206
SHALLOW: FATIGUED	212
SHALLOW: PAIN	217
SHALLOW: WARMTH	222
SHALLOW: THOUGHTFUL	227

SHALLOW: STUBBORN	233
SHALLOW: DOUBT	237
SHALLOW: CURIOSITY	243
SHALLOW: RELAX	248
DESCRIBE THE SENSES	253
DESCRIBE THE EMOTIONS	256
EMOTION: EXCITEMENT	260
EMOTION: FRUSTRATION	265
EMOTION: DISAPPOINTMENT	270
EMOTION: ANGER	274
EMOTION: SADNESS	280
EMOTION: WORRY	285
EMOTION: FEAR	290
EMOTION: UNEASE	296
EMOTION: NERVOUSNESS	301
EMOTION: RELIEF	305
EMOTION: SURPRISE	309
EMOTION: HAPPINESS	314
EMOTION: JEALOUSLY	319
EMOTION: EMBARRASSMENT	325
EMOTION: ANXIETY	330
EMOTION: PANIC	336
EMOTION: DISGUST	341
EMOTION: GUILT	345
EMOTION: RESENTMENT	349
EMOTION: PARANOID	354
CONCLUSION	359

Contents

HUMBLE REQUEST	361
FICTION WRITING TOOLS	362
ABOUT THE AUTHOR	365

INTRODUCTION

Dear Writer,

I've been writing most of my life, and even though I've studied the craft for years, I still love developing my skills as a writer, and I'm assuming since you purchased this book that you do, too.

First I thought I'd share a little about myself…I have over fifteen years of experience on all sides of the publishing business. I was a Creative Writing major in college, and I once owned an eBook publishing company where I edited over a hundred manuscripts. Then I worked as a developmental editor for another publisher, and in the last five years, I've even had the honor of editing books for a number of successful authors.

I've currently written eleven fiction novels and eight nonfiction titles, but it wasn't until 2015 that I became a bestselling author, and the road to success was a long journey. Many of my books have spent time on the 100 Kindle bestseller lists and some of my fiction has been chosen as top picks in the "Best Paranormal Romance" categories at several prominent review sites.

In this guide, I share some of the wisdom that I've gleamed from various workshops and online courses, along with the savvy advice from other bestselling novelists and professional editors with whom I've had the pleasure to work with in the publishing industry.

And this manual provides step-by-step instructions on ways to create realistic emotions, visceral responses, and body language, along with ways to deepen characterization that writers can easily and quickly apply to their own writing.

Even if you believe you've already mastered Deep POV, I challenge you to dig *deeper*. It doesn't matter if you are traditionally published, an Indie author, a self-published writer, or if you enjoy spending your weekends writing fanfiction. These tools can help anyone improve their storytelling abilities. Writers should use these tips as an arsenal of creative knowledge to include in their writer's toolbox.

This manual is not a "grammar do or don't" because honestly, mine is not the best, so please don't contact the literary police. My goal is always for writers to come away with stronger writing and editing abilities that they can utilize in their own stories and give their audience a more personal reading experience.

Happy writing and revising,

S. A. Soule

DEEP POINT-OF-VIEW

Quote: "In case you're unfamiliar, "show, don't tell" is the literary maxim that says stories should reveal through action (dialogue, scene, thoughts, and present conflict) instead of summary or a laundry list of descriptive details.

"Showing" is to reveal details by having your characters exemplify them, instead of the writer simply "telling" us those details outright. Done correctly, it's the difference between making your reader a participant in the story or delegating them a mere observer. Research papers and legal documents *tell*. Fiction *shows*." —*author, Jon Gingerich*

Deep Point-of-View (POV) is one of the best editing techniques that you can use to take your writing to the next level. This chapter will explain how you can revise filter words used in shallower sentences by transforming the narrative in much stronger and vivid ways.

Even if you believe you've already mastered showing vs. telling, I challenge you to absorb this handbook and go *deeper*. It doesn't matter if you are traditionally published, an Indie author, a self-published writer, or you enjoy spending your weekends writing fanfiction, these tools and techniques can help anyone improve their storytelling abilities.

Let's start with what many writers call: *Narrative Distance.*

A writer creates narrative distance (taking the reader out of the story or by reminding them that they're reading a book) when writers insert *filter words* into their writing. A Deeper POV (showing) is a much more direct and intimate way to describe a character's emotions, reactions, and actions. It will bring every scene in your novel instantly alive for your reader. And most importantly, it will keep you from using a weaker form of characterization.

Showing kicks writing up a notch by tightening, solidifying, and strengthening a manuscript. As a stellar side effect, many of those annoying problems with "show don't tell" will fade away like a bad memory.

What is Narrative Distance?

This means that the reader has been distanced, or in some cases, jolted out of the story by author intrusion. The more filter words a writer uses, the more distance they put between the reader and the story, and the less involved the reader will feel about what's happening.

Please study this example, where each sentence is *telling*…

SHALLOW:

Shawn <u>noticed</u> that the sky <u>looked</u> dark, and he <u>felt</u> a chill. He was <u>scared</u> and he wanted to go home. When he <u>saw</u> the shadows moving and <u>heard</u> a strange howling, he <u>started to</u> <u>run very fast</u> on the path.

The first scene is inert. It's too sluggish, right?

Here is a revision, where same information is *shown*…

DEEP POV:

The sky darkened and Shawn rubbed his arms against the sudden chill. His pulsed jumped. *I can't wait to get home!* The shadows shifted and the eerie howl of a wolf cut through the air. He spotted the porch lights glowing on the house and he sprinted along the path.

In the second version the reader has all the same information–dark sky, the feeling of coldness, the fear, seeing shadows, hearing the howls, introspection, and that he started running—but the revised example is vividly alive because the reader has been given something to clearly visualize rather than reading a bland report.

Personally, I'm a character-driven writer, so I *love* being inside my character's head. I want to experience their journey firsthand.

But writers often create a narrative distance when they consciously or unconsciously insert filter words into the narrative. This issue is also known as author intrusion. In my early drafts, I use a lot of filter words too, but I try to weed them out completely before my final draft. Once you start noticing them, they are easy to spot, and it becomes easier to stay in Deep POV by revising your narrative.

Deeper POV is vital to good storytelling.

This method immerses the reader so deeply in the character's skin that any external narrator simply disappears. That is, the scene is not only told from that character's perspective, but it exemplifies the character's thoughts, emotions and reactions. In other words, it's the ultimate way to *show*, not tell.

The number one reason that *showing* is more visual and appealing for the reader is that fiction is image focused, and *showing* usually generates a vivid image for the reader. Generally, *telling* doesn't produce a strong enough image on the reader's mind.

Please study this example, where the sentence is *telling*...

SHALLOW: Caleb felt hot in his wool coat.

That sentence isn't an image the reader can effortlessly imagine. It's an ambiguous fact.

DEEP POV: Caleb swiped a bead of sweat from his forehead and shrugged off his heavy winter coat.

The revised sentence puts a very powerful illustration in the reader's mind.

I realize that some filter words are mandatory in narrative, but not when you are describing the character's thoughts, emotions, or attitudes. Those should all be shown by using the Deep POV technique.

It's natural to include filter words in your early drafts. However, before you self-publish, send your manuscript off to literary agents, or post any of your short stories, you should always go back through your manuscript and revise as many filter words as you can.

By adding detailed descriptions of characters' emotions, thoughts, and actions, it will help the reader imagine the sights, sounds, smells, and textures of each scene, allowing you to take your writing to the next level.

Don't let filter words clog your prose—describe the emotion!

We feel emotions; however, we use expressions to *show* them. When you are furious, your face gets hot and your voice rises to a higher pitch. That is how people around you know that you are enraged.

You don't tell them: "Watch it. I am so mad!" No, you display it through actions, gestures, and body language. That's how real people behave.

Narrative distance also puts extra words in your sentences, which aren't needed. So, try to cut out all of the *telling* that states emotions such as: *love, hate, joy, grief, sorrow, sympathy, trepidation, fear, anger, irritation, hope, etc.* They can creep into your writing and weigh down your prose.

Over the course of this manual, I provide tons of examples from my own published novels and short stories to help you understand how to incorporate this amazing technique. Hopefully, they should spark your own creative muse and give you clever ideas on how to rewrite your shallow scenes.

Disclaimer: There are many, many ways to write in Deep POV. While this guide is only my personal opinion on this topic, it is not meant as a rule or a strict requirement. Remember, with any guides on fiction writing, trust your own instincts. Focus on the story and keep asking yourself what will make it better. As long as you do that, you pretty much can't go wrong.

So please take all of these suggestions to heart, and *only* make the changes that you feel will best suit your writing style and story.

SHALLOW WRITING

Quote: "Rather than report on emotions (i.e., he was angry, he was scared) *show* them. Yes, it's the old show don't tell. But it's true. Deep POV is the ultimate in showing. Use action, thought, and perception to show emotion and feelings. When you're annoyed, it colors your whole perception of the world. Everyone on the damn road is too damn slow and every traffic light is out to get you. Show that." —*author and editor, Ann Laurel Kopchik*

Deep POV is getting your reader so deeply submerged within the head of your characters that they experience—*really experience*—what the character is feeling. One way to stay in close-and-personal (*show*, don't *tell*) is to do this: try to reduce as many filtering references as you can from your writing.

Instead, simply *show* us what the main character *felt* and *saw* and *heard* and *decided*, without using any filter words.

If a writer overuses filtering words that clutter up each sentence and remove the reader from the experience the character is undergoing or feeling, it creates narrative distance. Anything that describes the narrator's thought or mode of perception is considered "telling" the reader. If you can revise those sentences as much as possible, the POV will feel deeper and your prose will be greatly enhanced.

Also, if a critique partner or beta reader comments on something that confused them over the emotional reaction of one of your characters, check to make sure the stimulus cause is obvious to the reader through Deep POV. I advise to always try to include some type of an emotional response and a physical reaction to intensify the moment of any scene. This helps to *show* the character's response to what is happening by using the Deep POV method.

***

To really help you understand what Deep POV is and why it will turn your novel into an unputdownable read, I have compiled examples from my own published novels.

This excerpt was taken from my book, SHATTERED SILENCE, to offer an example of how to use this wonderful technique.

The first example is what I call shallow writing and crammed with filter words. (The filter words are underlined.)

Please compare the two illustrations below…

SHALLOW:

I could <u>feel</u> my head throbbing, which <u>made</u> me reluctant to open my eyes. I <u>could tell</u> that my vision was blurry. I took deep breaths because I <u>felt</u> dizzy and I <u>knew</u> I wasn't strong enough to raise my head. I leaned on one elbow. My tongue <u>felt</u> like it was glued to the roof of my mouth.

A door opened, and I <u>saw</u> a tall woman, with short red hair, wearing dark blue scrubs and clogs. She was tough looking like a man, I <u>thought</u>.

"You're awake. I'm Nurse Gwen. Let me fetch the doctor." She turned around and closed the door, then locked it.

Collapsing on the thin mattress, I <u>looked around</u> at my foreign surroundings. I <u>noticed</u> stark white walls, a metal-framed bed, and a nightstand. <u>There was</u> a solitary window with security wiring. I <u>heard</u> a loudspeaker call out codes and someone yelled. I saw a fluorescent light near the ceiling. I could smell bleach from the bedding and the antiseptic scent made me feel nausea.

I have no memory of how I'd gotten here, I thought.

There were no shadows on the walls. But eventually I knew they'd come for me. I felt like I had no protection here. I felt weak and scared.

I pulled off the sheets, and swung my legs over the bed. I was dressed in a hospital gown that felt scratchy and I had a bandage wrapped around my right wrist. I noticed that I had scrapes and bruises on my arms and legs. I could see a puncture wound on my arm where someone inserted a needle.

I decided to raise one hand to touch the gauze at my temple and noticed a white band on my left wrist: *Valley Grove Psychiatric Hospital: Trudell, Shiloh*

I knew then that I was in the hospital.

Now this second version is written in Deep POV, but it does contain one or two filter words for better flow. *Here's a revised version that reveals (shows), instead of tells…*

DEEP POV:

My head throbbed and I was reluctant to open my eyes. My vision blurry. I took deep breaths until the waves of dizziness lessened and I was strong enough to raise my head. I leaned on one elbow. My tongue felt glued to the roof of my mouth.

A door opened, admitting a tall lady—at least six feet—with short fiery-red hair, wearing dark blue scrubs and clogs. She looked tough and very butch. Bet nobody messed with her.

"You're awake. I'm Nurse Gwen. Let me fetch the doctor." She whipped around and closed the door. Locked it.

Collapsing on the thin mattress, I surveyed my foreign surroundings. Stark white walls, a metal-framed bed, and a nightstand. Solitary window with security wiring. Somewhere a loudspeaker called out codes and someone howled loudly. Fluorescent light glared down from the ceiling. Whiffs of bleach wafted from the bedding and the antiseptic scent gave me nausea.

I had no memory of how I'd gotten here.

No shadows danced on the walls. But eventually they'd come for me. I had no protection here. I was weak. Defenseless. Vulnerable.

I yanked off the crisp sheets, and swung my legs over the cold metal bed. Someone had dressed me in a scratchy hospital gown and wrapped my right wrist in an elastic Ace bandage. I had scrapes and bruises on my arms and legs. My forearm had a puncture wound where someone had inserted a needle. I raised one hand to touch the gauze at my temple and gasped at the band on my left wrist that read: *Valley Grove Psychiatric Hospital: Trudell, Shiloh*

Oh, no! I was in the nut house!

***

When *telling*, the writer is making a statement. Readers are being told (telling) what to believe by the writer, rather than the readers discovering things for themselves.

Remember that these are just "guidelines" to help improve your skills as a writer. Occasionally breaking the 'rules' is what a story calls for. But don't do it too often. By trying to create meaningful, descriptive prose, it will naturally move the story forward and convey a richer experience for your reader. Don't weigh it down with filter words.

I'm assuming that since you purchased this handbook, it's because you want to improve your writing skills. If you use the Deep POV technique, I promise that you'll notice an amazing difference in your writing. And I bet your readers will, too!

SHOWING

Quote: "Like many other techniques, Deep POV cannot be perfected overnight. At first, a keen eye and a conscious mind must work together to keep the work from slipping back into typical shallow POV techniques. However, writing in Deep POV continuously will help the technique become a natural part of your writing style." —*Kristen Kieffer, writer and blogger*

So now you've written a remarkable story, and had your manuscript ruthlessly edited by your critique partners and read by your insightful beta readers…but is it ready to be self-published or submitted to literary agents yet?

First, ask yourself:

What are some of the generally overlooked mistakes writers make that send red flags to agents and publishers that their work isn't polished?

What common mistakes do many self-published writers make that instantly turn readers off?

Even an experienced writer like myself always needs to triple-check my work before sending it out into the world. I continuously need to go back and revise all those annoying filter words. *Showing* engages the reader in ways *telling* (shallow writing) often can't do as successfully.

For example, readers need details. They need to know the thoughts, feelings, and reactions to every occurrence. Instead of *telling* readers what those reactions and actions are, I would just let the reader figure it out for themselves. Readers need to smell the flowers, taste the apple, experience the fear, and feel the silky fabric of a dress. Anything less than that cheats the reader from deeply experiencing our fictional world.

Examine these two examples. The first is written in Shallow POV and the second is revised into a much Deeper POV and it includes a few of the five senses, and even "voice" to bring the scene to life. Please carefully compare these examples…

SHALLOW:

Simone saw the zombie shamble through the doorway. It had green drool coming from its mouth and the sight made Simone feel sick. The bad smell coming from the zombie's body caused her to cover her mouth and nose. She looked around for a weapon. She didn't notice anything handy, and realized that she was about to be attacked. She swallowed a frustrated scream.

DEEP POV:

The zombie shambled into the room. Toxic green saliva dripped from its mouth and she backed up. A sickly putrid stench of decay rose from the drooling brain-muncher. Simone almost gagged, pinching her nose with one hand. Her gaze quickly scanned the space. No guns. No real weapons. *This is not good!* Her heart rate tripled. She grabbed a baseball bat from the closet and faced the walking dead. *Game on.*

***

When a writer doesn't use Deep POV, it is called "telling." Most new writers use shallow writing, because they are not applying the Deep POV method.

A few common filter words include: *considered, regarded, wondered, saw, heard, hoped, realized, smelled, watched, touched, felt,* and *decided.*

These types of weak words are often used when the author wants to inform the reader of the character's reactions or emotions, rather than describing them directly. "Telling" is a method of expressing facts to the reader, but it is usually the *incorrect* way. In this handbook, I offer some practical ways to identify filter words and phrases.

When I was writing my new adult novel, SMASH INTO YOU, I used a lot of shallow writing and filter words in the first few drafts, and then I went back and deepened the POV to *show*.

Please study this example…

EXAMPLE (early draft): Everywhere I looked, I saw older, tall buildings.

It conveys the info about the setting in a dull and un-visual way, and it worked while I was stilling in the drafting stage.

Here is the revision, where the same information is *shown*…

EXAMPLE (final draft): All around me stood lofty buildings constructed of brick and stone, crowned by shingled rooftops and spires, tradition and pride oozing from every cornerstone.

Did you grasp the difference?

My point is, tell all you want in early drafts of a story. Then go back and revise with a deeper POV. For instance, if a writer states that a character is grief-stricken it is shallow writing.

SHALLOW: Megan was distraught over her husband's death.

That first example is *telling* the reader in a shallow way that Megan is grieving, which is fine. However, once the revision work starts, then that same statement should be revised into *showing*.

Please study this revised example…

EXAMPLE: Her heart seemed to spiral into a deep abyss followed by a hollow ache swelling inside her chest. The physical pain was suddenly too much to endure.

Which example had more impact?

The second example provides a deeper POV and a better visual, and it's for reasons of dramatic impact that *showing* is commonly encouraged over *telling*. When a writer does use "telling," it is to keep the pace of the story moving forward.

***

Here is an excerpt taken from my novel, LOST IN STARLIGHT that shows how using Deep POV correctly will enhance any scene.

DEEP POV:

Hayden glances in my direction and his extraordinary eyes lock onto mine. An unfamiliar thrill shoots through my veins. Even from a short distance, the boy looks mouthwatering good. His eyes harden into chips of ice.

Although I'm obviously busted, I can't look away. For a second, his gaze flares into the hottest flame. As though ignited by kerosene, my body temperature rises. There's a wariness lingering in his expression that I don't understand. Finally, I tear my gaze away and a fierce spark of panic hits hard.

Is my hair tangled? My pencil skirt unzipped? Lip gloss on my teeth?

Pulling a quick ninja hair check, I look out the nearby window, surreptitiously using the reflection to ensure that my flyaway hair looks tame. I sweep a hand around my waist to check my zipper and run my tongue over my teeth. All good. I grip the hem of my black tee under my leather jacket, the silver studded leather cuff on my wrist digging into my stomach, and yank it down. Much better.

Possibly embarrassing situation averted.

***

Did you grasp how I stay in Deep POV throughout that scene? Great!

Here is an excerpt written in Deep POV from the novel, "The Traveler" by John Katzenbach:

She felt suddenly overcome by heat, as if one of the spotlights had singled her out, covering her with a solid beam of intense brightness. She gulped a great breath of air, then another, fighting a dizzying sensation. She remembered the moment years earlier when she'd realized that she was shot, that the warmth she felt was the lifeblood flowing from her, and she fought with the same intensity to prevent her eyes from rolling back, as if giving into the blackness of unconsciousness would be as fatal now as it would have been then.

***

Within that excerpt, the author does use a filter word or two, but he still manages to stay close-and-personal with a tight POV.

Want to know how to become a powerhouse of a writer?

Simply, start using a Deeper POV. The right way to "show" is by revealing information through action, dialogue, and the five senses. Learn to be ruthless and revise any shallow sentences.

TELLING

Quote: "Telling speeds up the pace when we don't want to add another ten paragraphs…we can "tell" when we need to include a number of vital, yet minor events that aren't particularly dramatic. The purpose of those scenes is to bring readers up to the present without interfering with the pace…Or if our story moves along, and we introduce an unfamiliar element to readers, we interject a one or two sentence explanations and move on." —*author, Cecil Murphey*

While there are a lot of writing blogs and professional editors that offer advice on showing vs. telling, most of them don't explain when to "tell" and *not* show in writing. So I've listed a few in this chapter…

The contrasts of showing vs. telling:

Telling is when a writer provides the reader with direct facts, or explains a situation, or offers important information in relation to the storyline in a straightforward manner. This approach is considered passive writing that summarizes events that aren't really significant to the plot, but they are necessary to fill in plot holes or get the info across quickly to keep the story moving forward.

In general, telling requires using fewer words to convey details, but those sentences should still be written with "voice." (I go into much more detail about character "voice" and a writer's narrative style in book two, "The Writer's Guide to Deep POV," if you're interested.)

Also, *telling* is kind of an old-fashioned way of storytelling. Although, recently I read three traditionally published authors that still do way too much telling with info-dumps that made me put the book down while yawning, and then pick up a different novel…

Showing is sensationalizing and digging deeper. It vividly conveys more of a visual for the reader through visceral, impactful, and evocative writing that allows them to effortlessly imagine the story-world, as well as the characters you've created. A deeper POV is considered active writing, but it is typically more wordy and descriptive.

Also, (showing) Deep POV relates to almost every sentence in a story, and can be conveyed through the author's use of language, through the syntax and word choices.

When writing in Deeper POV, everything that happens in a scene is processed in a unique way by that POV character, so even the narrative (telling) must have "voice."

I know some of you are asking: So when is it okay to just *tell* the reader something?

While there are many different methods to *showing* in writing, there are just as many reasons to *tell* when needed.

Showing vs. telling is all about balance.

To me personally, *showing* is used when a writer wants a Deeper POV, and *telling* is needed when the reader requires certain information pertaining to the timeline or plot. *Telling* is for informing the reader in a passive way, like giving them the bare bones.

For instance, whenever the writer gives the reader information in a direct manner, it is considered telling. But it can also make the reader feel somewhat removed from the immediate experience of the moment.

In spite of that, if a writer showed *everything*, then it would cause a lot of overwriting and major pacing issues within the manuscript. Some parts of a story are so inconsequential that writers might want the reader to known a fact or small detail, without going into too much description. If the details or facts are only supplemental to the scene, then it's perfectly okay to just tell the reader. Because if a writer were to *show* every single thing, then the reader would consider the scene padded.

And there's nothing wrong with *telling* in early drafts of a manuscript. Most writers do it because the important thing is to get the story written, and then go back and fill in any plot holes. Using Deep POV comes later, after five or six drafts are finished, when it's time to *dig deeper* in some scenes and revise the characterization. There is no need to stop writing the first or second draft to include carefully detailed descriptions or a Deeper POV. That can wait.

There are no hard-and-fast rules when it comes to showing vs. telling, but a few instances where it would better to "tell" would be these:

1) To convey the passing of time

2) When a character travels from one location to another

3) When backstory is essential to a scene

4) When world-building is necessary

TIME

Let's discuss the first reason. When a writer wants to convey the passage of time to the reader, it is much quicker to just state that a few days have passed or even months. However, a writer should still *show* it through "voice."

In my novel, LOST IN STARLIGHT, I wanted to skip the duller parts of the story whenever the main character was in school, so I summarized when required.

Let's take a look at one example…

EXAMPLE: My afternoon classes zoom by like movie trailers. And then the theater goes dark right before the film starts, and mercifully the last bell rings. I'm finally free.

Did you grasp how I showed the passing of time?

The short paragraph lets the reader know that school has ended without a long info-dump of shallower writing.

Here's another example…

EXAMPLE: Miss Rogers had kept Charlene after school, giving the entire class a lengthy and dull lecture in French. When class finally ended, Charlene rushed out of the heavy doors, buttoning her strawberry-colored Agnes B. trench coat as she went outside.

Now if the paragraph above had gone into more detail about the teacher's longwinded speech, then the passage would've become a dull lecture for the reader as well.

Another example is in Stephenie Meyer's book, NEW MOON, where she states the passage of time by simply having chapters listed with the name of the month, but no other text or explanation is given. The reader infers that (spoiler alert!) months have passed since Edward left and how long poor Bella has been wallowing in her heartache.

TRAVEL

Now onto the second reason why a writer should tell instead of show. To speed things up in a scene, it might be better to just state that character got from point A to point B without being too descriptive.

Readers don't need specifics regarding a long drive, or a plane ride, or even exactly how a character managed to get from one place to another. In other words, if nothing vital to the plot happens, then just tell the reader.

TELLING

In my novel, IMMORTAL ECLIPSE, the character went from New York to California, but I didn't bother with boring details regarding the drive to the airport or about checking in at the airport, itself.

Let's take a look these examples…

EXAMPLE: It takes two trips to haul my luggage downstairs, which leaves me panting. Talk about a workout. I hail a cab for the airport and three hours later, I'm boarding the plane.

Please carefully study this next example…

EXAMPLE: After departing Matthew Rosenberg's office, I'm too jet-lagged to drive the two hours into Carmel, so I check in to the San Francisco Hyatt overnight and play tourist. I roam Fisherman's Wharf, snapping pictures of the neighborhood, and later I devour a scrumptious dinner at a Pier 39 waterfront cafe before falling into bed for the night.

Sunday morning I awake to a thick fog shrouding the city and order room service. I have scrambled eggs and a mocha for breakfast before starting the two-hour journey to Carmel.

Did you grasp how I told the reader that a day has passed? I needed to include those short paragraphs in the novel to fix a plot hole in my timeline.

The next paragraph taken from one of my novels basically states that the character drove from one location (school) to another (graveyard) without going into too much detail because nothing eventful happened plotwise.

Please carefully study this example…

EXAMPLE: But instead of going to study hall as I was instructed, I speed-walk to the school parking lot. Twenty minutes later, I park my VW Jetta near the arched entrance of Shadowland Memorial Cemetery.

Quick and to the point!

These examples should give writers a few clever ideas on other ways to convey that a character traveled from place to another without a long info-dump.

BACKSTORY

There's really only one way to let the reader get a *glimpse* of a character's past, and that's by telling them.

Now a writer could reveal it in a flashback, but that's a topic for another book. Or they could use common tropes like a diary, or even through dialogue, but it often comes across akin to, "As you know, Bob…" which can be annoying to readers.

Writers should disclose a character's backstory through "voice," action, and dialogue. And most importantly, it should just be sprinkled throughout the narrative—and *never* dumped.

In my novel, BEAUTIFULLY BROKEN (free to read and download for a limited time), the reader needed some background info about the main character's dysfunctional family.

Please carefully study this example…

EXAMPLE: After a heartbeat, I relaxed my shoulders and stared at the small trunk as though it contained all the hidden mysteries of the Underworld. I never had a chance to question Aunt Lauren about the trunk after she'd given it to me. To ask about either the books or the prophecy. After that, she wasn't allowed in our house. No one would explain why. But I'd heard. Statements hurled out like spears. Hurtful words that could never be taken back once spoken. A family divided by silence.

It majorly sucked because my family used to be close. Since my tenth birthday, Aunt Lauren and my grandparents, Grandma Naomi and Grandpa Samuel, didn't come around as much. I missed them. Their absence caused me to feel even more alone in the world.

Could you perceive how I included "voice" to the backstory to keep it from becoming too info-dumpy?

Backstory when done well can often deepen characterization and tie into the story's theme.

TELLING

Please carefully study this next example…

EXAMPLE: My ancestors had escaped the violent witch-hunts in England and France by coming to America in the middle of the 17th century. Rumor had it that they had brought magick with them to Ravenwood. Started over here. Away from persecution and prying eyes. They had tapped into the arcane power confined within nature and prospered. And I *had* somehow opened the blinds covering my bedroom window this morning. By my own sheer force of will…or by magick? It was still hard for me to believe.

"Maybe I'm a real witch," I said aloud, then shook my head with a smile.

Did you notice how the backstory unfolds with some interesting tension?

To avoid backstory becoming an info-dump, a writer should never include those dreaded chunks of backstory that are spewed onto to the page in one long block of text that can cause the plot to come to a skidding halt.

WORLD-BUILDING

Every story needs a solid and vivid fictional world for the reader to envision.

In certain genres such as, fantasy, historical, or science fiction, world-building is essential to the plot and for readers to understand and visualize the story-world. (I will dig deeper into the topic of world-building in another guidebook, but I do have a few chapters devoted to how to describe a setting in "The writer's Guide to Deep POV.")

These types of stories necessitate detailed settings and descriptions of clothing, modes of transportation, food, housing, etc. But a writer should always describe these types of specifics through sensory details even when doing an info-dump. In a way, world-building is like the backstory of the story. (I am not going to go into too much detail in this chapter about world-building or when to *tell* because I plan to write another book in this "Deep POV" series that will expand on this topic.)

As the narrative progresses, writers should introduce only the elements relevant to the scene, the theme, the characters, and the plot. Whenever a writer is describing the setting, they should include action and "voice" and sensory details.

Please carefully study this next example…

EXAMPLE: As I walk out of the quiet, air-conditioned comfort of the bookstore, I'm immediately hit by a blast of hot air from the street. I unzip my windbreaker and tie the sleeves around my waist.

Tall buildings with their concrete heads in the clouds crowd the business district, and the grumble of trucks and cars passing by resemble a congested river of vehicles rushing toward an unknown destination.

I maneuver around a hot dog vendor, wiping his sweaty brow, but bump into office-workers on their lunch break. Smartly dressed men and women hurrying in the direction of a cafe further down the street. The mixture of onion, garlic, pepper, and other spices create a potent combination that tingles my nose.

Holding my breath for a moment, I hurry past the Italian restaurant and cross the street. I've always wondered how the people working inside can stand the odor of garlic. *Ugh*.

At the next corner, I pause, shifting my weight from foot-to-foot while I wait for the signal to blink "walk" before I cross the busy street. The light changes to green and I step off the curb—right into the path of a big, black SUV. My body bounces on the hood, pain ripping through my limbs. Shards of glass from the windshield slash into my skull and torso.

When I woke up hours later in the hospital, my head is bandaged and I'm sporting a white plaster cast on my left leg. The sterile, white room reeks of disinfectant and strong soap.

TELLING

Could you vividly imagine the setting? Visualize the busy city streets? Smell the aroma of spices?

Whenever *telling*, try to avoid doing an info-dump (when information is being dumped in blocks of text onto the page without a break with action or dialogue) is a type of exposition that is particularly wordy and often dull. Although, some info-dumping can be done in a way that is interesting and even compelling, most exposition is noticeably intrusive. It usually makes a reader want to skim past the pages of wordy descriptions to get back to the action.

Another thing that writers should watch out for is any *showing* that becomes "Purple Prose." That's when the writing is so ostentatious, flowery, and overwritten that it breaks the story's flow and draws unnecessary attention to itself.

In fact, I used to be the queen of "purple prose" when I was a young writer. And I think I'm still guilty of it on occasion. But then again, I do enjoy reading some purple prose if the writer is skilled enough to pull it off.

As you revise your story, remember that Deep POV will help to lure the reader into each character's head so completely that your readers will feel as if they are experiencing everything that happens right alongside your narrator, so always try to *dig deeper*.

INFO-DUMPS

Quote: "Deep POV allows writers to do away with *he thought, he felt, he wondered, he saw*, all those phrases that unnecessarily encumber a story. At one time such phrases were necessary to let readers know we were in the character's head or seeing through his eyes. With deep POV, readers are in the character's head [almost] all the time, and so such intrusions aren't necessary." —*fiction editor, Beth Hill of "A Novel Edit"* (I had the honor of working with Beth on my novel, IMMORTAL ECLIPSE, and she's an amazing editor.)

An info-dump can be a way of "telling" a reader, instead of describing it. As you revise your novel instead of stating the emotion for the reader, resulting in long passages of exposition, try to include some action, emotion, and reaction within the scene. Make use of the five senses: hearing, sight, touch, smell, and taste. Try to include descriptive words and Deep POV to enhance everything you write. You don't have to use each sense in every scene; one or two in any given situation will transform an otherwise tedious scene into a tangible and vivid experience for your reader.

Plus, telling the reader everything the character thinks or feels is boring and not needed. Instead, try to *show* by using Deep POV, which can and will enrich your story.

Please carefully compare these examples. The filter words are underlined.

SHALLOW:

INFO-DUMPS

Jennifer <u>entered</u> her bedroom and frowned. She <u>smelled</u> her best friend's perfume and her husband's cologne. She <u>felt</u> <u>angry</u>. She <u>decided</u> that he must have been cheating on her.

DEEP POV:

Jennifer walked into her bedroom, planning to surprise her husband with a ten year anniversary gift. She stopped short and raised a trembling hand to her chest. *Oh, god. No!*

Her stomach lurched. The faint trace of her best friend's perfume lingered in the air, mingled with the musk scent of Jack's aftershave. *That lying, cheating jerk!*

***

Using Deeper POV will heighten every scene in your story and make your dialogue come to life.

This next example was taken from my novel, SHATTERED SILENCE. Again, the shallower words are underlined. Please compare these examples...

SHALLOW (before revision):

Just when I thought my night couldn't possibly get any stranger...

I <u>felt</u> pain hurting the scar on my forearm. It burned. I <u>felt</u> tremors throughout my body. The mark began to vibrate and <u>felt</u> feverish. I slightly screamed in pain.

My dad and my aunt Lauren, standing beside me, instantly became <u>concerned</u>.

Dad rubbed my back. "Honey bunch, are you okay?"

I <u>knew</u> I couldn't talk, but I could nod. Something bad was here. I <u>knew</u> it.

"Relax, Shiloh. Just breathe," Aunt Lauren said. "Do you feel sick?"

I heard the doorbell chime.

I took a step back, bumping an end table. A vase fell over onto the floor. I felt an unnerving expectancy in the room. I felt like I was being smothered.

I watched Aunt Lauren bend down to pick up the vase. I saw my mother—Darrah—cross the room to answer the door.

I was scared. I knew something bad was ringing the doorbell. I felt like screaming and telling my mother, no.

***

This revised version written in Deeper POV *shows* the different emotions that the character is experiencing in this short scene.

Deep POV (after revision):

Just when I thought my night couldn't possibly get any stranger…

Pain pulsed across the jagged scar on my forearm. My mark burned, sharp and quick, like it did whenever something dangerous was around. My chest hurt. Tremors raked my limbs. The mark on my forearm vibrated and became feverish. A short scream tore from my lips.

My dad and my aunt Lauren, standing beside me, instantly became concerned.

Dad rubbed my back. "Honey bunch, are you okay?"

I couldn't speak, only nod. Something bad was here. I knew it in my bones.

"Relax, Shiloh. Just breathe," Aunt Lauren said. "Do you feel sick?"

The doorbell chimed.

INFO-DUMPS

Little pig, little pig, please, let me come in…

I took a step back, bumping an end table. A vase crashed to the floor. The room brimmed with an unnerving expectancy. I felt smothered, like I was crammed into a dangerous and airless place.

Aunt Lauren bent down to pick up the shards of porcelain from the vase. My mother—Darrah—crossed the room to answer the door.

Oh, god. It was here. Now. Ringing my damn doorbell.

I wanted to scream, *No! Don't open that door!*

***

These examples should help you to revise your own story into a gripping read!

FILTER WORDS

Quote: "Filtering words are generally words that you add to a sentence when you are trying to describe something that your character is experiencing or thinking. These can be sense words like *feel, taste, see, hear*, and *smell*, or variations thereof. Writers don't necessarily have to avoid these words, but they should be aware of the effect that they have on your prose. Rather than describing a sensation outright, you are distancing your reader from the sense that you are describing." —*young adult author, Corrine Jackson*

Inner-monologue or internal exposition is one of the essential ingredients used to create a comprehensive story. But unfortunately, it's all too often one of the most misused elements in storytelling and can be weakened with too many filter words.

Since internal-monologue is slower and can be boring for the reader, find ways to bring it to life through Deep POV. Don't let your character's mental babble (long blocks of introspection) go on for pages at a time without a break by either dialogue or action.

Dialogue illustrates characterization quicker than any amount of exposition. If you disrupt the action and dialogue to include colossal chunks of description or introspection, it will remove the reader from the story.

Try to start each scene with a compelling bit of action, dialogue, and intrigue. Once the reader is "hooked," then go ahead and add in the necessary exposition. Too much introspection or shallow writing can hinder the flow of the scene and smack of author intrusion by yanking the reader out of the story. It is so much more powerful to be *shown* rather than *told* a character's thoughts, decisions, reactions, and feelings. In active scenes, interior monologue is also a powerful tool to make scenes more emotional and cause your dialogue to sparkle. Internal dialogue is a very effective technique, but one that should be used sparingly.

In almost every scene, I think it's important to stay in Deep POV. One way is to try to reduce the number of filtering references. So rather than: "he/she think or thought," or "he/she felt, he/she see or saw," or "he/she hear or heard," or "he/she noticed," or "he/she realized," or "he/she wondered," or "he/she decided," or even "he/she wished," simply describe the emotion or thought or feeling through Deep POV.

Examples of weak filter words are underlined, along with examples on how to revise your sentences into Deep POV. Please carefully compare these sentences ...

SHALLOW: I thought Tom was being a jerk.

DEEP POV: Tom was acting like a major jerkwad!

SHALLOW: Sammy felt the floor shake.

DEEP POV: The floor shook violently beneath Sammy's feet.

SHALLOW: Katie realized that she had forgotten her keys.

DEEP POV: *Oh, no!* Where did she leave her keys?

SHALLOW: I saw the cat pounce on the mouse.

DEEP POV: The cat crouched, tail swishing. Then the feline pounced on the unsuspecting mouse.

SHALLOW: Reed heard her mom's car pull into the driveway.

DEEP POV: Reed's ears perked up at the crunch of tires on the driveway.

SHALLOW: I noticed that Zander was angry.

DEEP POV: Zander's face reddened and he balled up his fist. *Ah, crud.*

SHALLOW: Sharon <u>wondered</u> if her daughter, Jill had passed her history test.

DEEP POV: Sharon frowned. *I sure hope Jill aces that test!*

SHALLOW: I <u>decided</u> to confront Zach during lunch.

DEEP POV: Instead of going to my usual table at lunch, I bypass my friends and their curious stares and storm right up to Zach.

SHALLOW: Max <u>wished</u> for a new bike more than anything for his birthday.

DEEP POV: Max put the ad for the bike in his mother's cookbook. That should be a clear hint!

***

I realize that writers cannot remove every occurrence of filtering, but they can revise those shallower words whenever possible. Just remember that Deep POV respects the reader's intelligence. Shallow writing (telling) presumes that your reader isn't clever enough to understand unless the writer states the emotion. But if you use the Deep POV method, it will immerse the reader into the story and induce an emotional response, which gives them a much deeper reading experience.

Another way to really use Deep POV effectively is to give each of your characters a distinctive "voice" that comes across in your narrative. Choose your words carefully, because they will reveal a lot about your character and vividly *show* their unique voice.

Please study these two examples from my published novel, IMMORTAL ECLIPSE:

SHALLOW (no voice):

I looked at the cream envelope on the kitchen table. Is it a wedding invitation? I thought. I hated being unmarried and having people give me a hard time about it. I didn't understand why being single and in my late twenties made my married friends give me odd looks. I was just independent.

DEEP POV:

My gaze rests on the cream envelope lying on the kitchen table. The one I'd first thought was a wedding invitation. Yet another nail in my unmarried-still-tragically-single coffin. Why does being single equate to being tossed in the bargain bin at Target? I'm a sophisticated and independent New Yorker, dammit!

***

Each sentence portrays the same scenario, but how the character reacts and is *shown* in the wording used to convey her thoughts and feelings is vastly different and gives the reader a Deeper POV. The first one is "telling" the reader info in a weak shallow way, but in the second version, we get a glimpse of her personality and "voice" and it is written in Deep POV.

To avoid filter words, a useful tool to help search out and eliminate repetitive or unproductive words is the FIND and REPLACE function in Microsoft Word. Either delete the weak word entirely or revise the sentence into actively showing. Alternatively, print the page and use a colored highlighter to single out needless words, and then re-edit the scene.

Don't let weak filter words distance your writing. Most of those words can be deleted, and by using Deep POV instead, it will give your writing greater impact. Just remember that you should always strive to *show* the emotion instead of telling the reader. The next few chapters will cover this in more detail with some great examples on how to revise your prose into a Deeper POV.

In the subsequent chapters, I have listed helpful examples on how to revise filter words.

*Note: All of the Deep POV examples in this handbook have already been used in my published books or short stories, so you'll need to come up with your unique variations.

DEEPER POV

Quote: "The difference between showing and telling can be set out in four words. Showing reveals. Telling explains." —*author, James Thayer*

In the early drafts of a manuscript, *telling* is expected. It is more important to get the story finished and the plot holes filled in, then to worry about if a writer is *showing* enough. It is during the revision stage of later drafts (more like draft five or six) when it's time to polish the storyline and start checking for red flags of *telling* and begin enhancing the characterization, along with the setting and dialogue.

Just stating that you need to "*dig deeper*" or having someone say, "don't show" can become confusing for a lot of writers. I think that's one reason that I wanted to share my knowledge and understanding of the Deep POV technique.

When writers are told to *show, don't tell*, they're frequently left without any step-by-step instructions on how to fix those problem areas in a story, and even when *not* to use Deep POV, so this guide should help shed some light on those issues.

The Deep POV method can be used in a lot of different ways besides the obvious ones, like *show emotions* or just *getting inside a character's head*. It can also create engaging dialogue, aid in describing characters and vivid settings through sensory details, and even strengthen characterization. We just need to understand *how* and *when* to apply it.

Showing merely means allowing the reader to deeply experience things for themselves, through the viewpoint and perception of a character.

Deep POV is just describing everything that your character is feeling, observing, and identifying, along with whatever they're seeing, hearing, touching, and smelling, etc.

Throughout this guide, I have included examples to demonstrate how writers can avoid narrative distance in easy to grasp methods that can instantly improve anyone's writing.

*Please note that while all of the examples in my guidebooks have already been used (mostly in my own novels published under Sherry Soule), but you can turn almost any of these Deep POV examples into new, unique phrases that fit your own stories. The purpose of the examples that I provide are to get your own creativity flowing enough to come up with innovative ways to describe your characters and settings in your own distinctive style.

Let's check one example below…

SHALLOW: Sara <u>realized</u> that she had forgotten the baby at home.

DEEP POV: The thought struck her like a punch to the gut. She'd forgotten the baby at home!

Now ask yourself: which example caused more impact?

If Deep POV (showing) demonstrates detailed proof to the reader and permits them to obtain their own conclusions, than *telling* (stating the emotion or details) states a fact to the reader, telling them what to accept as true.

For instance, stating (telling the reader) that a character "realized" something, like she was late for work, is fine, but it is also somewhat shallow. Instead, a writer can *show* that the character is late by her rushed actions.

Please carefully compare these examples…

SHALLOW: I woke up and looked at the clock. I realized that I was late for work. I quickly showered and got dressed. Then I ran out the door.

DEEP POV: The morning light seeping through the window burns my eyes. Rolling over, I check the alarm clock. It's after eight.

Groaning, I throw back the blankets and rush into the bathroom. I hurry through a shower without washing my hair, and then brush my teeth. Back in the bedroom, I go to the closet and dig through the trendy garments, ripping clothes from the hangers. I glance at the clock again.

Ten minutes left before I miss my bus.

Needing a jolt of espresso, I yank on a dress and slip on my shoes. On my way out the door, I grab my purse and dash outside into the bright morning sunshine.

Could you perceive the difference? One is telling the facts in a bland way and the other is showing in a visual way.

Please study this example, where each sentence is *telling*…

SHALLOW: Kate noticed that it was getting late and it looked very dark. She felt cold. When she saw the shadows moving and heard a strange howling, she felt scared. She saw the house and she started to run very fast on the path.

Although, the first scene states the facts, it's inert and sluggish.

Here is a revision, where the same information is *shown*…

DEEP POV: The sky darkened and the wind wailed through the stiff branches on the pines. Kate shivered and hugged herself. The shadows shifted and the eerie howl of a wolf cut through the air. Her pulsed jumped. Kate spotted the porch lights glowing on the house and she sprinted along the path.

The second scene is much more vivid and visual, right?

In the second version the reader has all the same information–dark sky, the feeling of coldness, the fear, seeing shadows, hearing the howls, introspection, and started running—but the revised example is vividly alive because the reader has been given something to clearly visualize rather than reading a bland report.

Showing is more effort than just *telling*, but that is part of a writer's job during revisions.

Please compare these examples…

SHALLOW: He looked depressed.

DEEP POV: Tears slid down his pale face.

SHALLOW: He felt angry.

DEEP POV: He clenched his fist and his mouth formed a thin, flat line.

SHALLOW: She looked happy.

DEEP POV: She jumped in the air, clapping her hands.

SHALLOW: She felt envious.

DEEP POV: Her gaze narrowed and one side of her lip curled upward.

SHALLOW: He looked nervous.

DEEP POV: He chewed his bottom lip and fidgeted with his keys.

Most of the time, using Deep POV to *show* is much better than *telling* because of the experience it provides for our readers.

Now just to be clear, *telling* isn't always the wrong way to describe an emotion or reaction. It doesn't always indicate flat, shallower writing. Please take into consideration that "show, don't tell" is *not* a strict writing rule. As a matter of fact, none of the self-editing tips in this Deep POV book should be deemed as actual rules. There are going to be times in a writer's story when *telling* will be needed, because sometimes *telling* can be much more effective if done correctly. However, whenever a writer can use Deeper POV in their stories, they should treat their readers with respect by *showing*.

So just keep in mind that showing vs. telling is all about balancing the two concepts.

SHOW DON'T TELL

Quote: "Every creative writing student has heard the rule that you should *show*, not *tell*, but this principle seems to be among the hardest for beginners to master." —*author, Robert Sawyer*

First let me say this…I get it. I *really* do. Your book is like your baby, and you love it and you've poured your sweat and blood and tears into it. But sometimes writers need a take a step back and look at the writing from a reader's perspective…

I've found that a lot of novice writers that I've worked with get confused by the whole "show vs. tell" concept, and I admit that it used to confuse me, too.

A few months ago, one of my critique partners said that she thought writers could only use the Deep POV technique about 50% of the time. I disagree. I think it can be used anytime a writer wants to avoid *naming the emotion* or they use sensory details to describe a scene. And describing a character's body language, facial expression, actions, gestures, or tones of voice are just some of the many ways that writers can *show*.

Most of the time when writers do not apply Deeper POV, it creates narrative distance. This means that the reader has been distanced, or in some cases, jolted out of the story by author intrusion. The more *telling* a writer does, the more distance they put between the reader and the story, and the less involved the reader will feel to what's happening or a real connection to the characters.

And if readers aren't connecting to your characters, then you've got a major problem.

The number one reason that *showing* is more visual and appealing for the reader is that fiction is image focused, and *showing* usually generates a much more vivid image for the reader, rather than stating facts. Generally, *telling* doesn't produce a strong enough picture in the reader's mind, and it often causes author intrusion, which reminds readers that they are reading a story—and that's not something a writer ever wants.

Please study this example, where the sentence is *telling*…

SHALLOW: Caleb felt hot in his wool coat.

That sentence isn't an image the reader can effortlessly imagine. It's an ambiguous fact.

DEEP POV: Caleb swiped a bead of sweat from his forehead and shrugged off his heavy winter coat.

The revised sentence puts a very powerful illustration in the reader's mind.

If you read a ton of fiction like me, you'll notice *telling* in almost every published novel, some more than others, but that doesn't mean you should "tell" if you can *show*. I realize that some telling is mandatory in narrative, but not when you are describing the character's emotions or internal-thoughts. Those should always be shown by using the Deep POV technique.

Fiction is a creative art, and writers need to use descriptions and senses, and not simply state emotions or continuously give direct facts.

Please look at one example below…

SHALLOW: Jane was a beautiful young girl.

That sentence is a form of *telling*, and although the sentence states a fact, it gives a rather weak visual.

DEEP POV: Jane swept into the room and her delicate lilac perfume wafted in the air, tickling my nose. When she spotted me sitting alone, her pouty, pink lips lifted into an amazing smile that lit up her azure eyes. A thick mane of ebony waves fell over one shoulder, and to me she resembled a painting of a Greek goddess brought to life. For a moment, it felt like my heart stopped beating in my chest.

Now ask yourself: which description was more powerful and visual?

Now, I'm not suggesting that a writer show or describe *everything* in great detail because that would be overwriting and create pacing issues. The key is to understand the difference so writers can intelligently decide when to use Deep POV and when to just tell. Finding a balance is necessary.

Here are four easy to master tips on writing in Deep POV and red flags:

1) Writers should try to reduce as many filtering references as they can from their writing. Words such as *felt, saw, heard, smelled,* and *noticed*, etc. that tell the reader what the narrator felt or saw or heard or noticed instead of just stating it.

Always strive to find new and active ways to describe a character's emotional state, or allow your characters to convey their emotions through action, facial expressions, internal-dialogue, and body language.

2) Naming the emotion can become a bad habit that writers easily fall into. Writers create narrative distance and author intrusion when they deliberately or unintentionally insert shallower POV and telling sentences into their scenes.

Anything that directly states the narrator's thought, emotion, or mode of perception is considered *telling* the reader about whatever the character is experiencing.

Writers should have more respect for their readers by *showing* instead.

3) Be more specific when describing places, settings, people, clothing, objects, cars, etc. so you don't create a weak visual. The easiest way to stay in Deeper POV is to try to be much more specific whenever possible by including sensory details.

By writing with precise and detailed words, and avoiding vagueness, writers will remove most of the "tells" from a story and breathe new life into any scene.

4) One way to rid your fiction of shallow writing is to use the "look through the camera lens" method, which is an excellent tool for helping writers begin to notice any *telling* within a manuscript.

Imagine this: the character is standing behind the camera, and everything in the scene, is perceived through that POV character's eyes and then reported through their perspective.

But the camera can't view any of the five senses, like sounds, touch (the way something feels), smells, temperatures, or tastes. In addition, interior-dialogue—the character's internal thoughts and emotions—cannot be viewed by a camera, and so it is not (usually) considered telling.

***

There are times when *telling* will add to the rhythm of your sentence and it is simply necessary. Telling shouldn't be completely removed from your manuscript because that would be impossible and some of your prose could become particularly awkward.

Do I use filtering word/references on occasion?

Yes, because I mostly write in first-person POV and sometimes they are hard to avoid without creating awkward sentences. However, my advice is this: if you can rewrite the sentence without it and stay in Deeper POV, then do it. If some of the time you cannot, then go ahead and leave the shallow word in the sentence.

SENSORY DETAILS

Q uote: "Place matters to me. Invented places matter more." —*best-selling author, Alice Hoffman*

Deeper POV removes bland storytelling by including sensory details and cranks it up a notch. It pulls readers deeply into the heads and hearts of our characters by allowing the story to be seen, experienced, and felt through the close-and-personal POV of the character.

If done correctly, Deep POV rids a story of unneeded phrases like *he thought, he knew, he heard, he smelled, he felt* (when it applies to emotions), *he wondered, he saw* that cause author intrusion. (Reminder: it is always okay to use shallow "telling" words in dialogue.)

Another huge advantage of applying the Deep POV method to your writing is offering the reader direct access to the character's moods, emotions, and perceptions. A character needs the ability to describe what she/he experiences as it occurs.

The most obvious way of *telling* and the number one red flag is to state the emotion or reaction. A better way is to show them through facial expressions, internal-monologues, and body language.

Please carefully compare these examples…

SHALLOW: The smell was awful and made me feel sick.

DEEP POV: I covered my nose and tried not to gag at the offensive stench.

Remember that "stating the emotion or reaction" for a reader is *telling*. The correct way is to *show* by describing what is unfolding in every scene by the use of action, "voice," dialogue, facial expressions, and the five senses, etc.

Writers can *tell* a reader that when Harry steps into the kitchen, he notices a stinky smell, but it is much more creative to *show*. Sometimes showing is more descriptive and wordy than just stating the facts, but where's the fun in that, right?

Please examine these examples…

SHALLOW:

When Harry went into the kitchen, he noticed there was a stinky smell coming from the sink. He realized that it was apparent that no one had washed the dishes in a very long time.

Sure, the shallow example gets to the point and states the facts, but let's be honest, it's bland and flat. Now compare this one written in Deeper POV.

DEEP POV:

The second Harry stepped through the kitchen doorway, a raucous odor wafted from the sink and made his nose wrinkle. "*Gross!* When was the last time anyone cleaned the dishes?"

The second example was more impactful, right?

Please examine these next examples…

SHALLOW:

While I changed into my gym clothes, I watched my best friend Dana carefully. I noticed that she looked overly excited to go workout with weights and gym equipment. I knew something was going on with her, and I decided to find out.

SENSORY DETAILS

That example was too bland and gives the reader a weak visual.

DEEP POV:

Grunting, I yanked on my tight gym clothes, while my best friend Dana was humming to herself and prancing around the stuffy locker room.

Once she'd finished dressing in a brand-new workout outfit, she turned to me all smiles. "Ready to get sweaty?"

"Since when do you like cardio?" I propped a hand on my love handle, protruding over the waistband of my sweats. "Are you crushing on that new trainer, Sergio?"

Dana twirled around like a ballerina in her glaring white tennis shoes. "Oh, yeah…"

***

Showing (Deep POV) makes your readers become even more emotionally invested in your wonderful story. One way to do that is for writers to use specific words to describe how things smell, how certain foods taste, how objects feel, how the setting sounds, and looks through your character's eyes.

Why keep your readers at arm's length, when you can pull them in close-and-personal?

Recognizing the difference between *showing* and *telling* is the most crucial skill a writer needs for stronger storytelling.

DIALOGUE SCENES

Quote: "Perhaps it's a lack of confidence on the writer's part, perhaps its simple laziness, or perhaps it's a misguided attempt to break up the monotony of using "said" all the time, but all too many fiction writers tend to pepper their dialogue with ly adverbs…" —*Renni Browne and Dave King, Self Editing For Fiction Writers*

The Deep POV method is an amazing tool that can immediately turn your dialogue into stronger, more emotive scenes. This is frequently a difficult skill to master for some writers, but it's so effective that it will amplify any area of a manuscript. Deep POV can put the reader so firmly into the character's head that the writer basically vanishes.

One of the best ways to avoid *telling* in your writing is through dialogue, which can help deepen characterization, reveal emotions, and even accentuate mood and theme. Reading an engaging dialogue scene makes a reader feel as if they're actually eavesdropping on a real conversation.

What disappears in a Deeper POV dialogue scene are the need for lots of intrusive dialogue tags with the "ly" adverbs (emotional qualifiers) attached to them, which are the "John said <u>angrily</u> or Jane asked <u>sadly</u>" or "Max said <u>mysteriously</u>, or Ashley said <u>wryly</u>".

Dialogue tags used as emotional qualifiers like "yelled," or "said crossly," or "cried out," as a description of the character's emotional state can often cause author intrusion. Author intrusion is only one drawback with using "ly" adverbs in our dialogue because it also tacks on an "emotional qualifier" that often creates shallower writing.

So try to avoid the overuse of emotional qualifiers in conversations. A few are okay, but don't overdo it because these types of tags *tell* and don't *show*, which take writers out of Deeper POV.

Please examine these examples…

SHALLOW: "Do you know where the treasure is hidden?" she asked anxiously.

DEEP POV: She clenched her jaw. "Do you know where the treasure is hidden or not?"

SHALLOW: "This is private property and you're trespassing," I yelled coldly.

DEEP POV: I crossed both arms over my chest. "This is private property and *you're* trespassing."

SHALLOW: "Charles never takes me anywhere fun," she complained bitterly.

DEEP POV: Clenching her teeth, she muttered, "Charles *never* takes me anywhere fun."

The dialogue tag should allow the reader to know who spoke without *telling* them the emotion behind the words. Most "ly adverbs" can be revised by using Deeper POV, which will give your dialogue scenes greater impact. Learn to be ruthless and omit those emotional qualifiers.

Please compare these examples…

SHALLOW: "Give it back," Amber shouted threateningly.

DEEP POV: "Give it back!" Amber's hard stare bore into me like two heat seeking missiles.

SHALLOW: "Please don't hurt me," Thomas pleaded miserably.

DEEP POV: He recoiled and his voice sounded weak. "*Please* don't hurt me."

SHALLOW: "Don't be such a jerk," Samson said scornfully.

DEEP POV: "Don't be such a jerk," Samson said through gritted teeth.

SHALLOW: "Stay back!" he yelled loudly in anger. "Or else."

DEEP POV: "Stay back!" His voice rose and his body tensed. "Or else."

If writers use other types of tags like *roared, implored, wailed, hollered, suggested, noted, remarked, answered, begged, crooned,* or *complained*, it will almost certainly take them out of Deep POV and be distracting to the reader.

To use Deeper POV in your dialogue scenes, writers should try not to use dialogue tags other than "he/she said" or "he/she asked" most of the time. These tags are invisible to the reader, yet they let the reader know which character is speaking. Some editors state that it is redundant for a writer to use "asked" after a question mark, but I think it is fine if needed to identify the speaker.

I encourage writers to study how to properly use a combo of action tags, emotional responses, and dialogue tags in their conversations.

ENHANCE CONVERSATIONS

Quote: "Dialogue in fiction has five functions. One or more of the following must always be at work, or you're just taking up space: 1) Reveal story information. 2) Reveal character. 3) Set the tone. 4) Set the scene. 5) Reveal theme…" —*bestselling author, James Scott Bell*

One of the best ways to *show* is through dialogue, which is usually the most interesting aspect of fiction for any reader. But so often, writers don't create engaging dialogue scenes that arouse the reader's attention.

Most writers have heard or been told that the use of adverbs is considered a major writing offense because it is often a way of *telling* rather than *showing*.

In dialogue heavy scenes, writers need fresh ways to describe emotions directly to the reader instead of just "stating the feeling," which causes the dreaded *narrative distance* that I talked about in book one.

The examples below are ones frequently found in fiction that will demonstrate why it is better not to *state the emotion* in dialogue tags. (I have underlined what I consider to be shallower writing.)

Please carefully compare these examples…

SHALLOW: "I don't want to go to the dance this Friday night, Lucas!" I said with frustration.

DEEP POV: I threw my hands up and sighed. "For the hundredth time, Lucas, I *don't* want to go to that stupid dance on Friday."

SHALLOW: "Come here now," he said menacingly.

DEEP POV: When he spoke, his tone was low and hard. "Come here now."

SHALLOW: "My puppy ran away and I can't find him," I said sadly.

DEEP POV: Tears clouded my vision. "My puppy ran away and I can't find him anywhere," I said, my voice cracking on the words.

SHALLOW: "Stop harassing my girlfriend," he said angrily.

DEEP POV: His hands formed fists at his sides. "You'd better *stop* harassing my girlfriend."

SHALLOW: "Get away from me!" I shouted boisterously.

DEEP POV: "Get away from me!" I said, my voice high and shrill.

SHALLOW: "Never enter my room without permission," she said hotly.

DEEP POV: Her expression turned cold and unyielding. "*Never* enter my room without permission."

SHALLOW: "Where were you between the hours of six and seven o'clock last night?" I asked suspiciously.

DEEP POV: I eyed him closely. "So, where were you between the hours of six and seven last night, huh?"

Those examples illustrated how writers can eliminate the "ly adverb" from their dialogue and express the emotion instead to strengthen the dialogue. It is okay to use an adverb occasionally, but *only* sparingly.

I advise writers to insert visual descriptions of facial expressions, body language, and gestures to convey emotions and reactions within the dialogue to make it come alive for the reader.

Please carefully examine this example…

ENHANCE CONVERSATIONS

SHALLOW:

My best friend Candace looked furious as she walked over to me. She expressed that she was angry because I had told her crush that she liked him. I felt really bad. A crowd of girls gathered around us to watch the fight. Then I was scared that this misunderstanding would get out of hand. I did not know how to fix this, I thought.

DEEP POV (no dialogue tags):

Candace marched over to me with her nostrils flared. "I'm going to kill you! How could you tell Devin that I had a crush on him?"

Oops! I took a step back. "I'm sorry—"

"Save it." Candace rolled up the sleeves of her purple hoodie.

A group of our classmates made a tight circle around us as if waiting for an epic showdown. My best friend lifted her hands, curing her fingers into claws.

A girl from my Bio class shoved me from behind. "Cat fight!"

My heart rate tripled. I had to figure out a way out of this mess—and *fast!*

***

Some writers depend on the same one or two descriptors or adverbs to repeatedly describe an emotion or expression, but I encourage you to be creative and find fresh and unique ways to describe them.

This first scene has too many "emotional qualifiers" and the speech reads too formal. (I have underlined the shallower and clichéd writing.)

Please carefully examine these longer examples…

SHALLOW:

"Get ready!" Lucas shouted vociferously as he ran into the house in a big panic. "They are coming."

Ava looked up in surprise from her seat on the sofa. "Is it the vampires?" she asked intensely.

Lucas looked at his friends and his face was white with terror. "Yes. They have found our hideout!" he yelled vehemently.

"How many are there?" Oliver asked fearfully.

"There are twelve vampires," Lucas answered nervously.

"Did you see the vampire slayer, too?" Oliver said impatiently.

Lucas looked thoughtful. "No. But I do hope that she is on her way," he answered pensively.

***

*Note: In all of the Deeper POV revised examples, I rewrite the shallower example to combine both "voice" in the dialogue speech and in the characterization.

DEEP POV (only 1 dialogue tag):

The front door burst open and Lucas raced into the house. "Get ready!" His eyes were wild and he was breathing heavily. "*They're* coming."

Ava jumped up from her seat on the sofa and placed a hand over her thumping heart. "Is it the vampires?"

Lucas nodded, his face bleached of color. "Yes. They must've found our hideout."

"How many?" Oliver asked, his voice slightly trembling.

Lucas wrung his hands. "Twelve nasty blood suckers."

Oliver nodded. "Did you see the vampire slayer, too?"

Lucas scratched his head. "Um, no. But let's hope that she's on her way."

ENHANCE CONVERSATIONS

***

The second version is much more immediate and engaging. It *shows* the emotions and has more "voice" in the narrative.

Please carefully study this next example…

SHALLOW:

"I saw your ex-boyfriend today," she said with concern. "He said that he missed you."

"I do not accept that as true," I said in surprise. "Because it is hard to believe that when he broke up with me on Valentine's Day," I said bitterly.

DEEP POV:

"I ran into your ex…" My best friend gently rubbed my arm. "He even had the nerve to say that he missed you."

"*Seriously?*" My eyes widened and I bitterly laughed. "That's hard to believe since the jerk dumped me on Valentine's Day."

***

Now this much longer scene is crammed with too many distracting dialogue tags that cause major author intrusion.

Please carefully study this extended example…

SHALLOW:

Mia went over to the Thompson's house and she was very distressed when she arrived and went into the kitchen where she saw her friends.

"I know Eddie is cheating on me!" Mia declared. "I saw him at *her* house today."

"Maybe he was just driving through the neighborhood," Isabella suggested.

"Sure," Logan agreed. "Ed is a good guy and he wouldn't be having an affair."

"I followed him from the office and he drove over there, and then parked on her street," Mia insisted. Then she drank some wine that was on the counter. "He's definitely having an affair. I mean, face it," she observed. "Eddie is handsome and an influential doctor, and I have gained a lot of weight and gotten flabby. So I know he is having an affair," she claimed sadly.

"You don't know that for sure," Logan responded sympathetically.

"He might have been going by the nanny's house to visit the kids," Isabella offered. "Mia, you said that sometimes the nanny takes the children back to her place."

"Maybe…but he did mention that he was going to be in a meeting all afternoon when I called this morning," Logan confessed.

"It must be true. He is even lying to his friends. Now I am going over there to confront him," Mia announced.

Then her friends watched as she lifted her purse, and reached inside, and then removed a handgun.

Now please compare this revised version with some "voice" and sensory details added…

DEEP POV:

Mia marched through the Thompson's house and entered the bright yellow kitchen. She tossed aside her leather handbag and slumped onto a stool. "I know Eddie is cheating on me!" Tears clouded her blue eyes. "I caught the lying jerk at *her* house today."

Her best friends, Isabella and Logan, had been happily married for ten years. Both slim and blond, they looked like the perfect couple.

Isabella frowned, holding a bottle of wine in one hand. "Well, maybe he was just driving through the neighborhood." She poured the liquor into her crystal wineglass.

"That has to be why." Logan nodded, leaning back against the counter. "Ed is a good guy and I doubt that he's having an affair."

"I followed him from the office and he drove straight over to her house." Mia sniffled and snatched a glass of wine off the counter, gulping the burgundy liquid down. "He's *definitely* having an affair. I mean, let's face it," she said, taking another sip of wine, this time from Logan's half-full glass. "Eddie is totally hot and he's an important doctor, and I've gained twenty pounds over the last year. Now I've got varicose veins and a flabby ass. Of course he's having an affair!"

Logan grunted. "You don't know that for sure."

"He might've been going by her house to visit the kids," Isabella said, her voice thick with sympathy. "Mia, you've mentioned that sometimes the nanny takes the children back to her place."

"Maybe…but Eddie told me that he was going to be in a meeting all afternoon when I called this morning," Logan said, fiddling with the wine bottle and avoiding Mia's stare.

Mia shook her head and fresh tears lined her eyes. The idea of her muscular-tanned-golf-loving husband having sex, let alone in the middle of the afternoon, with the skinny-designer-knock-off-wearing nanny made her want to rip the hair from her own head.

"*See!* He's even lying to his friends! I'm going over there to confront him." Mia squared her shoulders, then removed a handgun from her purse.

***

Which scene did you find more exciting and interesting? The revised scene in Deeper POV with the added details makes the example much more vivid and engaging. Those last two examples demonstrate how writers can revise any heavy dialogue scenes with a Deeper POV to make them more intimate for their readers. When writers stay close-and-personal with their audience, it can easily enhance the dialogue.

DESCRIPTIVE EXCHANGES

Quote: "Dialogue has only two purposes: (1) to enhance the character, and (2) to further the plot." —*Othello Bach*

Writing realistic dialogue does not come easily to everyone. Well-written dialogue advances the story while providing a respite from lengthy sections of introspection and it also helps to avoid author intrusion.

In James Scott Bell's guidebook, "*How to Write Dazzling Dialogue*," he advises this for any novel:

1. Make a list of your cast. Give each character a one or two line description.

2. Step back and make sure the descriptions are sufficiently different from each other.

3. Give each character one quirk. Make them irritating to at least two other characters.

4. Write a few "practice scenes" pairing two of the characters at random.

***

Another way to make dialogue more powerful is to include character "tics" or gestures throughout, and make sure that the characters have the correct responses and that they're reactions are clearly shown.

Here are a few quick tips to revise dialogue and connect the conversation with the setting, senses, and Deeper POV.

1) Briefly describe the setting at the start of each new scene: an urban city, a coffee shop, a desolate farm, a graveyard, a dark forest, a high school bathroom.

2) Give the characters moving body parts

3) Show reactions through expressions and gestures

4) Share the character's internal-thoughts

5) Weave some connections to the setting and any objects by having characters interact with them

6) Include the five senses: *what are the characters seeing, hearing, smelling, touching, etc.?*

7) Add a flourish of color. Mention the shade of the car, the paint on the walls, the color of the trees, etc.

***

Dialogue is a place where "voice" is vital to revealing personality and character traits, along with making your characters seem more multi-dimensional. Weave a character's inner-thoughts and emotions into the narrative, and you'll notice an immediate difference.

This next excerpt (condensed) was taken from my new adult novel, SMASH INTO YOU, and gives another example on how to incorporate Deep POV by including "Voice," sensory details, description, and dialogue.

Please closely examine this example…

DEEP POV:

DESCRIPTIVE EXCHANGES

When the stranger stopped beneath the lamppost, the stream of incandescent light struck his body and shone on a head of unruly waves. He stood with his thumbs hooked into the loops of his jeans, with the strap of a backpack drooping from one broad shoulder. I caught the glint of a silver ring piercing his left eyebrow.

Fan-friggin'-tastic. I was alone in the quad with a dangerous-looking, pierced stranger. One who probably carried around a backpack full of paraphernalia used to torture innocent young women.

"You okay?" He took a step toward me. "You look kinda spooked—"

"Stop!" I aimed the pepper spray at him, holding one finger on the trigger. "Give me an extremely good reason not to blast you right now."

His hands went up in surrender. "Whoa! Don't shoot." He gazed steadily at me, his eyes bright under the streetlight. "I'm a student here, just waiting for someone."

Okay. So, it wasn't an insane-asylum escapee or a bloodthirsty murderer. Only another college student. The tension in my shoulders unwound, along with the muscles in the back of my neck.

He transferred the backpack from one shoulder to the other. "Sorry. I didn't mean to scare you."

My attempt at a smile felt forced. "And I didn't mean to almost blind you." I lowered my arm, but kept a wary eye on the guy.

***

There are no dialogue tags in that entire excerpt, but it is clear which character is speaking and that the emotions are "shown" rather than "told" by what the first-person narrator is seeing and feeling and interpreting.

It's very important for readers to be able to clearly imagine a character's facial expressions or reactions in a scene. In some scenes, a writer might need to *dig deeper* to describe emotional reactions and responses through body language without always having to use emotional qualifiers or adverbs.

TALKING HEADS

Quote: "Unless a dialogue exchange is grounded in a physical place, and I can see the physical bodies doing the speaking, what we have on the page are two talking heads." —*author and editor, Ramona DeFelice Long*

I love reading dialogue. Dialogue done correctly can quicken the pace of any novel, reveal characterization, add tension, or reveal the motives and/or goals of your characters. It can show two characters exchanging in witty banter, falling in love, or even add a dash of conflict and intrigue into a scene without *telling* the reader what's happening.

First, I'd like to discuss what some professional editors and writers refer to as "talking heads" in dialogue heavy scenes. The term refers to any dialogue where it reads as if two or more heads are just floating around in space without any real connection to the setting or the scene itself. To correct this, writers should try adding in some sensory details (like the five senses) and action beats, which can substitute for a dialogue tag, as well as some internal-monologue.

Please compare these two examples…

EXAMPLE of "TALKING HEADS":

"How long have you and Amanda been in a relationship? A long time?" Brenden asked.

"Yes, we have," Nick replied. "Why do you ask?"

"Did you sleep with her yet?"

"Do you mean have sex? No," Nick answered. "But we have only been dating for a few months."

"My girlfriend wants to wait. Nonetheless, I would like to do it right away."

"It might be too soon to have sexual intercourse."

"I disagree," Brenden told Nick. "We have been dating for a very long time."

"Then why do you not just ask her why she wants to wait?" Nick questioned.

"I am fearful of scaring her off….Because I love her."

"That is very good to hear, Brenden," Nick said. "Now can we please finish our lunch?"

***

In the first scene above, the reader has no idea where this conversation is taking place, what the characters are feeling, or their reactions.

Anytime dialogue is placed on its own, it creates a lot of narrative distance and even confusion. Readers can't visualize, or experience, or know what the characters are thinking, or even where the scene takes place. Readers are distanced from the story-world when there's no connection to the setting or visual interactions.

EXAMPLE REVISED:

The Chinese restaurant was quiet with only a few patrons. Rain pattered against the front window, beating out a dull symphony of taps. Nick sighed. The grey weather seemed to match his somber mood. A plump waitress wearing a stained apron came by the table to take their order, then scurried off.

Brenden leaned back in the leather booth. "You and Amanda have been going out a long time, right?"

Nick raised an eyebrow, but didn't reply. When Brenden had sent him text about meeting up for lunch, Nick had *not* expected a chat about relationships.

"Well?"

"Yes," Nick said, twisting his napkin around one finger. "Why?"

Brenden took a swig of his beer and set the bottle back on the table with a clank. "You sleep with her yet?"

"Have sex? Not yet." Nick squirmed in his seat and the napkin in his hands tore in half. "But we've only been going out officially for like, three months." He slouched in his seat and his untouched glass of iced tea sweated on the crumb-coated tabletop. The tangy scent of fried onions and spicy foods flowed from the kitchen doorway and made Nick's stomach grumble.

"That's a long time, dude. My girlfriend keeps telling me that we need to wait." Brenden grunted and reached for his beer again. "But, dude, if I had my way, we'd be doing it right now!"

This conversation was becoming way too chick-flick for Nick. The food couldn't get here fast enough. A few tables over, a baby in a stroller furiously waved his little arms and legs like a capsized beetle.

"So any advice?" Brenden's tone lowered.

A waiter dropped a heavy tray and the metal clatter rang out like an explosion. The paper napkin was in shreds. Nick dropped it on the seat beside him.

He shrugged. "It might be too soon."

"Nah." Brenden shook his head, gulped down the rest of his drink, and then wiped his mouth with the back of his hand. "We've been dating for over a year. It's *way* past time."

"Then why not just ask her?"

"I don't want to scare her off…" He rubbed the back of his neck with stiff fingers. "I love her, dude."

"Good for you." Nick sighed again. "Now can we please just get through lunch without all the *touchy-feelies*?"

***

If you've compared the two examples, then you can grasp how I wove in all the key elements needed to make a scene more tangible by adding Deeper POV, which includes "voice," setting, and sensory details. Even dialogue heavy scenes need some type of connection to the setting, so the reader can visualize the world in-which your characters populate. When describing the surroundings, I would include some visual elements, like the weather, or some of the five senses, or colors to make the setting come alive for the reader.

Some of you might've noticed that I added internal-thoughts to the second example too because when a writer is *showing* rather than *telling*, it helps to heighten the scene with additional context to make the scene more visual.

Writers can easily revise any dialogue scenes with "talking heads" in their current manuscript by inserting facial expressions, gestures, actions, and tones of voice within the conversation to make it more vivid and realistic. Also, the way a character speaks is an important part of making the story more lifelike and *show* the character's personality, so try not to be too formal in the speech.

Also, I'm not stating that writers can't use dialogue tags. Just in moderation. Remember that dialogue and Deep POV and action accelerate the story, while introspection (internal-babbling) and exposition slow it down. Action, tension, and dialogue are the best solutions to revising any pages of straight exposition that go on for longer than a page in your manuscript.

INTERNAL EXPOSITION

Quote: "Dialogue is a key part of any story and it's usually what readers find most engrossing. They might skim long descriptions, but when they get to someone speaking, that's where they'll get pulled back into the narrative."—*Moody Writing blog, mooderino*

Internal exposition is when a character is busy having a discussion inside their own head. It can provide vital information on how a character is reacting or feeling in regards to what's happening within the story, but it's a skill that if done incorrectly, often causes shallower writing.

Dialogue illustrates characterization quicker than any amount of exposition. If you disrupt the action and dialogue to include colossal chunks of detailed description or introspection, it will remove the reader from the story.

Yet, if I'm being honest, I have to admit that I've written a couple of bad novels, and had them published under a pen name many years ago. But that was long before I sharpened my writing skills and studied the art of fiction writing with a crazed intensity. I read articles on editing and revision, books on the craft, and studied style guides. I love learning new ways to improve my writing, so hopefully you gleam some insight from this chapter.

Long blocks of introspection can be dreary and slow down the pacing of a novel because it is passive, and often robs the reader of getting to know a character's personality and/or personal struggles by *showing* them.

INTERNAL EXPOSITION

While dialogue usually quickens the pace of the story, internal exposition slows it down.

So anytime a writer can revise introspection into dialogue, they should. Especially, when there are two or more characters in a scene.

Why have the character say it in his/her head, when it would be much more impactful to be shown in conversation?

Please carefully study this example…

SHALLOW: Henry said that he wanted to quit school. I wondered what Henry meant by that remark. Was he serious about dropping out of college?

DEEP POV: "I'm thinking about quitting school next semester," Henry said, shuffling his feet.

"Why would you do that?" I leaned back to stare into his face. "Are you serious about dropping out of college?"

Henry stared out the window and didn't answer.

***

The Deep POV example reveals more insight into the characters, rather than having the main character just thinking about it in his/her head.

Inner-monologue is one of the essential ingredients used to create a comprehensive story. Unfortunately, it's all too often one of the most misused elements in storytelling. Since internal-monologue is slower and can be boring for the reader, find ways to bring it to life through Deep POV, action, and dialogue. Don't let your character's mental babble (long blocks of introspection) go on for pages at a time without a break by either dialogue or action.

Whenever possible, I encourage writers to revise introspection (also known as internal exposition, interior monologue, inner-thoughts, or inner dialogue, etc.) into dialogue when there are more than two characters in a scene. I feel that dialogue is naturally faster paced and much more interesting to readers than long blocks of narrative.

I have included some examples on how to stay in Deep POV by turning boring exposition into attention-grabbing dialogue between two characters. (In the shallow example, I did not underline the obvious areas of shallower writing, but see if you can easily spot it.)

Please carefully compare these examples…

SHALLOW: I saw the pirate give me a mean look as he asked about his gold.

DEEP POV: The pirate's bushy brows furrowed. "Where be my gold, wench?"

SHALLOW: Martha McCray was angry and glared at me. I told her that I wasn't scared of her, but that was a lie.

DEEP POV: Martha McCray gave me the evil eye and I gave it right back to her. "You don't scare me," I lied.

SHALLOW: Damon wore a furious expression, and then he told Tyler that he was going to beat him up.

DEEP POV: Damon's eyes darkened and he rolled up his sleeves. "I hope you realize, I'm about to kick your ass, Tyler."

SHALLOW: Klaus stared at Stefan and he looked upset when he called him a liar and accused him of dating Caroline.

DEEP POV: Klaus gave him a hard, unblinking stare. "You lied! You *are* dating, Caroline."

SHALLOW: Emily felt angry. Why did he have to be such a jerk?

DEEP POV: Emily's lips flatten and she gets right in his face. "Why do you have to be such a jerk?"

SHALLOW: He seemed unsympathetic when he said that he would not help me with the corpse.

DEEP POV: His expression turned stony. "I'm *not* helping you bury the body. You're on your own this time."

SHALLOW: He was exasperated with the cops and demanded that they locate his daughter.

DEEP POV: He ground his teeth. "Find my daughter—*now!*"

SHALLOW: Amber looked indifferent when she complained that I always got my way.

DEEP POV: "Fine. Have it *your* way. You always do," she said, her tone laced with bitterness.

SHALLOW: Dorian was mad at her for asking if they could eat pasta again this evening.

DEEP POV: Dorian clenched his mouth tighter. "I do *not* want to eat pasta again tonight."

***

Writers never want the reader to feel removed from their story by too much introspection, instead of being deeply emerged within the fictional world that the author has worked so hard to create. Now I realize that writers can't turn all introspection into dialogue, but I encourage you to find clever ways to change the ones you can.

REALISTIC SETTINGS

Quote: "Don't tell me the moon is shining; show me the glint of light on the broken glass." —*playwright and short story writer, Anton Chekhov*

This chapter explains why Deep Point-of-View is one of the best editing techniques that you can use to create a realistic setting through sensory details without giving readers a weak or bland visual. The tools and tips in this section will demonstrate how writers can revise filter words used in shallower descriptions by transforming the setting into a much stronger visual.

By incorporating sensory details into a setting, along with vivid descriptions, writers can easily stay in Deeper POV. So, don't tell me that the house was on fire, instead *show* me the blaze and let me feel the heat on my skin.

Here are four simple techniques to make a setting more visual:

1) Make the landscape active by having characters interact within it.

2) Use color to add an extra depth to the scenery.

3) Make the setting a vital part of the scene.

4) Use the five senses to make the backdrop more realistic.

Sometimes writers need to simply and quickly convey details or information to the reader and move on, but if a writer applies Deeper POV on occasion, then they can bring the reader into the scene as intimately as possible.

For instance, when depicting a location/setting, describe things the way only your unique character sees them through their unique "voice" and include a few significant sensory details.

But when writers use "There was" or "There are" at the beginning of a sentence to describe an object or a setting, it creates a weak visual. These words add nothing to the scene, and sentences with these phrases can become wordy and flavorless.

Look at some examples…

WEAK: There are many witches living in the woods.

GOOD: Many witches live in the woods.

WEAK: There was a desk and a bed and lamp in the bedroom.

GOOD: The room contained an unmade bed, a dusty desk, and a tall brass lamp.

***

What usually draws a reader deeply into a story is the use of language and the way a writer describes a setting through the head and heart of their characters. One way to do that is to include a few of the five senses in every scene by describing them for the reader.

Please compare these next two examples…

SHALLOW:

There was a big table in the dining room and it looked like the wood was rotting. When I touched the surface it felt rough and dusty.

Now, the next example states the facts while giving readers enough of a visual to "see" the table in their mind's eye and experience the "touch" through sensory details without describing it in a boring way.

DEEPER POV:

A wooden table, its surface peeling away like brown bark, sat in the unused dining room. As my fingers trailed along its uneven surface, specks of dust coated my fingertips.

***

Quote: "…[if the writer] gives us such details about the streets, stores, weather, politics, and details about the looks, gestures, and experiences of his characters, we cannot help believing that the story is true." — *author "The Art of Fiction" John Gardner*

***

Showing is always much more powerful and explicit than just *telling* the reader, but it can often be more wordy. Yet I wouldn't let that hinder your use of this amazing tool. Sure, simply *telling* the reader can be a faster way to convey a lot of details about the setting, or things like a character's backstory and events; however, it is usually written in a way that is nondescript and slow and inelegant. It often creates long blocks of text without much "white space," or even "voice" within the narrative.

When readers see more than a page of thick text, they know it is straight exposition. That means no action or dialogue, which equals no forward movement of the plot. Which usually means: *boring*.

Have I made this offense? I'm sure I have, but I try very hard to avoid it.

My advice is to never push "pause" on your story to dump out long rambles of introspection or tedious facts about the setting. Although, I realize with some genres like high-fantasy or science fiction lots of world-building is needed, the descriptions can still be cleverly woven within the narrative.

Let's start with the description-dump. (In my guidebook, *The Writer's Guide to Vivid Scenes and Characters*, I provide even more examples on how to avoid doing an info-dump of description.)

When describing a room don't just catalog items or furniture like a monotonous list of inventory. To successfully create a visual scene, you need to balance the action of your characters with the description of the scene, along with the sensory details. Do not give your readers a weak visual through shallower writing.

(In the shallow example, I did not underline the obvious areas of shallower writing, but see if you can easily spot it.)

Please carefully compare these examples…

SHALLOW:

Sarah entered the room. There was a lamp, a couch, a tall grandfather clock and some letters on the table in the living room. Sarah saw some blood on the floor. She also observed a really bad smell. When she noticed the lifeless corpse, she got scared. When she heard the clock rang out the hour, she loudly screamed.

DEEP POV (sensory details):

Cautiously, Sarah tiptoed toward the dusty antique lamp and switched it on. Muted light illuminated the space. The stench of decay assaulted her senses as she weaved around the velvet sofa and past an oak table, which held a stack of unopened mail.

On the Oriental rug lay a bloody butcher's knife. Her eyes widened and her pulse thumped. Sarah backed up slowly into a towering grandfather clock. Her gaze followed the trail of blood over to a body, still and pale.

When the clock bonged midnight, she screamed.

***

Explanations of events are much more dramatic if your readers are directly involved and experiencing them along with the character. Readers may skim long pages of unbroken description; however, if it is slipped in as part of the action, then it is absorbed by the reader almost without being noticed, and enhances the scene. Always try to mix description with dialogue, actions, and the emotions of your characters.

VIVID DESCRIPTIONS

Quote: "...setting is more than a mere backdrop for action; it is an interactive aspect of your fictional world that saturates the story with mood, meaning, and thematic connotations." —*veteran writing instructor, Jessica Morrell*

I strongly recommend that writers briefly describe the setting at the beginning of each new scene or chapter to help the reader get a visual of the location. Also, writers should include a few vital details about the location by lacing the description throughout the dialogue and action to remind the reader where the scene takes place.

This excerpt should help writers get a clear idea on how to write a descriptive scene using the five senses (sensory details), action, dialogue, and Deep POV. And whenever you can describe something, try to see if it can be revised more effectively through the character actions, like in the example below from my paranormal romance novel, IMMORTAL ECLIPSE.

Please study this example…

DEEP POV:

As we finish touring the second wing, Mrs. Pratt finally opens a door to the left and switches on the light, illuminating a quaint bedroom. It's richly furnished and decorated in a startling, opulent blue softened by the flowered wallpaper.

The fireplace is flanked by a duo of overstuffed armchairs. Heavy damask curtains tied open with braided tassels cover the bay window that has a cushioned window seat. The huge bed looks soft and warm. With my gaze lingering on the stack of decorative pillows, I almost trip over my luggage and the boxes already placed beside it. My fingers trace the plush velvet comforter; I'll enjoy reading by the fire or snuggled in the bed on cold winter nights. The huge walk-in closet is, hands-down, the best feature of the room.

"This is the Blue Room. It has a private bathroom," she said.

"The Blue Room, huh? Wonder why they call it that?" A giggle erupts. Mrs. Pratt clucks her tongue, so I flatten my lips to stifle the laughter.

I wouldn't ordinarily choose blue, yet the color seems calming, like an antidote to the strange feelings I've been experiencing since arriving at Summerwind.

She moves to the door. "We thought it would be better if you were close to the staff's quarters in this wing. On the other side of the house, otherwise there'd be no one around to hear you scream in the darkness. At night..." She frowns and looks away.

I stare at her. *As if that doesn't sound ominous.*

***

Could you grasp how the scene from my novel is vivid and inciting? It lures the reader into the scene with a mixture of description, action, dialogue, and "voice."

Now these longer scenes below are both very different. The first is shallow and bland, with too much *telling* and gives readers a weak visual

Please examine these examples...

SHALLOW:

VIVID DESCRIPTIONS

I went into my father's vast bedroom that had been decorated in an historical style, and I saw a gold mirror over the headboard of the really big bed, and then I noticed a black and golden colored comforter. There was some red curtains hung in the windows. The walls were adorned with flowery wallpaper and there were some pictures of our family's home in the Hamptons.

Then I smelled my mother's perfume, but I realized it was just coming from the flowers that were placed in the room. I knew that my mother would have hated all the money wasted on this room. There was an expensive Persian rug bought for my father's new wife for their wedding anniversary on the floor.

I noticed there was a big screen TV on the far wall and it was the only contemporary exclusion to the bedroom's antique furnishings.

That shallow scene is boring, passive, and just states the facts. But this second Deeper POV scene has "voice" and action and stays in close-and-personal.

DEEP POV (sensory details):

Sighing heavily, I hesitated in the doorway of my father's gaudily redecorated suite. I rolled my eyes as I took in the vast bedroom decorated in the style of Louis XVI, with a gilt-framed mirror hanging over the headboard of the king-sized, black-and-gold-upholstered bed.

Is he for real?

I stepped inside, my fingers lightly trailing along the flowered wallpaper, and paused to study the photos of the family's beach house in the Hamptons. At least my father hadn't removed those…

When I turned, my shoulder brushed against the red velvet curtains covering the windows. When the fragrance of lilacs drifted over from the flower arrangement on the dresser, my heart stuttered. The scent reminded me of my dearly departed mother. And she would be turning over in her grave at all the money my father had wasted on this luxurious room.

I shook my head when I caught sight of the Persian rug bought at auction from Sotheby's as a gift to my father's gold-digging third wife for their fifth wedding anniversary.

Glancing upward at the wall, I grunted at the lone modern exception to the room's historical décor—a fifty-inch plasma TV.

***

Now ask yourself: which example caused more impact?

Words and phrases with powerful sensory connotations always increase the chances of producing an empathic response in the reader. Some things to continuously consider whenever you're revising the setting:

Do the word choices paint vivid images in the reader's mind?

 Do the descriptions place the reader in the scene?

Do they make the reader an active participant in the story instead of a mere observer?

It's easy for writers in early drafts to depend on simple, straightforward descriptions of rooms and settings. Using Deep POV does add more words to your scenes, but the experience you'll give your readers will be well worth it.

DRAMATIC SCENES

Quote: "Let your description unfold as a character moves throughout the scene. Consider which details your character would notice immediately, and which might register more slowly. Let your character encounter those details interactively." — *columnist, Moira Allen, editor of Writing World*

Deep POV just means painting a more vivid picture for your readers through your POV character. How they "see" the world and describe it for the readers is what gives a writer their own unique style and the character its "voice."

When writing in Deeper POV, a writer should always include the five senses and other sensory details to make the scene very visual and more *real* for the reader.

Here are two different scenes of a girl walking through a residential neighborhood that were taken from one of my short stories. The first is written in a *telling* style (weak visual). Telling does convey the facts and details, but it does so in a flavorless and nondescript way. (I have underlined what I consider to be shallower writing.)

Please carefully study this longer example...

SHALLOW:

Andrea <u>noticed</u> that Elm Street <u>looked</u> deserted. The residential houses <u>looked</u> very quiet and unoccupied inside. <u>There were</u> no other people around her, and it made her <u>feel uneasy</u>.

She realized the sky was a very white color. Andrea was feeling more anxious as if someone was watching her. She walked quickly down the street and she heard the fallen leaves crunch.

She saw a woman hanging clothes on a line. The woman noticed Andrea walk by and lifted her head. Andrea could smell the scent of laundry. Andrea realized the smell reminded her of her mother.

"Hello," Andrea said timidly.

The woman looked at her and she said coldly, "Good morning."

Andrea saw big truck drive past with a gassy smell from the exhaust. It made her cough. Andrea looked around. She realized that the woman hanging the laundry was gone.

I need to get to Rachel's house, she thought. Before they find out that I left.

She turned around and felt her body collide into a tree. She hurt her arm on a branch. She walked faster until she saw her best friend's house further down the street. Andrea stopped and let out a heavy sigh of relief. Her friend lived near the high school. There was a lot of houses that looked the same.

Andrea heard a car turn the corner at a slow pace, and she suddenly felt scared so she ran to the house. She felt herself trip and fall down. She was feeling apprehensive when she stood up and then she tasted blood because she had bitten her lip.

Suddenly, the driver started to drive very fast toward her.

She got frightened and she ran to the porch, then she knocked on the door. "I need help!" she shouted fearfully.

***

Now please compare the next example revised with Deeper POV. And remember that applying any of the five senses to a scene will deepen the experience for the reader, and in some cases, even induce an emotional response. Also, try to include emotional reactions, internal-dialogue, and physical actions to spice up your descriptions and avoid a boring list of details.

DEEP POV:

Elm Street seemed deserted. The suburban homes appeared strange and silent, like houses in an abandoned ghost town. Andrea hurried down the sidewalk, her dirty sneakers crunching on the crisp autumn leaves. The sky was not cerulean, but milky and opaque, like a giant sink turned upside down.

She slowed her steps, a cold tremor racing up her spine. She glanced over her shoulder for the hundredth time.

Just get to Rachel's house. No one is following you. They don't know that you've escaped…

Her gaze darted left, then right. From someone's backyard, a big dog barked, the noise echoing off the vacant-looking homes. Andrea quickened her pace, shoving her hands into the pockets of her winter coat.

A woman hanging clothes on a line, glanced up as she passed by, and the scent of fresh laundry and fabric softener polluted the air. Andrea smiled. The floral scent brought back memories of helping her mother with the housework.

"Hello," Andrea said with a slight smile.

"Good morning," the plump woman said, her tone cold and unfriendly.

A delivery truck rumbled down the tree-lined street, spewing noxious exhaust. Coughing, Andrea peered behind her again. The street remained empty. But the woman hanging laundry was gone.

Andrea turned so abruptly that her body smacked into a tree. The rough bark of the birch chafed the tender flesh of her arm.

Rubbing the spot, she quickened her steps until the house came into view. The tension in her shoulders slightly diminished. She was safe now. Her best friend only lived two streets away from the high school, but the walk felt like it had taken hours. The cookie-cutter house resembled all the others in the neighborhood, except for the shabby porch swing and the flaking yellow paint.

A car slowly turned the corner, and Andrea's heartbeat ramped up. *They had found her!*

She sprinted toward the house. Tripping on a loose shoelace, she fell forward onto her knees. Shakily, she stood and ran her tongue over her lips, the coppery tang of blood filling her mouth.

The driver hit the gas and the car flew down the street, coming straight at her.

Dashing up the rickety steps, she pounded a fist on the door. "Help me, please!"

***

After reading the second scene, which do you think painted a more vivid picture for the reader?

Incorporating Deeper POV in your fiction writing is a great way of making any scene multi-dimensional.

Here are a few more examples of Deeper POV and how it applies to setting. The shallower sentences are considered *telling* the reader information by writing descriptions in a straightforward manner, which is fine on occasion if needed, but I want to inspire writers to *dig deeper* to make their fictional world as three-dimensional as possible.

Please take a look at these examples…

SHALLOW: I thought the forest looked tall and huge.

DEEP POV: Within the vast forest, the towering trees swayed in the breeze, their spindly branches waving hello.

SHALLOW: He noticed that the room was sparse and it felt cold.

DEEP POV: A chill shivered over his skin. The vacant room seemed lonely and unused.

SHALLOW: There were very tall buildings in this part of the city.

DEEP POV: The soaring buildings with their concrete heads in the clouds cast long shadows on the sidewalks below.

SHALLOW: The hillsides looked enormous and they had dry grass.

DEEP POV: The rolling hills resembled an endless expanse of balding grey heads.

SHALLOW: There was a bad storm coming.

DEEP POV: The horizon lit up with white light followed by the loud grumble of thunder.

SHALLOW: The night looked dark and it had a big moon.

DEEP POV: The darkness fell quickly like a shadowy blanket over the land and moonlight struck the sleeping homes like cold silver.

SHALLOW: There were big homes that looked affluent and expensively furnished in this area.

DEEP POV: The area was dominated by impressive mansions with fluted Corinthian columns on the lower and upper stories.

***

Here is another excerpt taken from my NA series, *Sorority Row* that shows writers how to describe a setting by adding sensory details through Deeper POV.

Please closely examine this "setting" example…

DEEP POV:

My new roommate and I were polar opposites. Her name was Vanessa Carmichael and she apparently guzzled energy drinks by the gallon, and her tousled copper hair looked like the "before" picture in a Pantene commercial. At least she seemed nice and normal. I wouldn't have to worry about her doing anything weird like stealing my underwear or taking cell phone pictures of me while I slept to post on Instagram.

Our shared room was enormous compared to my old dormitory. Stevenson Hall had an ancient brick façade, but they'd remodeled the interior to create larger rooms. Apparently, not all dorm rooms resembled dank prison cells with painted cinder block walls. The rooms were more like an expensive apartment than regular campus housing. Even better, the dorms had single-gender floors.

While Vanessa talked a mile a minute, folded clothes on her bed, and sipped a Red Bull, I inspected her—*incredibly* cluttered—side of the room. I flicked a glance at the red poster with that lame phrase "Keep Calm and Carry On" in white lettering over her headboard. Vanessa had fastened a corkboard to the wall above her desk, pinned with snapshots of her high school debate team and blue ribbon awards for science and math. Piles of Old Navy hoodies and graphic shirts and bell-bottom cords were scattered on her dark green comforter.

***

After reading that last scene, did you notice how I weaved a combination of description, introspection, and "voice" into the narrative?

DRAMATIC SCENES

So instead of just describing something in bland detail, writers should try to lace in some of the five senses, emotional responses, "voice," and action to make the description of a setting even more powerful and visual for their readers.

Please remember as you revise your own work that these are only guidelines and examples meant to help writers develop their own style in crafting dynamic settings and locations.

CHARACTERIZATION

Quote: "...Voice is the "secret power" of great writing." —*Bestselling author, James Scott Bell*

Using the methods outlined in this chapter will help writers create three-dimensional characters who will come alive within their complex fictional worlds by captivating their readers with deeper layers of characterization.

One of the critical elements to differentiate good writing from just average storytelling relates to how the writer handles the point-of-view. That's why, I strongly feel that Deep POV is tightly connected to *voice*, which is a big part of characterization in my opinion.

In this chapter, I'll try my best to explain "voice" in the terms that I understand them, and clarify how important it is to convey that through Deeper POV.

I consider the phrase "show, don't tell" to primarily specify going deeper into a character's POV. It isn't just stating the facts or information, but giving the reader a glimpse of the world through the senses of the POV character. It allows the reader to become more immersed within the storyline and feel a stronger connection to the character(s).

A lot of manuscripts that I've edited over the years were lacking any "voice." So it is my belief that some writers don't fully comprehend what it means, or how it can deepen the characterization and give your writing a distinctive style.

So let me put it this way…just as everyone has their own characteristic way of speaking or expressing themselves, a writer's characters should also have a distinctive "voice" that clearly comes across in the narrative.

I advise the writers that I work with to strengthen "voice" by using phrasing that reflects the overall tone of their book, along with the POV character's unique personality. How the character reacts or responds in any given situation should be distinctive to their individuality. So choose your nouns and verbs carefully. Being specific about even small details like the weather, description of settings, or objects can create a stronger impression of that character's POV.

These next two longer scenes were each taken from one of my novels, UNDER SUNLESS SKIES. The first one lacks any real emotional descriptions and has no "voice." (I have underlined what I consider to be shallower writing.)

Please carefully compare these examples…

SHALLOW:

I really hate my boring math class. I'm not listening to Mrs. Brooks talk about angles and measurements because I do not care. I will never use this type of math in the real world. I look up at the clock. There is fifteen minutes before the bell rings.

I feel bored and sleepy. I put my elbows on my desktop, and then I put my forehead into my hands and I close my eyes. Mrs. Brooks continues to talk about equations and her loud voice is irritating.

"If Miss Masterson paid attention in class," Mrs. Brooks says, "I wouldn't have to re-explain how the trigonometric ratios are derived from triangle similarity considerations today."

I don't glance up, because I don't want to see her ugly face.

"Are you paying attention, Miss Masterson, or are you in a world of your own again?"

I hear several students laugh. I feel my cheeks heat with embarrassment.

I still do not look up at her unattractive features. "No, I'm not preoccupied," I say sullenly.

"Then would you like to share with the class what you were doing that is more important than listening to my lecture?" Mrs. Brooks asks impatiently.

Now I feel enraged as I lift my head. My classmates laugh, and I hear them move in their seats as they turn to look at me.

***

The revised scene has been revised with Deep POV and it has "voice," tension-soaked dialogue, introspection, and characterization. It is much longer and more detailed, but creates a much more vivid scene in the reader's mind.

Please study this rewritten example…

DEEP POV:

Now I'm trapped sitting in class, not really listening to Mrs. Longwinded Brooks drone on about angles and measurements. I glare at the back of Hayden's head, silently willing him to turn around and acknowledge me. It feels like I'm a minor character being faded out of a TV series, as if I've had one minute of total screen time with Hayden.

Clenching my jaw, every muscle in my body feels taut. I *hate* how he just blew me off. I *hate* that my parents aren't trustworthy. I *hate* Zach and his fat-shaming slurs. I *hate* the mysterious person leaving threats in my locker. And I *hate* this uncomfortable metal desk with gum stuck to the side of it.

The seconds tick by. I glance at the clock hanging on the wall. Thirty-nine tortuous minutes before class ends. I want to be anywhere but here.

CHARACTERIZATION

I almost wish demons would attack the school and drag me to Hell, or worse…somewhere where there's no chocolate. Now that would be pure evil!

Mrs. Brooks lectures on equations and her shrill voice sounds like braying sheep in heat. A sharp throbbing spreads across my forehead. I rest my elbows on the desk, then lower my head into my palms and close my eyes.

"If Miss Masterson would be more attentive…" Mrs. Brooks walks down the aisle, the rubber soles of her cheap pumps squeaking on the floor. "Then I wouldn't have to waste everyone's time by re-explaining how the trigonometric ratios derive from triangle similarity considerations." Her footsteps pause at my desk.

I keep my head down, my eyes squeezed shut. If I lift my head and look at her, I'll be compelled to stare at that mole on her chin. The one with the long, black witch hair sticking out of it.

"Are you paying attention, Miss Masterson?" She taps an impatient foot, then moves further along the aisle. "I do *not* tolerate sleeping in my classroom."

Jeez. Adults think they're *so* superior all the time. Just like my lying-deceiving parents.

"You do know that it's not Halloween, right?" Emma says in a loud whisper, twisting in her seat. "You look like a wannabe vampire in that strange getup."

The sarcastic edge in her voice grates on my last nerve.

With my head still cradled in my hands, I'm feeling the height of bitchiness coming on strong. So my style's dark with a side of edgy? What's the issue?

Slowly, I lift my head and shoot Emma a heated glare. "If you must know, it's Halloween *every* day at my house."

Emma's pink mouth gapes, then snaps shut. Most of my classmates turn in their seats to watch the impending showdown. Several kids even stop scribbling in their notebooks. Hayden hangs his head and shakes it as if in disapproval.

"You call *that* style? More like chubby couture." Emma snickers. "You must've read one too many Anne Rice novels. Unless you're praying you'll never come in contact with direct sunlight."

My cheeks heat, my skin piping so hot it feels as if I've stuck my face in an oven.

Several students giggle. Hayden's shoulders stiffen. Emma smiles and her best friend Kaitlyn rolls her squinty eyes.

I wonder if Emma is the blackmailer. Or maybe it's her evil sidekick, Kaitlyn. Their combined Sloane-hate places them on my *Do Not Trust* list. I size Emma up. She's wearing what might be the most preppy outfit I've ever seen outside an 80's Brat Pack movie, a white button-up shirt under a pink cardigan and capris with plaid flats. She almost looks too innocent to be a suspect, but her bitchiness is singeing through her good girl persona.

"Emma, cut it out," Hayden says under his breath.

Mrs. Brooks crosses both arms over her chest, obviously expecting me to apologize. "Are you quite done disrupting my class, Miss Masterson?"

Usually, I'm incapable of making people feel bad. Even if they're in the process of mocking me. Not today.

"Yeah, can I go back to taking my nap now?" I yawn, then mumble, "As if I'll ever use this stupid math anyway."

"Get out of my classroom!" Mrs. Brooks points an index finger at the door. "Go to the principal's office."

***

CHARACTERIZATION

Besides all the other key ingredients a writer needs to enhance a scene, "voice" is among the most vital to Deeper POV. Spend some time getting to know your characters. Fill out character interviews and profiles to gain some insight into their temperaments and personalities, and then let that shine through in your narrative by use of the Deep POV technique.

Each character's voice personifies more than their speech or internal-thoughts. The narrative should express it as well. When you write a scene in a certain character's POV, each sentence in that scene has to read as though it is being experienced, felt, and expressed by that character.

One easy way to add "voice" to any character is to incorporate a few personal quirks, or unique phrases, rather than impersonal or formal syntax. Strive to include words meaningful to the character's personality and world views within the storyline.

CHARACTER VOICE

Quote: "Clichéd, superficial characters are the mark of a poor writer. A great character can save an overly simplistic plot, but no amount of action will make up for unbelievable or shallow characters. A good character has the same kind of depth, complexity, and believability as an interesting person." —*author Magdalena Ball*

Like I mentioned in the last chapter, realistic "voice" is the characteristic speech and thought patterns of your narrator, like a persona. Because voice has so much to do with the reader's experience of a work of literature, it is one of the most important elements in any piece of writing to create three-dimensional characters.

I have included two scenes to show writers the difference between "voice" and bland narration. The first one has shallow writing with lots of *telling* and hardly any "voice" or sensory details. (In the shallow example, I did not underline the obvious areas of shallower writing, but see if you can easily spot it.)

Please carefully compare these examples…

SHALLOW:

Sam Harrington heard the door open and he looked up from his comic book where he worked at the Book Shark. He saw a fat man with brown hair and eyes and a big nose walk into the bookstore. Sam noticed that the man was wearing jeans with socks and sandals and a T-shirt. He watched him walk past the bookcases and then he went toward Sam.

"Can I help you?" Sam asked in curiosity as the man approached.

"Here to pick up my book," he said loudly. "My name is McGrath."

"Sorry, this week's order hasn't come in yet. Do you wanna give us a call next—" Sam started to say but McGrath cut him off, so he stopped talking. (*None of this is needed at the end of the dialogue.*)

McGrath leaned across the counter and Sam thought he looked very angry. "What do you mean my book is not here in the store?" he asked raucously.

Sam opened his mouth to respond but stopped. He was nervous because the man was so furious and Sam didn't know what to do.

McGrath's face looked red and he tried to relax. "Where is my book?" he repeated more calmly.

Now, this second scene has been rewritten to clearly reveal "voice" in the speech, internal-thoughts, and the narrative, and it even shows a Deeper POV.

Please compare this revised example…

DEEP POV:

It was a slow day at the *Book Shark*. Sam Harrington stood at one end of the bookstore in the self-help section, stuffing last week's shipment of books onto the shelves.

The bell over the door chimed and Sam glanced up. A waft of car exhaust and brewing coffee from the Starbucks next door entered the room as the door creaked opened.

A customer entered the shop and maneuvered around the bookshelves with a heavy limp. When Sam caught a glimpse of the man's clothing, his eyebrows rose. It was the middle of summer and the guy had on jeans with socks and leather Birkenstocks. *Crazy.*

Sam hurried past a pimply teenager sitting on the floor, reading a book and an old lady with blue hair—*well, it looked blue*—scanning the covers of the romance novels on sale.

Sam walked behind the counter and faced the new customer. "Can I help you, sir?"

"Here to pick up my book," the man said in a gruff tone. "Name's McGrath."

"Sorry, this week's order hasn't come in yet. Do you wanna give us a call next—"

"Whaddya mean my book didn't arrive?" The stocky man leaned over the glass counter, and glared at Sam. His dark brown hair fell into his beady hazel eyes, and McGrath pushed the strands aside with a pudgy hand. He lowered his head, and blew out a breath soured by stale beer and cigarettes.

Sam's shoulders slumped. *Great. Another pissed off customer. It's not my fault the shipment is always freaking late.*

McGrath straightened, tugging at the collar of his faded Aerosmith T-shirt as if in an attempt to collect himself. His bulbous nose twitched. "*Now.* Where's my book on ritual human sacrifices, boy?"

***

Each example presents the same scenario, but how the character relates it to the reader and the way the scene is *shown* through the words used to convey the character's reactions and views is what reveals "voice." The first one is *telling* the reader in a bland way, but in the second version, we get a glimpse of the character's unique personality through Deeper POV.

"Voice" can add an extra layer of characterization to any novel, and it can avoid making your character seem like the dreaded Mary-Sue type.

CHARACTER VOICE

Yes, writing with Deeper POV and "voice" often adds more words to your prose, but it is far more interesting and reveals a character's personality aka "voice."

Let's use another example in order to clarify what I mean. Here's a snippet from my science fiction novel, LOST IN STARLIGHT, before revision (no "voice"). The heroine has lost her cell phone and she suspects that the new guy at school has stolen it. (I have underlined what I consider to be shallower writing.)

Please study and compare these examples…

SHALLOW:

The next day, I go past my typical lunch table. I disregard my friends as they watch me I walk across the cafeteria. I am furious with Hayden Lancaster. I had no phone last night and I felt weird without it. This is the first chance I've had all day to talk to him. If I'd known where Hayden lived, I would've gone to his house in anger last night.

How did he take my iPhone? He must have removed the device from my purse while I was talking to Devin, I thought.

Viola sees me walk by, and says silently, *Where are you going?* And I point a finger in Hayden's direction.

I notice sunlight shines through the windows. I smell pizza and I hear the sound of a soda can opening

Hayden is sitting alone with a bowl of pasta. Two drumsticks are near the bag. I'm still so infuriated with him. I see that he is wearing pants and a black shirt.

I set my lunchbox on the table and then sit down. I hear the loud sound it makes and see how it causes people to look at us, but it doesn't bother me.

"Where's my phone?" I ask angrily.

I watch Hayden sit back. "What's up, Emo Chick?" he asks casually.

"Emo? Really?" I say with irritation.

I watch him look at me in my outfit. Why is he staring at me like that? What is wrong with my fashion sense?

"Okay, then, Goth Girl," he says flippantly.

I hate stereotypes, I think to myself.

DEEP POV ("voice" and characterization):

The next day, I bypass my usual table at lunch, ignoring my friends and their curious stares as I storm across the cafeteria, swinging my Monster High lunchbox like a weapon. I have an animalistic urge to destroy Hayden Flippin' Lancaster. Being without my phone all night felt like I was missing an actual limb. I even tried calling my cell, but no one answered.

This is the first chance I've had all day to confront him. If I'd known where Hayden lived, I would've been kicking down his door last night.

I just don't know exactly *how* he managed to steal my iPhone undetected. But he must've snatched it out of my purse when my back was turned while I was talking to Devin in the hallway. I should've expected this when I stupidly blabbed about filming his epic dog rescue.

Viola watches me march past, mouthing: *Where are you going?* And I stab a finger in Hayden's direction.

Super Boy thinks he's so smart. *Well, he's just met his Kryptonite!*

Sunlight trickles through the windows, dancing over the tables and the tacky orange chairs. The nauseating odor of greasy pizza wafts from the kitchen area, and the hiss of a soda can opening resonates throughout the crowded space.

Hayden's sitting alone with his sack lunch and a plastic bowl of pasta. Two grungy drumsticks rest against the bag. Guess where I'd like to

CHARACTER VOICE

stick those. I try not to think about how hot he looks in urban decayed pants and a black V-neck shirt. He might be the silent, stoic type of man candy, but I'm about to crack his tough guy shell.

I drop my lunchbox on the table with a *bang* and slide onto an empty seat. The clatter draws attention, but I don't care about making a scene.

"Where's my phone?" I demand.

Hayden nonchalantly leans back and crosses his legs in that dude-*esque*, one ankle-over-the-opposite-thigh. "What's up, Emo Chick?"

"Emo? Really?"

He checks me out from head-to-toe in my aquamarine dress with a white skull pattern, black knee-high socks, and riding boots. My cute Rock Rebel studded chain purse rests on one shoulder, and my hair is styled in a high ponytail. I am *so* looking glam-rock today!

"Okay, then, Goth Girl."

Even worse.

* * *

Now one last piece of advice, I think even secondary characters should have a distinct personality that separates them from other characters.

The subsequent excerpt is taken from my new adult romance novel, SMASH INTO YOU, and it shows how even a secondary character has her own personality. Vanessa (the secondary character) has a very unique voice, as well as my spunky narrator.

Please closely examine this example with "voice" for both characters…

DEEP POV:

"…then I laughed so hard, I nearly peed in my hemp underwear…*Hello? Are you even listening to me?*"

I glanced up. "Oh. Yeah. Sorry. What were you saying?"

Vanessa pushed up her glasses. "You don't care that I took the right side? Because I like being closer to the window and you came a day late—"

"It's fine," I said, shifting on my bed and lowering the novel I'd been reading.

My new home. This square, off-white room with its squeaky wooden floor only had two closets that barely fit all my clothes and shoes. My gaze swept over my side of the room, which resembled an ad from an IKEA catalog, decorated in girly pastel colors of turquoise, white, and pink, with two prints of Vincent van Gogh's artwork gracing the walls. Over my headboard, I'd hung a string of twinkle lights.

I fluffed the row of pillows behind my head and stretched out my legs. I'd loved shopping for all my new stuff. My dad just handed over his credit card with a warning not to go *too* crazy. It allowed me to imagine a completely different life to go with my brand-new persona.

"If it's gonna be an issue, I can move my stuff," Vanessa said.

"I don't care. Honest."

Vanessa took a swig of her drink. She blinked her big owlish eyes behind square-framed glasses. "Awesome. My roommate last year was *sooo* picky. She was always borrowing my stuff without asking, and making out with her emo boyfriend…"

Chatty Vanessa would be my cellmate for the next year. *Oh, yay.* I already wanted to duct tape her mouth shut.

* * *

This additional chapter on "voice" should help writers to really understand how to depict a character's distinctive personality within the narrative.

FIRST-PERSON POV

Quote: "Emotions are critical to making a character feel *real*, but describing them from afar can sometimes leave a reader feeling a little disconnected from that character. The descriptions don't feel like a character feeling, but like the author *telling* the reader how the character feels."
—*author and blogger, Janice Hardy*

As requested by a number of writers, I have included a chapter on writing Deep POV through the eyes and ears and senses of a first-person narrator.

When you're writing in first-person point-of-view always strive to stay in Deeper POV. Actually, most editors and bestselling authors would agree that first-person narratives are the easiest way to avoid *telling*.

While writing in deep first-person POV, try to make sure that each scene is intimate and detailed for your readers by being specific whenever possible and revising any filter words.

Even with first-person POV, you're never limited in describing a character's facial expressions or emotions. Although, the first-person narrator can't see his or her own face, a writer can still vividly describe the character's expressions and emotions and body language.

There are many ways to "show" reactions or emotions for a first-person POV narrator, instead of just *telling* the reader what the character's emotions are directly. Writers should revise any shallow words like "felt / feel" to describe an emotion.

Please compare these examples…

SHALLOW: Staring into the utter darkness, I <u>felt</u> my palms grow damp.

DEEP POV: Staring into the utter darkness, my palms grew damp.

SHALLOW: I <u>felt</u> my face get hot in embarrassment.

DEEP POV: My cheeks burned at his rude remark.

SHALLOW: I <u>felt</u> sweaty and nervous before the talent audition.

DEEP POV: Sweat beaded my forehead and I restlessly paced backstage.

SHALLOW: I <u>felt</u> sad on my long walk home.

DEEP POV: My lips pulled downward at the corners and I blinked back tears while I drudged home.

SHALLOW: I <u>felt</u> really angry at Amy for forgetting my birthday again.

DEEP POV: I stomped my foot. "Seriously, Amy? You forgot my birthday day *again*?"

SHALLOW: I <u>felt</u> lust fill my body when I <u>saw</u> Kenneth.

DEEP POV: A burst of sizzling desire heated my body as Kenneth entered the room.

***

I mainly write in first-person and that's why most of the excerpts are taken from my own work as examples of Deeper POV.

Here is another one with too many filtering references…

SHALLOW:

I could not see in the darkness as I moved through the brambles.

This is really creepy, I thought.

There was an old farmhouse somewhere near Maple Drive. I thought I would be okay if I could just find the path. Suddenly, I saw headlights, blinding me. Then I heard a car on the road and I felt my body freeze. My legs felt wobbly and I knew my breathing had increased. I heard the car rev its engine and it sounded scary.

I knew I had to move out of the way when I noticed the old car drive past.

Here is the scene revised without the filter words…

DEEP POV:

I stumbled in the darkness through the brambles.

This is really creepy.

An old farmhouse sat somewhere near Maple Drive. I'd be okay if I could just find the path. Suddenly, headlights shone in my eyes, blinding me. The crunch of tires on the gravel road caused me to freeze in my tracks. My legs wobbled and my breathing sped up. The car revs its engine ominously.

I leaped out of the way just as the rusty Buick rumbled past.

***

Since I primarily write in first-person POV, I don't think it's necessarily incorrect for my characters to "interpret" the expressions or body language of another character as long as they aren't too specific.

This next excerpt is from, LOST in STARLIGHT, which will show writers how to lace "voice" with action and humor into your first-person descriptions. This example shows embarrassment (along with other emotions) without stating the feeling.

Please study this first-person POV scene…

DEEP POV:

"It's just…" His voice is soft. "I want to be clear, we can't be anything more than friends, Sloane…you'll only end up collateral damage."

I frown. "Collateral damage? What the hell does that even mean?"

Hayden takes a shallow breath. "Dammit, I'm saying this all wrong."

"Ya think?"

"It's to protect you."

I arch an eyebrow. "From?"

"I can't…" He groans and his long bangs flop onto his forehead, nearly obscuring his anxious stare. "I want you to be safe and I can be really impulsive. It's just that when I catch the way you look at me sometimes, I get the feeling you'd like something more than friendship."

Oh. My. God.

Am I that obvious?

An even hotter flush steals across my face and sweeps down my neck. I am beyond mortified. This is bad. So bad. I need to take my fragile, wounded ego and go hide. For, oh…like a decade.

For a moment, my vision goes black and red. My body shudders. I need to get away from him. *Now.* I step stiffly forward and trip on my shoelace, staggering off the curb and onto the pavement…

***

FIRST-PERSON POV

Here are more examples of writing Deeper POV from the first-person perspective. Please carefully compare these examples…

SHALLOW: I felt light-headed and I wanted to throw up.

DEEP POV: A bout of nausea struck my senses and my body swayed.

SHALLOW: I was scared of the dark and I forgot my flashlight.

DEEP POV: My heart rate kicked into overdrive. The light switch didn't work, and I had stupidly forgotten to bring a flashlight.

SHALLOW: I was shocked to discover that I won the contest.

DEEP POV: The breath caught in my lungs. *I'd won the contest!*

SHALLOW: I became thoughtful. "Tell me more," I inquired.

DEEP POV: I frowned, tapping a finger on my chin. "Tell me more."

SHALLOW: My face had a panicked look on it.

DEEP POV: Every molecule in my body turned icy, and my expression froze.

SHALLOW: I'm really worried about Karen's illness.

DEEP POV: My palms are sweating. The doctors just *had* to find a way to save Karen.

SHALLOW: I knew my face was pinched in disgust. (Cliché)

DEEP POV: My lips turned downward and I turned away.

SHALLOW: I heard Janice running up the driveway.

DEEP POV: Janice's sneakered feet pounded the gravel on the driveway.

SHALLOW: I saw Hank stealing a candy bar.

DEEP POV: Out of the corner of my eye, I caught Hank stuffing a candy bar into his pocket.

SHALLOW: "You are a liar," I said, my facial expression turning into a scowl.

DEEP POV: "You're such a liar!" I said, rolling my eyes.

***

Could you grasp how removing filtering references can instantly deepen the POV?

Here is an excerpt taken from the first chapter of my young adult paranormal romance novel, BEAUTIFULLY BROKEN, (free to download or read on wattpad for a limited time) to give writers another example on how to cleverly write Deeper POV from a first-person narrator. The character becomes nervous and frightened when she suspects that she's not alone in her bedroom, but the emotions are never blatantly stated in this short scene.

Please carefully examine this example…

DEEP POV:

For as long as I could remember, I'd heard whispers in the shadows. Black, twisting shapes that chilled my blood. Slithering through the night, their greenish skin, crimson eyes, and sharp claws were illuminated even in the dark.

Sunlight often meant the difference between life and death.

I normally felt safe during the day, with the heat of the sun brushing my skin, so that morning, when the shadows showed up in my bedroom, I barely recognized their eerie whispering.

The desk lamp flickered, startling me. I stared at the last line I'd typed on my essay for English class, one hand hovering over the keyboard.

Homework could wait.

I raised my head and closed the laptop. My heart hammered. A hint of chilling menace climbed up my spine. Finishing homework was the last thing on my mind.

The spooky, inhuman whispering grew more intense.

Setting the laptop aside, I jumped off the bed, nearly tripping over my long nightgown. I scanned the dark bends and edges of the room. The swirling azure colors of the witch-ball suspended over the bed rotated in a slow circle. I got down on my hands and knees to check under the bed. Nothing.

The closet door was open a crack. I stood up and wavered, shoulders hitching.

I hesitated for a second before walking over to the closet and kicking the door open. On tiptoes, I leaned over the threshold, stretching to grasp the brass chain, and then gave it a yank. Light bled across dirty laundry, illuminating metal hangers scattered on the floor. Dusty board games littered the shelf, and haphazardly hanging clothes swayed on the bar. My fuzzy bunny slippers stared upward with glassy button eyes. Nothing unusual.

So why was I so freaked?

The feeling, indistinct but ominous, lingered like the remnants of a bad dream. I couldn't isolate the source. But something felt *wrong*.

The closet light and lamp blew out. As I turned around, my peripheral vision caught a maelstrom of shadows. Things withered within it. Something snaked past my leg….

***

There is one rhetorical question in this scene, but besides that, it stays in a very tight and close viewpoint.

Now I challenge you to rewrite a scene in your own story and use Deep POV to get inside the head of your first-person narrator and keep your readers in close-and-personal.

One last word of advice, the first-person narrator can *only* reveal his/her own thoughts and feelings and reactions, and then merely assume or guess the responses or meanings of facial expressions of the other characters. A first-person character is <u>not</u> a mind-reader, so be careful of this POV violation.

The next few chapters will cover on how to revise "stating a feeling or reaction" instead of *telling* the reader what the character is feeling. All of the Deep POV examples in this handbook have already been used in my published novels or short stories, so you'll need to come up with your own unique variations.

CHARACTER DESCRIPTIONS

Quote: "The characters in our stories, songs, poems, and essays embody our writing. They are our words made flesh. Sometimes they even speak for us, carrying much of the burden of plot, theme, mood, idea, and emotion. But they do not exist until we describe them on the page. Until we anchor them with words, they drift, bodiless and ethereal. They weigh nothing; they have no voice."—*excerpt from "Word Painting" by Rebecca McClanahan*

This chapter focuses on ways that writers can describe a character's physical appearance though Deep POV. (Some of these topics are also covered in my handbook, "*Craft Vivid Scenes and Dynamic Characters,*" but I have expanded some of that information in this guide.)

Character descriptions can be tough to write and so many writers neglect to add physical descriptions to the narrative. When we describe a character's physical appearance, sometimes precise facts about their features, or height and weight, are not quite visual enough.

How you ever read a book and visualized the main character as a lanky, brown-haired nerd, only to discover fifty pages into the story that the character was a brawny, tan, blond guy?

And if writers use clichéd, colorless descriptions they can be too generic, and they don't really help the reader get a clear image of the characters. Writers should describe the characters as early as possible in a manuscript, but avoid creating a boring list of attributes by using weaker descriptive words. Now, I know some of you will argue that other published writers do this, but most professional editors will consider this to be lazy writing. So avoid using descriptors that simply label a character, *short, fat, young, old,* or *ordinary,* which do not create a clear image.

Readers need vibrant images and physical details to envision fictional characters. So I suggest thoughtfully selecting only those descriptors that evoke the clearest, most revealing impressions. Also, writers should allow their descriptions to multitask to also reveal (*show* rather than *tell*) more about a character's personality and background.

Please take a look at these examples…

SHALLOW:

John was slender and he had very long legs. He had messy brown colored hair. John's lips looked really thin. He usually wore baggy clothes and a baseball cap. He hated to go to work meetings. His boss gave him a dirty look when he yawned at one of the meetings.

DEEP POV:

Man, I hate these boring sale's meetings.

John stretched his long legs under the table and loudly yawned.

When the boss paused in his speech and glared at him, John immediately straightened in his seat and tugged at the drooping waistband of his pants.

Once the meeting concluded, he darted back to his desk. John slouched in his chair, running his slender fingers through his tousled brown hair, and then flipping a baseball cap backwards on his head. He caught sight of his reflection in the laptop monitor and wiped a smudge of mustard from the corner of his thin lips.

***

CHARACTER DESCRIPTIONS

A clever writer applying the Deep POV method can learn to skillfully tuck the physical characteristics into the narrative by lacing it through action and dialogue. Writers need to make all characters as three-dimensional as possible, so that the reader sees them as real people.

If writers can describe what the character(s) look like, how they feel, and how they react to situations and events unfolding around them, it will make the writing much more powerful.

The best technique is to present just enough relevant details to help your reader instantly "see" the character without doing an info-dump, because the right blend of description, dialogue, and introspection, along with some action can create a stronger image for the reader.

Telling descriptions create weak illustrations that can leave the reader grappling for a visual and feeling disconnected from the characters and the scene.

I have included some examples on how to describe physical characteristics to show you what I mean.

Please take a look at these examples...

SHALLOW:

Cole wore tan pants, and leaned against a car. He had blond hair and blue eyes. His full lips grinned at me. I really liked him.

DEEP POV:

Cole stuffed his hands into the pockets of his wrinkled khakis, reclining his large frame against a shiny black Mustang. The breeze ruffled his blond hair, and I yearned to brush the gold strands out of his cerulean eyes. When those generous lips tipped into an arrogant grin, I knew my heart was in big trouble.

***

These next two scenes are longer, and the first is a bland example with intrusive dialogue tags and wordy sentences. (In the shallow example, I did not underline all the obvious areas of shallower writing, but see if you can easily spot it now that you're more aware of *showing* vs. *telling*.)

Please study and compare these examples…

SHALLOW:

Tad noticed a tall woman in a skirt with bare legs and high-heels enter through the front doors of the building. She had green eyes. He saw that the woman was clutching the handle of a purse very tightly as she examined the lobby. He watched her lick her lips, and then she frowned. She had medium-length blond hair. He noticed that she was wearing an ivory shirt, and there was some blood on the sleeve. He watched as her eyes looked back at the parking lot.

Then she saw the security desk and she walked across the floor toward Tad. He felt nervous, so he sat up before she made it to the desk.

"May I help you, miss?" he asked politely.

She placed her hand on the top of the desktop. He looked down and he saw that she had long red fingernails. Her eyes looked into his, and Tad felt very nervous.

"Can you please tell me what floor I can find Stanley Martin's office?" she asked coldly.

This second scene has been rewritten with "voice" and sensory details.

DEEP POV:

A tall woman wearing a striped skirt, with the longest, smoothest legs, Tad had ever seen entered the building. Her icy blue gaze searched the lobby, her hands clutching the handle of her Fendi purse. She licked her red lips, the corners of her mouth tipping downward. She half turned,

CHARACTER DESCRIPTIONS

staring at the parking lot through the sliding glass doors, before muttering a curse. When she pivoted back around, her silk blouse became partially untucked.

Spotting the security desk, she glided forward, her flaxen hair styled in a feathery bob that bounced off her slim shoulders. Her stilettos clacking against the marble floor echoed like a shotgun going off in the quiet room.

Tad sat up, quickly adjusting his wrinkled uniform and straightening his tie. A waft of her exotic perfume reached Tad before she did.

Damn, she's even sexier up close.

He gave her a toothy grin. "May I help you, miss?"

She studied him for a long second, one long ruby fingernail tapping the polished surface of the desktop. A splatter of blood stained her ivory cuff.

"Can you please tell me what floor I can find Stanley Martin's office?" Her voice was low and cold. The woman withdrew a 38. Special from her purse and pointed the gun at him. "And don't make me use this."

***

These three excerpts were taken from my novel, IMMORTAL ECLIPSE. They both illustrate how writers can describe a character through Deeper POV and "voice" and emotional reactions.

Please closely examine this example…

DEEP POV:

I blink several times at the dark-haired man standing in the doorway, trying not to stare at his eyes, an intense shade of blue. Damn, he was better looking than most male fashion models I've photographed. Mr. Tall, Dark, and Yummy tilts his head as his eyes lock on mine. Even from a distance, I can tell he'll tower over me, and I'm no midget. He's even dressed similar to the man in the portrait: a soft, white linen shirt —bulging biceps stretching the fabric—under a black vest paired with snug pants and chunky boots. Although, he appears to be only in his late twenties, he looks reserved and intimidating.

Conclusion: no sense of style, but still smoking hot.

Please closely examine this next example…

DEEP POV:

Compared to the décor in Pauletta's posh office, the furniture is frayed and outdated, with a stack of law books dusting the desk. The room overlooks the Bay Bridge and smells of day-old cigar. *Yuck.*

Matthew Rosenberg glances up, surprising me with how much he's aged. His wrinkled skin—probably from all those afternoons spent negotiating cases on the golf course—with teeth that flash yellow when he smiles, and pants drooping beneath a gut that strains his shirt buttons. The years spent in California have added bloat and wrinkles that accentuate his every flaw.

Please closely examine this third example…

DEEP POV:

Behind her glass-top desk, Pauletta sits in a sleek black leather chair, which reclines to an almost obscene angle as she crosses her smooth brown legs. She's wearing a silk Hermès scarf draped over a gray blouse, a matching rayon skirt, and *really* cute pair of Bettye Muller heels.

***

Now describing a first-person narrator is a bit trickier, but not impossible if you have the tools and know how.

CHARACTER DESCRIPTIONS

This next passage was taken from MOONLIGHT MAYHEM in my young adult series, and it should give you a pretty good idea on how to describe a first-person narrator.

Please closely examine this example…

DEEP POV:

I flicked my gaze to Ariana. She stared out the window, her expression pensive. I reached over and gave her hand a squeeze. Glimpsing my skin next to hers reminded me that Ariana and I were total opposites, like sunny skies versus somber clouds. An optimist compared to a pessimist. And not only in personality, but in looks, too. She had blond ringlets, winter pale skin that had a sparkly glow in direct sunlight, and a curvaceous figure.

Me? Well, I'd inherited unusual looking features due to my Sioux lineage on my father's side: an athletic body, high cheekbones, olive complexion, bronze eyes, and thick hair the color of midnight. Yup, she was light to my dark. Even in how we viewed the world.

These next two excerpts were also taken from my novel, MOONLIGHT MAYHEM, to give writers an idea on how to describe a character's hair.

Please carefully examine these two examples…

DEEP POV:

My ex stood at the counter with his friend and ordered a pizza. His hair tapered in the back and across both sides, but left heavy on top was styled into a spiky mess.

DEEP POV:

Every time I caught sight of my reflection and my unevenly cut, shoulder-length black hair, it reminded me of the wickedness that my crazed mother was capable of doing. Last month, she'd hacked off my long, straight hair in an attempt to break me. It hadn't worked. She'd done other things—*awful things*—which I would never understand. Chopping off my hair had only been one of them. And I hated how it looked now. Taking the scissors, I trimmed the ends so they looked more even and rested on my shoulders. Much better.

***

Here are a few more examples of shallow sentences that "tell" the reader the physical characteristics instead of *showing*. I realize that using Deep POV in descriptions can make the prose wordy, and just *telling* the reader might be a quicker way to reveal a character's personality or describe their looks, but it always creates a weaker visual.

Please take a look at these examples…

SHALLOW: Charles was a fat man who couldn't fit his bulky body onto the lawn chair. His pants ripped in the back when he sat down and his huge belly hung over his pants.

DEEP POV: Charles' cheeks burned red as he squeezed himself down into the lawn chair. *Rippp!* His polyester golf pants split up the back, and his bulging stomach hung over the waistband.

***

Below is an excerpt from one of my novels, SHATTERED SILENCE to illustrate how to describe a character's clothing and personality.

Please closely examine this example…

DEEP POV:

Trent shrugged off a worn leather jacket and draped it over an armchair, displaying a long-sleeved black shirt. The guy was the epitome of hip. With artfully mussed hair, low-slung jeans, motorcycle boots, and model good looks, just a glimpse of Trent Donovan caused female hormones to rage, teenage girls to swoon, and mouths to drool.

CHARACTER DESCRIPTIONS

***

Here's another character description taken from my Sci-Fi romance, LOST IN STARLIGHT. Please closely examine this example…

DEEP POV:

Hayden turns his head and his light brown fauxhawk falls over his forehead in a messy yet somehow deliberate way, landing over his one strikingly blue eye. The other one is green. Besides the rare heterochromia iridis, he seems to be just another smokin' hot brainiac.

I add to my notes: *Weird eye color and member of the Amazing Hair Club.* Check.

***

Don't forget to describe your characters by weaving in descriptions of clothing, age, hair and eye color, height, weight, visible scars, and even nationality, etc. into the scene. Writers should do it by lacing the physical characteristics throughout the action and dialogue.

Adding descriptions of hair may seem silly to some of you, but if you write young adult novels, it will add an extra layer of depth and realism to your storyline.

If a writer learns to sprinkle physical characteristics into a scene mixed with the action, dialogue, and introspection, it will enhance the storyline and enrich the reader's experience. And I strongly suggest that each time a new character is introduced to the storyline, that the writer provides the reader with a visual illustration. Now, it doesn't have to be a lengthy description of the character, a few well-placed descriptive words or action tags should be enough.

FACIAL EXPRESSIONS

Quote: "One of the most difficult problems plaguing writers is how to describe facial expressions. The problem arises if the writer does not describe facial expressions at all, or if they provide cliché, or overused descriptions…" —*freelance writer and English teacher, Roger Colby*

Expressions are one of the universal languages of emotion, because just a *look* can instantly convey whatever a person might be feeling, such as joy, sorrow, anger, or fear, etc. And how your POV characters interprets these expressions is essential to page-turning prose. But for some writers it can be hard to find the right verbs or adjectives to describe facial expressions or emotional reactions, so use this chapter as a handy resource for ideas on describing the expressions of the characters, without *stating the emotion.*

In my opinion, using the filter word: *felt* or *feel* is the weakest way to depict an emotion. If a writer uses shallower writing like, *he felt miserable* or *she felt livid*, or *he was traumatized* or *she was excited* it takes the narrative out of Deeper POV. As writers, we should always be exploring new ways to describe character emotions and expressions.

One way to avoid shallower writing is to express a character's moods, responses, and emotions by describing their reactions and body language. There are endless creative ways to describe expressions and elicit a reader response.

Please take a look at these examples of facial expressions…

FACIAL EXPRESSIONS

Suspicion: Eyes hooded or narrowed

Surprise/shock: Eyes wide or open

Fear/sorrow/disappointment: Lip quivering

Disgust/abhorrence: Nose wrinkles or lips turn downward

Thoughtful/confused: Brow furrows or lips puckered

Sadness/shock: Tears or shaky movements

Annoyed/frustrated: Eye twitching or eye rolling

Inquisitive/doubtful: Raised eyebrow or long stare

Hesitant/uncertain: Biting lips or tugging on ear

Rage/displeasure: Pursed lips or flushed face/ears

Calm/happy: Smiling /body relaxed

***

When describing facial expressions, one thing that a writer can mention is the character's eyes. Eyes are very expressive, and they can tell a reader a lot about what a character is thinking, feeling, or trying to communicate. Eyes that dart around usually indicate a character that is lying or nervous. If a character is lying, then show the reader a slight twitch at the corner of the mouth. The character might avoid eye contact too, if he/she is trying to hide something. Eyes that are big and round can convey surprise. Or eyes that are droopy or lowered can indicate sleepiness or boredom. (But please don't over use "eyes" to convey emotions.)

A writer can also describe a character's mouth to reveal emotions or even a strong reaction. If the character is grinning, it shows that he/she is feeling joyful, content, or satisfied. Sometimes, a character might be hiding a negative or painful emotion behind the mask of a smile. A slight twitch of the upper lip may indicate amusement, or even disgust. When a character is frowning it shows the reader that he/she is unhappy, angry, or even thoughtful. Or if the lips are pulled downward, it could show annoyance.

Writers can show a melancholy expression with tear-filled eyes, slumped posture, drooping mouth, and loud sighs. Or a flushed face with tense shoulders and flashing eyes indicates an angry character.

Please review this list of common facial expressions...

ANGER: Eyebrows squeezed together, brows knitted, eyes squinty, pupils flared, lowered head, nostrils flared, looking upward through a scrunched brow, tight facial muscles, flat lips, flaring nostrils, or an penetrating gaze.

CONTEMPT: Squinty eyes, mouth snapped shut, mouth set in a hard line, or lips pressed together, grinding teeth, muscle in jaw twitching, face turns crimson, ears red or hot, or hardened expression.

EXCITEMENT: Smile shows teeth, eyes wide, flushed cheeks, eyebrows high, twinkle in eyes, tears in eyes, dimples showing, or raised eyebrows.

FEAR: Pale skin, eyebrows are drawn together, trembling mouth, brows furrowed, creased forehead, eyes wide and huge, blinking rapidly, mouth opening and closing, or tense, white lips.

FRUSTRATION: Slanting eyebrows, jaw tightened, face reddened, chin raised, deep frowning, gnashed teeth, tense eyebrows, squinty eyes, lips pulled back, or mouth twisted to one side.

REVULSION: Frowning, gritted teeth, lips drew back in a snarl, lowered head, tense lips, eyebrows drawn together, wrinkled forehead, or pursed lips.

SURPRISE: Wide eyes, mouth hanging open, huge smile, flushed face, gaping, raised eyebrows, pupils are huge, and head held back, intense gaze, and eyebrows lifted.

SADNESS: Pale face, lower lip quivered, tears shimmered in eyes, frowning of lips, head hangs low, pouty expression, or gaze downcast.

HAPPINESS: Smiling big with teeth visible, flushed cheeks, crinkle at corners of the eyes, the corners of mouth turned upward, eyes lit up, tears shone in eyes, face glowing.

***

Another great way to describe a character's expression is to avoid using an "external camera" to catalogue facial expressions or body language as an impartial description. Writers should *dig deeper* to show the emotions because these are indications that readers can use to determine how a characters feels or reacts. Sometimes a more complex description of someone's posture, expression, or mannerisms is needed, and on occasion, it's better to just simplify the description by *telling*.

REDUNDANT PHRASES

Quote: "Writers need good descriptions of facial expressions in their stories to help the readers picture the characters, to convey emotions, and to set up lines of dialogue without having to write "said" or any of its synonyms. However, it's easy for us to rely on the same descriptions over and over again." —*author, Bryn Donovan*

A redundant phrase is one used repeatedly to describe an expression, gesture, or emotion.

Please keep in mind that clichés are the enemy of good writing.

I strongly advise the writers that I work with to avoid describing facial expressions by using overworked clichés. If writers resort to using clichés, like *His smile was dazzling* or *Her eyes shone like diamonds* or *His face was red as a beet*, readers will understand the meaning, but the phrases are so unoriginal that it won't have much impact.

By using a stale cliché or redundant phrase, a writer is actually telling the reader that they lack originality. So I encourage writers to craft a more unique description, rather than relying on a cliché.

In this chapter, I have provided helpful alternatives to overused gestures and facial expressions (not saying mine are terribly original) that should inspire writers to describe a gesture, action, or expression in a different way.

I have put together a list of ways to rewrite certain redundant phrases and clichés…

REDUNDANT PHRASES

Alternatives for nodded / bobbed head in agreement:

SHALLOW: Spike nodded his head. "That is what I am talking about."

DEEP POV: Spike punched me in the shoulder. "Yeah, man, that's what I'm talking about!"

SHALLOW: He bobbed his head in agreement. (cliché)

DEEP POV: "Uh-huh," he said, his head bobbing like a yo-yo. "Go on."

SHALLOW: Denise gave him a nod. "Yes, I want to go skating."

DEEP POV: "Hell, yeah." Denise's head bounced up and down like a basketball. "I'd love to go roller skating this weekend!"

SHALLOW: Her head nodded. "Yes, I agree."

DEEP POV: Her head fell back, and then her chin tipped downward in quick, jerky movements like a puppet. "Yeah, that sounds good."

SHALLOW: The man agreed and said that he wanted to do it.

DEEP POV: The man put his hands flat on table. "Let's do this!"

Alternatives for smiled:

SHALLOW: He smiled, looking pleased.

DEEP POV: His mouth curved upward, the outer corners of his eyes crinkling.

SHALLOW: She wore a big smile.

DEEP POV: Her mouth widened, the corners lifting heavenward.

SHALLOW: Betty grinned at me. "I would like to go to the dance."

DEEP POV: Betty's lips stretched sideways. "I can't wait to go to the dance."

SHALLOW: Maxine looked happy and she was smiling because Charles wanted to marry her.

DEEP POV: Maxine floated into work. Finally, Charles had asked her to marry him.

SHALLOW: He had a quick grin that made the attraction more intense.

DEEP POV: His lightening grin made my insides turn into mush.

SHALLOW: I liked Sammy's grin, but it upset my calm demeanor.

DEEP POV: Sammy's grin was irresistibly devastating to my calm reserve.

Alternative examples for laughed:

SHALLOW: The villain had an wicked laugh and he glared at the hero, and then told him that he couldn't stop his evil plans.

DEEP POV: His head fell back and acerbic laughter spewed from his lips. "*Muahahaha!* Even you can't stop me, Marvelous Man."

SHALLOW: Sharon laughed hard and bent over at the waist.

DEEP POV: Sharon doubled over, bursts of breathy vowel sounds escaping her mouth. "Heh-heh. Ha-ha…Stop you're killing me."

SHALLOW: Craig chuckled rowdily and then asked if I was serious.

DEEP POV: Craig slapped his knee, hooting loudly. "Are you serious, man?"

SHALLOW: I saw her expression shift into a humorous one.

DEEP POV: A flash of humor crossed her face.

SHALLOW: Dyson had a loud laugh and his eyes were laughing now, too.

DEEP POV: Dyson chortled, and the teasing laughter was back in his eyes.

SHALLOW: Jeanie was giggling and tried to hide her mouth by lifting her hand and covering her mouth to stop the laughter. (*too wordy*)

DEEP POV: Jeanie tittered, covering her mouth with a slim hand.

Alternative examples for shake / shook head:

SHALLOW: Bo did not agree and she shook her head. "Be quiet."

DEEP POV: Bo wagged her blond head. "Shut up."

SHALLOW: She shook her head vehemently. (*cliché*)

DEEP POV: Her dark head swung from side to side like a tennis ball. "*No!* Please, don't hurt Jimmy."

SHALLOW: The woman shook her head and told him about the voices.

DEEP POV: Her head moved left, then right several times before she blurted, "The voices are telling me to steal your car...*and* your wallet."

SHALLOW: She kept shaking her head.

DEEP POV: Pushing the glasses up the bridge of her nose, she said, "I don't see your point."

SHALLOW: Kenzi shook her head in disbelief. (*cliché*)

DEEP POV: Kenzi's eyebrows rose. "Am I supposed to believe you?"

SHALLOW: He was shaking his head.

DEEP POV: He narrowed his eyes and frowned.

SHALLOW: She shook her head in denial. (*cliché*)

DEEP POV: Looking down, her face turned away. "How could this have happened?"

SHALLOW: With a slight shake of her head, she said incredulity, "I do not understand."

DEEP POV: She slightly rubbed her nose. "I need a minute to absorb this info…"

SHALLOW: Eric did not agree with the suggestion and shook his head.

DEEP POV: Eric leaned back further in his throne-like chair. "Are you for real?"

Alternatives for "made a face" / grimace:

SHALLOW: Winifred made a face at me and then showed me that she was going to punch me in the face, and then she told me that she was going to hurt me. (*too wordy and telling*)

DEEP POV: Winifred ground her knuckles into her cheek, squishing one side of her face. "*This* is what's gonna happen to you—if you're not real careful!"

SHALLOW: She made a face of disgust. (*cliché*)

DEEP POV: Her face twisted in ugly, savage glee.

SHALLOW: Sandra was mad and scowled at Tommy White.

DEEP POV: Sandra stuck out her tongue and squashed her eyes. Then she stomped on Tommy White's foot.

SHALLOW: She stared at me with hatred in her eyes. (*cliché*)

DEEP POV: Her head tilted to one side and her eyes narrowed as if I was a bug that needed to be squashed. And squashed *quickly*.

SHALLOW: Sookie wore a scowl on her face.

DEEP POV: Sookie narrowed her eyes before turning away.

SHALLOW: She felt disgusted with me and scowled in my direction.

DEEP POV: She wrinkled her nose and sneered.

Alternatives for shrugged shoulders:

SHALLOW: Tara felt unsure and shrugged her shoulders in dismay.

DEEP POV: Rubbing around her ear, Tara said, "Well, I don't know."

SHALLOW: Jodi shrugged her shoulders. (*What else can a person shrug?*)

DEEP POV: Jodi lifted her shoulder blades, then let them drop. "I don't *why* I stabbed Kenny—I just did."

SHALLOW: He gave off a shrug and told me whatever and that it wasn't a problem.

DEEP POV: He raised and lowered his shoulders. "Whatever. Not my problem, Liz."

SHALLOW: Ryan was shrugging as he told the police he was innocent.

DEEP POV: Ryan's right shoulder rose and fell, his palms upraised. "You can't bust me. I gotta an alibi."

SHALLOW: She gave him a dismissive shrug. (Cliché)

DEEP POV: Her eyes rolled upward. "Whatever."

Alternatives for frowning:

SHALLOW: Stefan deeply frowned. (Cliché)

DEEP POV: Stefan's face flushed, puffing out his cheeks.

SHALLOW: Lend was frowning at me and I became nervous.

DEEP POV: The muscles in his forehead were constricting, and I knew Lend well enough to know that this was when he was most dangerous.

SHALLOW: He frowned and looked confused.

DEEP POV: "That doesn't make sense…" His lips flattened together. "The magic spell should've worked."

SHALLOW: My boss looks angry and he's wearing a frown.

DEEP POV: His bushy brows squeeze together, and he jabs his index finger at my desk. "Have you accomplished anything today?"

SHALLOW: He frowns at me.

DEEP POV: His lips turned downward. "Oh."

SHALLOW: She wears a long frown.

DEEP POV: The corners of her mouth drooped.

SHALLOW: Elena frowned, looking thoughtful. (Cliché)

DEEP POV: With hunched shoulders, Elena slumped in the chair.

SHALLOW: Her expression frowned.

DEEP POV: She hesitated, blinking rapidly.

Alternatives for grimaced:

SHALLOW: I felt my face grimace.

DEEP POV: With my lips compressed, my heartbeat thundered in my ears.

SHALLOW: Anna grimaced when I touched her and demanded my money.

DEEP POV: Anna flinched when I gripped her arm. "Pardon me," I said, my sharp nails slicing into her soft flesh. "But you still owe me two hundred bucks."

SHALLOW: He had been shot and his face grimaced.

DEEP POV: He rubbed his collarbone, his breath coming in quick, whining gasps. "I—I've been shot."

Alternatives for wince / flinch:

SHALLOW: Heath winced when I startled him.

DEEP POV: Heath recoiled, his hand clutching his chest. "Sheesh, don't sneak up on me like that."

SHALLOW: Grant flinched.

DEEP POV: Grant gritted his teeth, cringing at the sight of all the blood.

SHALLOW: Clara's whole body flinched in revulsion.

DEEP POV: Clara recoiled, stumbling over her feet in an effort to get away.

Alternatives for pouted:

SHALLOW: Jackson wore a pouty expression. (Cliché)

DEEP POV: Jackson's shoulders slumped. "Fine. Kill the girl."

SHALLOW: Ruby looked disappointed and her bottom lip pouted.

DEEP POV: Ruby rubbed her hand over her face and turned away. "I didn't wanna go bear hunting anyway."

SHALLOW: Kent was pouting about the cookies.

DEEP POV: Kent's bottom lip thrust upward. "Can I have another cookie, please?"

SHALLOW: She moped, wanting to buy the ring.

DEEP POV: Her sexy lower lip extended just slightly past the top. "C'mon, luv, buy me that diamond ring."

Alternatives for sighing:

SHALLOW: Christian sighed with disapproval. (Cliché)

DEEP POV: Christian exhaled through tight lips.

SHALLOW: She let out a long, heavy sigh of defeat. (Cliché)

DEEP POV: Her whole body sagged. "Just drink my blood, Edward."

SHALLOW: Bella released a sigh of relief. (Cliché)

DEEP POV: Bella's tense posture relaxed. "Okay, you win."

SHALLOW: She was sighing and looking defeated.

DEEP POV: Her long, lowered eyelashes emanated a kind of surrender, and she let the breath swoosh from her lungs.

Alternatives for blushed / flushed:

SHALLOW: Buffy was blushing when she told us that she only killed vampires.

DEEP POV: Wringing her hands, Buffy leaned forward. "I swear I *only* kill vampires. They're not even really people."

SHALLOW: He blushed hotly and said Amanda was a liar.

DEEP POV: He twisted the pen between his index finger and his thumb, heat blazing in his cheeks. "Amanda's a liar."

SHALLOW: Drake's face looked flushed.

DEEP POV: Drake's forehead was damp with sweat and both his cheeks had red splotches like a circus clown.

SHALLOW: She looked nervous and her face was flushed red.

DEEP POV: She let out a nervous peal of laughter, then covered her mouth. "Sorry. I don't know what came over me."

SHALLOW: I was nervous and my I felt my face blush because I hated first dates.

DEEP POV: I fidgeted with zipper on my jacket. "Um, well, I'm not real good at first dates."

SHALLOW: I felt embarrassed and my face blushed.

DEEP POV: Blood flowed into my face, reddening my neck all the way up to my hairline.

SHALLOW: Julianna felt her face flush with color.

DEEP POV: Julianna's face colored fiercely, and her voice sounded edgy. "I, um, knew that."

SHALLOW: She felt her neck and ears blush.

DEEP POV: Her neck and ears turned scarlet like a sunburn.

***

This chapter should inspire you to create your own alternatives to overused facial expressions and gestures.

RHETORICAL QUESTIONS

Quote: "Deep POV is simply a technique that strips the author voice completely out of the prose. There is no author intrusion, so we are left only with the characters. The reader is nice and snuggly in the "head" of the character." —*editor and author, Kristen Lamb*

If Deep POV is done well, then the thoughts, emotions, moods, and experiences of the character(s) are interweaved so invisibly into the scene that the reader can almost experience everything along with the narrator, rather than having it itemized or stated for them. But much too often whenever a writer wants to express some kind of emotion, like confusion in their characters or add tension to a scene, they will include several rhetorical questions.

While a rhetorical question can focus on a particular character's inner-struggles, it should not be used instead of actually *showing* the characters' emotions and/or reactions.

Rhetorical questions shouldn't be used as a substitution for internal-dialogue or as the primary method for getting inside a character's head. There are much more effective and subtle ways to reveal a character's reaction or wonderment about an event or conversation, rather than using an internal question.

When I critique a novice writer's work, I often find that when they want to express some kind of uncertainty or curiosity or self-doubt in a character, they will overuse rhetorical questions. These interrogatory instances

RHETORICAL QUESTIONS

are a shallow way of establishing tension, and letting the reader know an internal debate is taking place by stating the obvious. The problem is that the misuse of rhetorical questions can become intrusive if the character asks multiple questions on the same page, or every time the author wants the reader to question something along with the narrator, which can become blatantly repetitive.

While rhetorical questions can raise tension, only use them if necessary when you cannot describe the reaction any other way.

Basically, a rhetorical question can be a way of *telling*.

Here are a few examples that should help you revise your own writing…

SHALLOW: I looked at my best friend with anxiousness. Why was Mary so mad at me? What had I done?

DEEP POV: I stared at my BFF and chewed on my lip. For the life of me, I couldn't understand why Mary was so pissed. I hadn't done a damn thing!

SHALLOW: Kent went down the stairs and into the basement and looked around the room that was dimly lit. What was Harold doing in the basement? Kent wondered.

DEEP POV: Kent crept to the bottom step of the basement stairwell and squinted into the dimness. Harold was up to *something* and Kent was going to figure out what.

SHALLOW: I went into the house very late past my curfew. Would my mom be waiting up for me? Would I be grounded for a month? I wondered.

DEEP POV: I snuck toward the house with my heart thumping. It was *way* past my curfew. If my mom was waiting up, then I was gonna be grounded for a month!

SHALLOW: She'd told the wizard that she only needed one wish, but he insisted on giving her three. *Why would he do that? Was this some type of* *trick?* Rainbow pondered to herself. *What would she do with three wishes now?*

DEEP POV: Rainbow scratched her head. She now had three wishes to use instead only one. Yet she wasn't sure if that was a good thing or bad. Or if it was some type of wizardly trick.

I have included a few longer examples to further illustrate this point. (In the shallow example, the questions are in italics.)

Please carefully examine these examples…

SHALLOW: I saw a ghostly shape in the doorway. I tried to hold back a silent scream as I stepped backward. *Why was there paranormal activity going on in my new home? Was I being haunted by a ghost?*

DEEP POV: A ghost floated in the doorway. With a silent scream stuck in my throat, I backed up into the wall. Okay, so there was some *obvious* paranormal activity going on in my new home.

Please carefully examine these examples…

SHALLOW: Shelton had asked me a lot of dumb questions on our first date. *Where better for an interior decorator to live than in one the most high-class cities in the United States? And what is it about guys that made them give the coldshoulder to a woman who says that she likes to wander around bookstores? Doesn't anyone like to read anymore?* Then he doesn't even ask me out again! *Why even ask about my hobbies if he wasn't interested in dating me?*

DEEP POV: I rolled my eyes and took another sip of wine. My first date with Shelton hadn't gone as well as I'd hoped. All those dumb questions about why I had moved to the city, and about my hobbies, and then snubbing me for being an avid reader.

I still wasn't sure what the point of asking me all those questions was—if the jerk wasn't even interested in a second date!

RHETORICAL QUESTIONS

***

Too many rhetorical questions can deflate the tension of the moment. Writers should revise them whenever possible so that they are not in the form of a question. One clever way to do that is, if there two or more characters in a scene, then revise some of the inner-questions into actual dialogue. And it's an awesome way to add tension and create turn-paging prose!

Please carefully examine these examples…

SHALLOW: Damon shook his head. He deliberated to himself as he put down his keys angrily on the table. *Why was Jane so insistent on going to dinner tonight? Didn't she understand that he was exhausted after a long day at work? Would it be too much to ask for Jane to think about his needs first for a change?*

DEEP POV: Damon threw his keys down onto the table with a loud *clang*. He was being ambushed by Jane again.

"Damn it, Jane! Why are you so insistent on going to dinner tonight? Don't you understand that I'm exhausted after a long day at work?" Damon shook his head. "Would it be too much to ask that you put my needs first for a change?"

***

Were the examples helpful?

Have you read a story were the author endlessly pestered the reader with internal questions laced throughout the narrative like an interrogator?

Or writers who are trying too hard to show doubt about something that happens or they question another character's motives?

Or even strive to be funny or colloquial by using lots of inner-questions? Or breaking the tension by inserting questions every couple of paragraphs?

Were all those questions above getting redundant?

Of course, they're annoying!

Prose littered with rhetorical questions can be really irritating for the reader. Consider it this way: inner-questions are not *real* questions, but rather a way to "tell" the reader what the character's thought process is in the form of a question.

The exception to this guideline is when a writer wants to indicate sarcasm or humor. A few rhetorical questions laced into the narrative can really enhance a scene and strengthen a humorous "voice" when needed. And it can even be a necessity in some scenes where any other type of sentence just wouldn't fit the moment.

There are no hard-and-fast rules regarding where or even when it's appropriate to use a rhetorical question in your narrative. But it becomes rather clear when it's one of the instances of *telling* rather than actually "showing."

Experienced writers should understand that you need to do both, so I'm not stating that all rhetorical questions are wrong, but in my opinion they should be used with caution. And definitely don't ask more than two rhetorical questions on the same page.

If you limit the use of internal questions and only include them on occasion, then it's just another tool for your fiction writing toolbox.

Now I challenge writers to consider revising almost every question into *showing* a character's doubt, confusion, unease, etc., or turn it into actual dialogue whenever possible.

SHALLOW: FELT

Quote: "A skill that leads straight into strong, emotive writing is Deep Point Of View. And I mean *deep*. This is often a very hard skill to conquer...Deep POV is an art, because it's putting yourself so totally into the character you [the author] basically don't appear because it's *all* the character. What also disappears in deep POV to a great extent is "tags" —the "he thought/ pondered/ wondered" that jerk readers out of the character's head, reminding them that they are not the hero or heroine—and that's what we, as writers, don't want!" —*author, Melissa James*

In my opinion, *felt / feel* is the weakest word there is to describe an emotional reaction to something. In this chapter, I will show you examples on how to eliminate the biggest "telling" offender of filter words: *felt / feel / feeling / feels* from your writing, and how to transform the sentences below into vivid sensory details by using the Deep POV method.

Writing with filter words "I felt" or "He had a feeling" or "It feels so soft" or "I feel angry" is almost never necessary in Deeper POV. Instead of saying "he/she felt" something, simply describe the emotion instead.

So I strongly encourage writers to revise as many occurrences of filter words like *felt* as they can from the manuscript before self-publishing, posting an online story, or sending any work off to a literary agent or publishing editor. Writers cannot remove them all, but any shallow writing that directly describes an emotion *can* and should be revised.

Whenever possible revise these filter words: FELT / FEEL

SHALLOW: I _felt_ a hand slap me sharply across the face.

DEEP POV: My head snapped back from the hard slap, my cheeks stinging from the unexpected blow.

SHALLOW: I _felt_ angry, suddenly.

DEEP POV: Flaring my nostrils, I stomped forward and got right in Missy's face.

SHALLOW: He _felt_ queasy.

DEEP POV: His stomach lurched, his breakfast threatening to cough back up.

SHALLOW: Charles _felt_ his cheeks go red.

DEEP POV: Charles' cheeks heated, a red stain coloring his face.

SHALLOW: He _felt_ as though the top of his head would explode.

DEEP POV: His head pounded and his thoughts swirled.

SHALLOW: Jack _feels_ unsteady on his feet.

DEEP POV: Jack wobbles forward, his legs unsteady.

SHALLOW: Mary _felt_ a tightening in her stomach.

DEEP POV: Mary's stomach tightened.

SHALLOW: Scott _felt_ his chest go tight.

DEEP POV: A deep ache snapped through him.

SHALLOW: Her heart _feels_ as if it had just flopped over inside her ribcage.

DEEP POV: Her heart flops over inside her ribcage.

SHALLOW: She _felt_ drowsy.

DEEP POV: Unable to stifle a yawn, she pulled up the blankets and closed her eyes.

SHALLOW: Lisa <u>felt</u> so disappointed and mad.

DEEP POV: Lisa's bottom lip trembled. She kicked at the ground with her sneaker. *This sucks!*

***

FELT / FEEL are filter words that will convey obvious information, while neatly inserting the dreaded narrative distance. The fact that the character *felt* whatever happens is understood by the reader without being told.

Please carefully compare these examples…

SHALLOW:

Max <u>felt</u> a flare of <u>jealousy</u> when he <u>noticed</u> his ex-girlfriend, Tammi with the new guy at work. Then he <u>calmed down</u> a little, <u>deciding</u> Tammi wasn't worth wasting his time.

He took a breath and pulled on his suit jacket. Then he <u>looked</u> over again and <u>saw</u> them kissing near the front counter.

Max <u>felt</u> so <u>enraged</u> that he <u>felt</u> his body tense up. The <u>rage</u> in his heart <u>felt</u> like it would explode. He moved closer to the office window and <u>felt</u> like he wanted to kill that guy.

He <u>watched</u> the new employee hitting on his girlfriend. Max <u>knew</u> Tammi belonged to him.

DEEP POV:

Max's mouth dropped open at the sight of ex-girlfriend, Tammi, flirting with the new guy at work. Heat boiled his insides. Then he relaxed his shoulders and blew out a breath.

Calm yourself, Max. She isn't worth wasting your time.

He tugged on his jacket, preparing to sell more cars today then the dirtbag chatting up his ex. But when he glanced over at them again, his chest tightened. The new guy had his tongue down Tammi's throat near the receptionist's desk. At work. In front of everybody.

Eyes narrowed and nostrils flared, he stomped closer to the office window to glare at them through the glass. Every muscle in his body tensed up.

Tammi's my girl! That new dude was gonna be nothing more than an oil stain when he was done plummeting him into the ground.

***

After reading the two different examples, could you see how *naming the emotion* and using filter words creates narrative distance?

The second example is a perfect illustration on how to describe a character's emotional state without *naming* the feeling.

In the succeeding chapters, I have listed tons of helpful examples of filter words that take you out of Deep POV. Again, all of these examples have already been used in my published books, but they should help spark your own creative muse and give you some ideas on how to modify your own wonderful stories.

SHALLOW: SEE

Quote: "Going through 100,000 words and looking at every use of "saw," "see," "seeing," and "seen" is time consuming and tedious. On the other hand, I think the search function forces writers to stop on things that we would otherwise miss in our writing. You can't gloss over something without noticing it when it's highlighted in yellow. When I'm stopped like that, I find I'm much more objective about my sentences."
—*writer and blogger, Michael J. McDonagh*

"Sight" is one of the main senses that a character would use to describe something, since people depend on sight more than any of the other senses.

When a writer states that a character "saw something" or when a character describes a place (setting) or an object, use the sense of sight to vividly describe it with colors, shapes, and an emotional reaction. Be detailed, yet have fun with the description!

Now I feel that it is perfectly okay to use "watch" in a sentence if it adds to the scene. For example, *As I watch him walk away, the cold night swallows him and a dark flutter strikes my chest, like a bird smashing itself against a window.* However, if the word "watch/watched" gets overused in your manuscript, or if it is being used as a filter word, than I would revise that sentence.

Always strive to revise filter words like *see / saw / could see* in a scene, and instead just describe whatever he/she saw.

Whenever possible revise these filter words: SAW / SEE

SHALLOW: I see the moon lift overhead.

DEEP POV: The moon hung in an inky sky overhead.

SHALLOW: He saw things moving, shifting.

DEEP POV: Things were moving, shifting.

SHALLOW: He saw nothing that threatened danger.

DEEP POV: He sensed nothing that threatened danger.

SHALLOW: She saw something out a window.

DEEP POV: Moving closer to the window, she peered through the glass.

SHALLOW: He sees the blue glow of the stars, and a milky ring around the moon.

DEEP POV: Glancing upward, he stares at the blue glow of the stars, and a milky ring around the moon.

SHALLOW: Sarah saw that he was wearing a black ski mask.

DEEP POV: Sarah stumbled back when he stepped forward wearing a black ski mask.

SHALLOW: He sees her sleek body moving through the water.

DEEP POV: He admires her sleek body moving through the water.

SHALLOW: I could see glints of gold in his blond hair.

DEEP POV: Glints of gold shone in his blond hair.

Whenever possible revise these filter words: WATCH

SHALLOW: He watched the bird bobbing its head up and down.

DEEP POV: The bird was bobbing its head up and down.

SHALLOW: He <u>watched</u> as she walked back into the kitchen.

DEEP POV: She walked back into the kitchen, her hips swaying, and he smiled faintly to himself.

SHALLOW: I <u>watched</u> my father walk into the motel.

DEEP POV: I moved out of the way as my father strode into the motel.

SHALLOW: He <u>saw</u> Melanie put the lipstick into her purse and head out of the store.

DEEP POV: Glancing down the aisle, his eyes popped wide. Melanie slipped the lipstick into her bag, and then walked out of the store.

SHALLOW: Cary <u>watched</u> her car drive away and <u>felt</u> his heart sink in his chest.

DEEP POV: Cary stayed on the porch as she drove away, his heart sinking lower in his chest.

SHALLOW: Maggie <u>could see</u> the snowcapped mountains from the window of her hotel room.

DEEP POV: Throwing back the curtains, Maggie had a clear view of the snowcapped mountains from the window of her hotel room.

***

Effective Deep POV requires that you take your readers through the emotional experiences of your character as your character actually experiences them.

Using filter words like *watched / see / saw* only distances your reader and takes you out of Deeper POV, which is not what you want.

Again, let's use another example in order to clarify what I mean. Here's a snippet from my book, LOST IN STARLIGHT, before revision (shallow) and after revising with the Deep POV technique. The heroine is writing a story for the school paper on a new guy at school, and she is confused by her attraction to him.

Please compare the two examples…

SHALLOW:

When my last class ends, I go to my locker to get my Trig textbook. I hear the doors at the end of the hall bang open, releasing students for the day and I feel it letting in a gust of air. I notice obtrusive fluorescent lights flicker overhead.

Across the hallway and a few lockers over from mine, I can see Zach and Hayden. I look at a red spray-painted slash on the metal door. I decide that someone must've spray painted Hayden's locker again.

While opening my locker, I notice Hayden's blatantly staring at me. I discern that he is taller than most boys.

I can see he has a messenger bag in one hand, and I notice drumsticks in his back pocket. I lift my hand to wave.

As I watch him, he doesn't return my gesture. He just continues gazing at me with unique eyes. I feel my head go woozy. It even makes my limbs feel jittery. Frustration and confusion are warring inside me for having *any* feelings whatsoever for someone like him. And I wonder why he is staring.

I feel a wave of nervousness because he is watching me. I wonder if there is something wrong. From the corner of my eye, I see him lean into the wall.

I think Hayden's stare is unsettling. I know there's something about that guy's rare smiles that draw girls to him. I decide that no one can resist Hayden Lancaster. Maybe not even me.

I see him watching me, and I feel heat on my skin. I notice Hayden isn't looking at my chest like most boys, which I know will only complicate my feelings for this boy.

So from the first shallow example, could you can see that those extra filter words clogged up your sentence structure?

Now study the revised version…

DEEP POV:

When my last class ends, I stop at my locker to get my Trig textbook. The doors at the end of the hall bang open, releasing students for the day and letting in a gust of warm air. Several obtrusive fluorescent lights flicker overhead.

Across the hallway and a few lockers over from mine are Zach and Hayden. An angry red spray-painted slash taints the metal door. Some jerk must've tagged Hayden's locker again.

While opening my own locker, I'm suddenly aware that Hayden's blatantly staring at me. Hard to miss. He's like a man among boys, at least in his flawless physique. His messenger bag is in one hand, and drumsticks stick out of his back pocket.

I lift my hand in a hesitant little wave. He doesn't return my gesture, just continues gazing at me through those thick lashes that frame his unique eyes. My head goes all woozy. Even my limbs feel jittery. Frustration and confusion are warring inside me for having *any* feelings whatsoever for someone like him. And what's with the stare?

A wave of nervousness hits hard. Is there toilet paper hanging out of my jeans? Food stuck in my teeth? Or have Frankenstein bolts suddenly sprouted from my neck?

Being on Hayden's radar is a little unsettling. I admit there's something about Mr. Puppy Hero's rare smiles, lopsided with an edge, that draw girls to him like insects buzzing a bug zapper. For better or worse, no one can resist Hayden Lancaster. Not even me.

Our gazes lock for just one second, and heat rushes beneath my skin. Hayden isn't gawking at my chest like most boys. He's only looking at my face, which further complicates my feelings for this strange guy.

***

In the second example, I left only one filter word for better flow.

Once you start applying Deep POV to your own writing, you'll know that there are times to use a "tell" word if it reads awkwardly when omitted.

SHALLOW: HEARD

Quote: "Filter words can be difficult to see at first, but once you catch them, it becomes second nature. "I heard the music start up, tiny and spooky and weird," vs. "The music started up, tiny and spooky and weird." One is outside, watching him listen; the other is inside his head, hearing it with him." — *bestselling author, Ruthanne Reid*

"Hearing" is one of the most common senses to use in fiction. When your character hears a noise or the scene changes to a new location, the sense of hearing should be applied for a Deeper POV while describing the scene.

And the sense of hearing can give a character information vital to survival. For instance, it can alert the character to an angry mama bear stomping over crunchy leaves that they might encounter while hiking in the woods, and enables them to get the heck out of harm's way. Writers should use the sense of "hearing" whenever describing a new setting to provide the reader with more sensory details.

Common filter words are *heard / hear / could hear*, which instantly take the writing out of Deep POV. And if your reader already knows in whose POV the scene is written, then why would you need to explain what he/she is hearing?

Whenever possible revise these filter words: HEAR / HEARD

SHALLOW: I hear a scream from the kitchen—it sounds like Amy is scared.

DEEP POV: An earsplitting scream echoes through the house. I guess Amy must've seen Michael's ghost.

SHALLOW: She <u>heard</u> the sound of the car coming.

DEEP POV: The Ford's tires screeched, kicking up gravel on the road.

SHALLOW: Kate <u>could hear</u> the crackling of burning wood.

DEEP POV: The burning wood crackled and spit.

SHALLOW: She <u>heard</u> a strange whoosh <u>sound</u> and looked up.

DEEP POV: A strange *whooshing* came from overhead.

SHALLOW: He <u>heard</u> the stubbornness in her tone of voice.

DEEP POV: There was a distinct stubbornness in her tone of voice.

SHALLOW: They <u>heard</u> another scream, high-pitched and frightened.

DEEP POV: Another high-pitched scream echoed throughout the woods.

SHALLOW: He could <u>hear</u> the roaring of his own pulse.

DEEP POV: His pulse roared in his ears.

SHALLOW: She <u>heard</u> the howl of a wolf.

DEEP POV: The lonely howl of a wolf resonated in the night air.

SHALLOW: I <u>heard</u> the sob in his voice.

DEEP POV: His words faded, but the sob in his voice remained.

SHALLOW: Everyone looked at the field when they <u>heard</u> the whistle blow.

DEEP POV: The game was about to start. When the whistle blew, everyone looked at the field.

SHALLOW: We heard the thunder rumble in the distance.

DEEP POV: Thunder rumbled in the distance.

SHALLOW: I heard the bedroom door slam down the hall.

DEEP POV: The bedroom door down the hall slammed shut.

SHALLOW: Ian heard the soft murmur of voices.

DEEP POV: The soft murmur of voices reached Ian's keen ears.

***

I have included another excerpt from the fourth book in my YA series, RECKLESS REVENGE, which will give you an idea on how to eliminate *hear / heard* filter words from your own writing. The first example has very little "voice" and too many shallow sentences that clutter the narrative and distance the reader.

Please carefully compare these examples…

SHALLOW:

For a moment I thought about casting a spell that would illuminate the yard, but I decided not to. I forced my fingers away from the gemstone and took a deep breath.

Until I heard loud howls from the woods. I didn't think it was coyotes or wolves. I knew this was Northern California. Then I thought that maybe I *should* use my witchy superpowers.

I felt the hairs on the back of my neck stand up. But I decided to stay there on purpose to test myself. I hated letting fear get the better of me.

The night air felt cold and crisp. I could hear the weeping willow tree sway in the breeze. Beyond the back fence, I could see the forest with giant redwoods that soared to heights that seemed to touch the clouds.

Staring into the utter darkness, I <u>felt</u> my palms grow damp. As I <u>watched</u>, every shadow seemed to shift and stretch.

Maybe it was just my fear of the dark, but I <u>felt</u> that fight-or-flight response kick in. Maybe I should run into the house and lock the door.

I <u>heard</u> another howl come out of the forest, and I <u>felt</u> my skin crawl with gooseflesh on my arms.

I <u>knew</u> something nasty was roaming the woods, something angry and loud. I <u>decided</u> to back up while <u>watching</u> the yard for any threats.

DEEP POV:

For a moment, I considered casting a spell that would illuminate the yard, but fought the urge. Forced my fingers away from the gemstone and breathed deeply.

Until chilling howls emanated from the woods. Not coyotes or wolves. This was Northern California. On second thought…maybe I *should* use my witchy superpowers.

The hairs on the back of my neck stood up. But I stayed there on purpose to test myself. I hated letting fear get the better of me. And because I was a control junkie, I had the profound desire to conquer all the things that frightened me…well, to a certain extent, anyway.

The night air was cold and crisp. The weeping willow tree swayed in the breeze, leaves falling from the branches like autumn rain. Beyond the back fence, the forest with giant redwoods—ancient trees, thousands of years old—soared to heights that seemed to touch the clouds. Staring into the utter darkness, I felt my palms grow damp. Every shadow seemed to shift and stretch.

Maybe it was just my fear of the dark, but that fight-or-flight response was kicking in, begging me to run into the house and lock the door. No, more like it was screaming: *Forget being all heroic and fearless and get your butt back inside!*

SHALLOW: HEARD

Another howl came out of the forest, and my skin crawled, ripples of gooseflesh prickling my arms.

Something nasty was roaming the woods, something angry and loud. I backed up toward the house, my gaze scanning the yard for threats.

***

Could you tell the difference in the two scenes?

Did you notice how closely we stay inside the heroine's head throughout the passage, except for that one "felt" verb in the paragraph when I go shallow for better sentence flow?

Although, it is not describing an emotion, even that one shallow sentence could be revised into a much Deeper POV.

As you start to revise your own work, remember that it is easy to unintentionally violate the *show, don't tell* principle when you include filtering words into the narrative, but now I encourage you to weed them out.

SHALLOW: LOOKED

Quote: "Use of the five senses not only tells our reader the experience of our characters at any given time, but can also infuse an ordinary story with deeper layers." —*author, Victoria Houseman*

Decreasing the amount of filter words like "looked / look" from your writing will transform any narrative into an engaging read. The object of Deep POV is to secure the reader inside the character's head without using shallower words that litter your prose and distance your reader.

Also, writers should avoid using "looked" or "appeared" to describe an object, setting or character expression because it is considered filtering (shallow writing). As an alternative, I would describe by *showing* the emotional reaction or the character's expression, or object to keep your writing in Deeper POV.

Whenever possible revise these filter words: LOOKED / APPEARED

SHALLOW: He looked angry.

DEEP POV: His eyes bulged and his lips pressed into a thin line.

SHALLOW: Ally looked at Scott in horror.

DEEP POV: Ally gazed at Scott, her big brown eyes wide.

SHALLOW: Misty looked so stricken.

DEEP POV: Misty wrung her hands and tears welled in her eyes.

SHALLOW: Lydia looked as if she hadn't slept at all.

DEEP POV: Lydia yawned and rubbed at her sleepy eyes.

SHALLOW: She looked less than thrilled.

DEEP POV: Her mouth pulled downwards into a pout.

SHALLOW: Darla huffed and appeared to mull over the offer.

DEEP POV: Darla huffed and tapped her chin as if mulling it over.

SHALLOW: The house looked quiet, almost peaceful.

DEEP POV: The house was too quiet, almost peaceful.

SHALLOW: I looked around the park for David. (Overused "to view" word)

DEEP POV: My gaze swept the park for David. No sign of him on the swings or the slide.

SHALLOW: She looked contemplative.

DEEP POV: She puckered her lips and nodded.

SHALLOW: He looked at me, and I looked back. (Overused "to view" word)

DEEP POV: He gazed at me, and I stared back.

SHALLOW: Zayne looked really mad.

DEEP POV: Shaking a fist in the air, Zayne glared at Bobby.

SHALLOW: Monique was looking amazed.

DEEP POV: Monique's hand lifted to cover her heart and she squealed.

***

Here is another excerpt that will demonstrate how to use the Deep POV technique. The excerpt was taken from my own published novel the first book in the Spellbound series, BEAUTIFULLY BROKEN. The heroine, Shiloh, is sitting in the car with her mother and they're parked in front of a spooky mansion.

Please carefully compare these examples…

SHALLOW:

I noticed the ghost float away and dissolve, and then I looked at Darrah. Next, I noticed her gaze was still fixated on Craven Manor. But Darrah's face changed in an instant. I opened my mouth to speak as I looked at her, but the hatred I saw twisting her features made me feel cold. Some old memory seemed to put a wry smile on her lips as I looked at her face, a smile, which appeared painted, suspended over skin. As I watched, she shimmered like an illusion, her expression looked both shrewd and ominous. Her face looked altered, as though her disguise had been removed. It appeared as if her aura thundered.

Her aura made me scoot away. Since my muddled suicide attempt, I could view auras. Looking at my mother now, I could see her aura flare with darker hues. This woman appeared angry and looked like someone else.

DEEP POV:

When the wraith floated away and dissolved within the fog, I glanced at Darrah. Her gaze was still fixated on Craven Manor. But Darrah's face changed in an instant. I opened my mouth to speak, but the hatred twisting her features stopped me cold. Her aura thundered, rolling off her flesh in icy waves. Some old memory seemed to put a wry smile on her lips, a smile which appeared painted, suspended over skin. She shimmered like an illusion, her expression both shrewd and ominous. Altered, as though her disguise had been removed, yet her flawless beauty flickered beneath.

Her aura had me scooting away. Since my muddled suicide attempt—when I'd almost died—I could see auras. Echoes of souls, which revealed a person's true nature, bound in colors that held meanings. Her aura flared with dark hues. She was not the same woman who'd raised me. This was *not* my mother. This was an ice queen.

***

From that last example, you can see that I only used one or two filter words for easier readability, but even they could be revised into a Deeper POV to enhance the scene. Once you start noticing shallow writing, it will get much easier to revise your own manuscript.

Last Tip: Stating that a character "looks or looked" is a bland way to tell the reader that he/she is viewing or seeing something. It is overused, and in my opinion, it is nothing more than stage direction.

Did he/she *gaze, glare, peer, stare, study, glance, gawk, blink at, glower, frown,* or *gape*? Any of these convey more information to the reader. And sometimes "look / looked" or "appear / appeared" is okay to use in a sentence if it improves flow and creates easier readability.

SHALLOW: SOUND

Quote: "I actually like deep POV because I love tight pose. I loathe unnecessary words. Deep POV not only leans up the writing, it digs deeper into the mental state of the character. We probably aren't going to stay completely in deep POV, but it's a nice place to call "home"…" — *author and founder of WANATribe, Susan Dennard*

This chapter will cover ways to eradicate filter words like *sounds / sound* from your writing that "tell" instead of "show." In my opinion, the word "sound" is extensively overused in fiction.

Did the character hear a *noise, hum, echo, thud, reverberation, crash, jingle, clatter*, or *vibration*? Any of which are more specific for the reader.

Not all filter words can be completely removed from your prose because that would be difficult and cause some of your writing to become awkward. If including a filter word like "sounded" in the sentence creates easier readability and avoids passive writing, then I would leave it.

Whenever possible revise these filter words: SOUNDS / SOUND

SHALLOW: There was a sound in the bushes.

DEEP POV: The bushes rattled with a menacing shake.

SHALLOW: I heard the sound of his boots echoing off the floor.

DEEP POV: The heavy thud of his boots echoed off the floor.

SHALLOW: A sound from inside the pantry startled him.

DEEP POV: A *crash* came from inside the pantry, and he flinched.

SHALLOW: The sound of thunder made the house shudder.

DEEP POV: The boom of thunder shook the house.

SHALLOW: He jerked at the sound of his father's voice from the doorway.

DEEP POV: His father's loud voice seeped beneath the doorway and his body jerked.

SHALLOW: The sound of the siren had receded.

DEEP POV: The siren's wail receded.

SHALLOW: He began striding toward the sounds of chaos.

DEEP POV: He strode toward the uproar of chaos.

SHALLOW: The only sounds were the muted muffle of my footsteps.

DEEP POV: The muted muffle of my footsteps were the only detectable noises.

SHALLOW: The smallest sounds resonated throughout the empty house.

DEEP POV: Throughout the empty house, slight noises echoed.

SHALLOW: The only sound I could hear were the rhythmic pounding of blood in my eardrums.

DEEP POV: Everything was muffled except the rhythmic pounding of blood in my eardrums.

SHALLOW: The sound of beating wings was like a balm to his soul.

DEEP POV: The resonance of beating wings was like a balm to his soul.

SHALLOW: I heard the sound of the garage door open.

DEEP POV: The garage door whirred open.

***

Here is another example that illustrates how to revise Shallow POV into a much Deeper POV for your readers taken from one of my short stories.

The first example is before revision and has a lot "telling." The narrative is also cluttered with filter words, and does not have enough "voice." The second example is written close-and-personal (Deep POV), with a more emotional punch.

Please compare the two excerpts.

SHALLOW:

The sound of students loudly talking makes me irritated. I notice Kevin Wells squirming in his seat, looking angry. The kid next to me smells like stinky feet and unwashed hair, making me want to throw up.

As I search my purse for a pen, a weird sound has me looking around. I see the teacher run his fingernails down the chalkboard to get everyone's attention. Finally, I find an uncapped pen, but when I go to start the test, I see the ballpoint only writes a faded blue line. I try it again, but it doesn't work. All dried up, I thought.

Then I hear the sound of the warning bell as everybody finally takes their seats.

Feeling frustrated, I feel a tap on my shoulder. I decide to ignore it, but I feel the person tap my shoulder again.

"Hey, Excuse me, but are you in need of a writing instrument" the boy asks. "Do you need a pen?"

I decide to turn around. It's the new guy from Bio class. I would have noticed the peculiar outfit—long coat, black boots—not to mention his blue eyes anywhere. He is close enough for me to touch if I want to. His eyes look so dark, they appear almost a black color. His eyeballs are looking at me with a frightening intensity. I <u>feel</u> my heart pounding, and <u>feel</u> frozen in my seat.

The <u>sound</u> of a book falling to the floor <u>makes</u> me flinch.

DEEP POV:

The students are making so much noise that I grind my teeth. My nerves are already frazzled from the pop quiz that Mr. Jenkins has sprung on us today.

Kevin Wells squirms in his seat, his ears bright red. Guess he isn't prepared for the test, either. The stench of stinky feet and unwashed hair comes from the boy across from me. My nose wrinkles and I try not to gag.

Ever hear of a shower, buddy?

As I dig through my purse for a pen, an ear-splitting noise echoes throughout the room. I want to cover my ears. The History teacher runs his fingernails down the chalkboard and instantly everyone quiets down.

My fingers touch an uncapped pen in my bag. *Whew!* But when I press the tip to the paper to write my name, the ballpoint only creates a faded blue line. I shake the pen and try again. Nada. Zilch. I slouch in my seat. Dang it.

The warning bell clangs loudly and everybody finally takes their seats.

Chewing my lip, I swallow hard. If I get up now and go to my locker, I'll get a tardy *and* might not have enough time to finish the quiz.

What should I do? Go or stay?

A hand taps my shoulder. I ignore it, but the person behind me taps harder. *Ouch!*

"Do you need a new pen?" someone whispers behind me.

I slowly turn around. It's that weirdly hot guy from Bio class. He's hard to miss, dressed in his usual outfit—black trench coat, scuffed combat boots—not to mention his strange eyes. He's sitting directly behind me. Near enough to touch. His dark eyes are almost black, and he gazes at me with an unnerving intensity. My heart races, and my butt feels glued to the seat.

Why is he staring at me like that? Like he can tell what I look like without my clothes on. I shudder, but I can't look away.

A textbook hits the floor with a resounding thud. My body jerks like a puppet and the noise breaks the spell.

***

The second example has rich details and uses the five senses. There are only one or two *filter words* in that excerpt, and it has "voice" and action and emotion. Even though it is mostly straight exposition, the Deep POV technique pulls the reader deeper into the story.

SHALLOW: SMELL

Quote: "Deep POV is a technique used to get inside the mind of a character and make a deep emotional connection with readers. To do so, the author must remove nearly all traces of authorship from the page. The less that the reader remembers that they are reading, the more effective the Deep POV." —*Kristen Kieffer, writer and blogger*

This chapter covers how to revise filter words from your sentences by using the five senses and omitting the offending words *smell / smelled* from your prose to avoid narrative distance. For Deeper POV, certain distancing words should be removed from your story as much as possible. (However, it is always okay to use shallow filter words in dialogue.)

The sense of "smell" can be a fun way to add depth to your descriptions. Smell can help a character to appreciate the aroma of a home-cooked meal, the whiff of freshly washed hair, or the scent of spring flowers. But it can also be a warning system, notifying a character to certain dangers, like smoke, rotten food, or dangerous chemicals.

One way to write in Deep POV is by incorporating the sense of smell into your settings. Smell is a natural reaction that can be included in almost every scene that you write. In Deeper POV, we experience what the character experiences. We smell the aromas, touch the same textures, and we experience the same emotions, so writer should include this vital sense.

Whenever possible revise these filter words: SMELL / SMELLED

SHALLOW: Suddenly he smelled smoke.

DEEP POV: Billows of smoke burned his nostrils.

SHALLOW: Her hair smelled really good.

DEEP POV: The heavenly scent of her hair—maybe roses—combined with the sunlight glittering on those gold strands caused his heart to thump.

SHALLOW: He smelled her perfume.

DEEP POV: The lingering trace of her flowery perfume invaded his senses.

SHALLOW: I can smell his clean, vital scent.

DEEP POV: His scent hits my nostrils, fresh linen and expensive bodywash.

SHALLOW: The room smells very clean when I go inside.

DEEP POV: The fragrance of leather, wood, and orange furniture polish surrounds me as I enter the room.

SHALLOW: I could smell his cloying sweet cologne.

DEEP POV: The nauseating stench of his aftershave made me want to gag.

SHALLOW: She smelled sweet, like strawberries or maybe peaches.

DEEP POV: A sweet aroma, like strawberries or peaches, wafted from her freshly washed hair.

SHALLOW: A thick sulfur smell was filling one corner of the gym.

DEEP POV: A thick sulfur odor filled one corner of the gym.

SHALLOW: He smelled like a campfire, and I buried my face in his chest.

DEEP POV: His skin and clothes held the scent of a campfire, and I hugged him close.

SHALLOW: The bedroom smelled of dust and thickness.

DEEP POV: The bedroom reeked of dust and a strange thickness.

***

Here is another example from one of my short stories. Try to avoid "telling" the reader how something *smelled / smells* with filter words.

Please carefully compare these examples…

SHALLOW:

Anne touched his shoulder and pointed with her nose. At first, Ryan couldn't figure out what she was trying to tell him.

Then he smelled it. The smell of gunpowder.

He headed toward the smell. He turned the corner down a dark alleyway—and saw his brother Peter lying on the ground with Nathan standing beside him.

Ryan and Anne hid behind a dumpster. The smell of rotting garage and old food made him feel sick. Ryan moved and took a quick look. Peter's aura was gone. He appeared dead. Nathan had murdered him.

DEEP POV:

Anne tapped his shoulder and jerked her chin, scrunching up her nose.

Ryan glanced at her with raised eyebrows. "What?" he whispered.

"Shhh," she replied quietly, putting a finger to her lips. "Do you smell that?"

Ryan shook his head, then the smoky odor of gunpowder filled the night air.

Sniffing, Ryan stamped in the direction of the offending stench. When he turned the corner down a dark alleyway—he halted in his tracks.

No, no, no!

His brother Peter lay on the ground in a pond of red with Nathan standing over him. A handgun rested in Nathan's closed fist. Sweat beaded his forehead. He did not look up.

Ryan and Anne quickly ducked behind a dumpster. The stink of rotting garage and decaying food wafted from inside and Ryan's stomach roiled.

This cannot be happening.

He leaned out and took another peek. Peter's aura gradually vanished. His brother was dead. And that evil jerk Nathan had murdered him.

***

Anytime that you can remove the sensory "tell" from your scenes and clearly state whatever it is the character *saw* or *felt* or *tasted* or *heard* or *smelled*, it will automatically put you into Deeper POV.

SHALLOW: KNEW

Q uote: "This [Deep POV] gives you an infinite possibility for characterization and a slew of ways to define character traits without so much as doing anything more than simply writing narrative. And you get all of this because the reader is privy to the characters thoughts and feelings because you've placed them so deeply inside the character's head….The result is prose that is much more snappy, responsive, clean, and clear."
—*author, Michael Hiebert*

In this chapter, we will examine filter words like *know / knew* that can take writers out of Deep POV in order to gain a stronger understanding of the purpose and nature of this awesome technique.

Some filter words can weaken your writing and bog it down such as "I knew" or "She/he knew something." Filtering is when you place a character between the detail you want to present and the reader. (I think, the term "filter/filtering" was first used by Janet Burroway in her book ON WRITING.)

Just because filter words tend to be weak doesn't mean they don't have a place in our writing. Sometimes they are helpful and even necessary. So if a writer must state that character *knew* something, then use "voice" and a deeper POV. However, eliminating the underlined words removes the filters that can often distance readers.

Whenever possible revise these filter words: KNEW / KNOW

SHALLOW: He knew his dad wasn't keeping up with the child support payments.

DEEP POV: His dad had stopped keeping up with the child support payments months ago.

SHALLOW: She sure knew how to kiss.

DEEP POV: *Wow.* His toes curled from the soft, erotic kiss.

SHALLOW: She knew he was lying.

DEEP POV: He glanced away when he told her he'd been at the office all day. A sure sign he was lying!

SHALLOW: I know Matt likes me a lot.

DEEP POV: The way Matt stares at me during Trig is an indication he wants more than friendship.

SHALLOW: Derek knew exactly how that would go down.

DEEP POV: Derek frowned. This would *not* go down well.

SHALLOW: When I touched his shoulder, I knew something was wrong.

DEEP POV: I touched his shoulder and he flinched as if something was wrong.

SHALLOW: I needed to know how awful my infraction was when it came to Thomas.

DEEP POV: Thomas might never forgive my infraction, but I had to find out.

SHALLOW: I know I haven't been a werewolf that long, but the full moon makes me twitchy.

DEEP POV: Although, I haven't been a werewolf for very long, my skin gets twitchy every full moon.

SHALLOW: I did not know who would come through that door.

DEEP POV: I had no idea who might come through that door.

SHALLOW: Shane knew his voice was low and angry, but he didn't care.

DEEP POV: Shane's voice was low and toxic, but he didn't care.

SHALLOW: I knew he wouldn't be in French class.

DEEP POV: The final bell rang, which meant he was ditching French class again today.

***

Here is another great example from my novel, DESTINY DISRUPTED, on how to avoid "telling" the reader that the character *knows / knew* something with filter words.

Please study these examples…

SHALLOW:

I knew it the second he walked into the room. Daniel, my boyfriend's best friend, was mad at me. I knew I couldn't really blame him after he'd caught me cheating on Trent. In my heart, I knew it was just one little kiss shared with a fallen angel and I'd regretted it the second it had happened. But I had to know if he told anyone about what he saw.

"You can't tell him, please," I said with a whine.

Daniel looked at me for a moment, then laughed. He chuckled and it was full of resentment.

"Okay, Shiloh," he said once he finished laughing. "But I have a request."

My heart felt sick. I knew what he thought of me now. "What?"

He looked thoughtful. "You can do my homework."

"I can do that," I said really fast.

We were both silent. I grimaced and looked around.

"I cannot believe you," he said, looking at me like I was a bad person. "You are not the same girl from last summer. But your secret is safe."

I felt tears on my face. I knew crying and begging would not work on Daniel. He was kind and levelheaded and the words hurt me. But at least I knew he would keep my secret. He was the most honest person I knew. However awful his tone sounded like, I knew the promise was just as strong.

Then he turned his back on me, and I knew he would always hate me.

DEEP POV:

My boyfriend's best friend, Daniel, strolled into the room and our eyes locked. His lips curled upward and his eyes became slits of hatred.

Oh, god. This is gonna be awkward.

He'd glimpsed me kissing that fallen angel, Raze last night, and I had to find out if he had told anyone yet. Mainly one person.

"You can't tell Trent, please," I begged. "It was a *huge*, really stupid mistake."

Daniel stared at me for a moment, then shook his head and laughed. He chuckled so bitterly, I'm not even sure the noise could be classified as a real laugh.

"Okay, Shiloh," he said finally, once his snickering quieted down. "On one condition."

My body relaxed a little, but my heart pinched. "Name it."

Daniel rubbed his chin and smirked. "Do my homework for a month."

"Fine. Anything," I said quickly and bit my quivering lip. "Just, please don't tell him. He's been going through so much lately. This would crush him."

An uncomfortable silence descended.

"Fine, but I seriously cannot believe you," he said, looking at me like I was lower than pool scum. "You're *not* the same girl I met last summer. But don't stress it—your slutty little secret is safe with me."

Tears spilled down my hot cheeks. Coming from Daniel—someone who was naturally so compassionate and even-tempered—the words and his ugly tone couldn't have stung more. But he'd keep my secret. He was the most decent, honest guy on campus. However hurtful his wording was, the promise was forever.

"Look, Daniel—"

"Save it," he said with a sigh.

Then he turned his back on me, and my stomach dropped into my feet.

***

Most of us have heard the saying "*show, don't tell*" many times. In order for a reader to become deeply involved in a story, they must be able to visualize the setting, hear the sounds, imagine touching the objects, and even smell everything within the scene.

These examples should help writers to revise your own stories into great reads.

SHALLOW: THOUGHT

Quote: "If you say, "She was stunning and powerful," you're *telling* us. But if you say, "I was stunned by her elegant carriage as she strode past the jury, with her shoulders erect, elbows back, eyes wide and watchful," you're *showing* us. The moment we can visualize the picture you're trying to paint, you're *showing* us, not *telling* us what we *should* see."
—author, Patricia Holt

Thoughts can either be shown in italics or plain text, which is a style choice made by the publisher or author. (But *never* use quotation marks for interior monologue.) While italics are most frequently used to convey inner-thoughts, they can become intrusive. Inner-monologue or internal exposition should only be used in moderation when writing in a deeper POV.

However, writers should ditch the filter words *he/she thought* or *she/he told themselves*, which will force the narrative into a Deeper POV. Remember that the objective of conveying character emotion through Deep POV is to anchor the reader inside the character's head without mentioning her/his thoughts.

And if the reader is already inside the POV character's head and reading their thoughts, then they already know what he/she is thinking, right? So writers don't need to include a filter.

Whenever possible revise this filter word: THOUGHT

SHALLOW: I'd better go to the store right after work, he thought.

SHALLOW: THOUGHT

DEEP POV: If Lacy was coming over for dinner, he'd better stop by the market after work.

SHALLOW: She was still <u>thinking</u> about the party and what went wrong.

DEEP POV: *The party was such a disaster!* Things could've gone smoother if she'd hired a DJ.

SHALLOW: Steven is such a jerk, she <u>thought</u> <u>angrily</u>.

DEEP POV: If Steven kept flirting with her best friend, he was gonna regret it!

SHALLOW: I <u>thought</u> that getting a promotion would solve all my problems.

DEEP POV: I sighed. That big promotion didn't help me financially liked I'd hoped.

SHALLOW: Maybe I should wear this green shirt today, <u>she thought</u>.

DEEP POV: Standing in the closet, she tugged a green blouse from the hanger. *This will go perfect with my new shoes.*

SHALLOW: Let him find out the hard way, she <u>thought</u>.

DEEP POV: She rolled her eyes. Her brother was so hardheaded sometimes.

SHALLOW: I <u>thought</u> I <u>saw</u> Danny cringe at the mention of his dad.

DEEP POV: Glancing over at Danny, I barely caught him cringe at the mention of his dad

SHALLOW: Except for the dragon tattoo on his chest, <u>she thought</u> with a smile.

DEEP POV: She smiled. Except for the dragon tattoo on his chest, he was unmarked.

SHALLOW: A terrifying <u>thought</u> occurred to me. (Cliché)

DEEP POV: My limbs shook and my pulse spiked. What if the killer came back before I escaped?

***

These next two scenes illustrate how to eliminate problems with shallow writing and revise the filter word: *thought*. Please study these examples…

SHALLOW:

Meg <u>thought</u> about what Evan had done. He could so easily lie about it, <u>she told herself</u>. And she almost <u>wished</u> he would lie, she <u>thought</u>, just so that she could walk away without any real heartache.

"Did you really kiss Carrie?" Meg asked, in a <u>jealous</u> tone. "Why would you do that?"

A smile crept over his face, and for a second she <u>thought</u> that he resembled the boy she once <u>knew</u> and loved before he broke her heart.

He shrugged. "Wouldn't you like to know. Sorry, but that's between Carrie and me."

Meg <u>felt</u> tears in her green eyes. "How could you do this to us?"

She never would've <u>thought</u> they'd end up this way—with her <u>feeling</u> so <u>bitter</u> and <u>dejected</u>.

DEEP POV:

Meg's face went deathly pale. She stared straight ahead, eyes fixed on Evan, as if begging him to tell her the truth.

Her stomach panged. *Maybe I don't want to know.* He might even lie about it. But that wasn't Evan's style.

"You kissed Carrie?" Meg's skin heated and warmth radiated from her pores. "*Why* would you do that?"

A smile touched his full lips, his usual smirk, and for a second he resembled the boy she once loved, before he'd met Carrie, before he'd broken her heart.

"Does it matter? We broke up two weeks ago, Meg." Evan shrugged and kicked at the ground with a dirty Converse. "Sorry, but that's between Carrie and me."

Tears sprang to Meg's green eyes. "How could you do this to us? I thought we were going to try and work things out."

"It's too late for that. I'm with Carrie now," he said coldly.

Meg's heart sank lower in her chest and sobs build up in her throat. *It can't end like this. It just can't!*

***

Did those examples spark your own creative muse? I hope so!

As you rewrite certain scenes where information is being revealed between characters, remember that they should still be moving, reacting, and *showing* emotion to keep the pace of the scene flowing smoothly.

SHALLOW: CAUSED

Quote: "First writing rule: Do not use semicolons. They are transvestite hermaphrodites representing absolutely nothing. All they do is show you've been to college." —*author, Kurt Vonnegut*

One common issue with narrative distance is the tendency to try to convey emotional reactions through weaker sentence structures by using filtering words such as "made / making" or "caused / causing" which *tell* how the character reacts after something happens. If you use Deep POV instead, you'll avoid slipping into this kind of shallower "telling" style.

Do I use these filtering words on occasion?

Yes, because I mostly write in first-person POV and sometimes they are hard to avoid without creating awkward sentences. However, my advice is this: if you can rewrite the sentence without it and stay in Deep POV, then do it. If some of the time you can't, then go ahead and leave the filter word in the sentence.

Examples on how to revise shallow writing:

SHALLOW: My heart pounded loudly and it made it hard to breathe.

DEEP POV: My heartbeat pounded in my chest. Now it was nearly impossible to breathe.

SHALLOW: "You look cute in pink," he teased, making me genuinely smile.

DEEP POV: "You look cute in pink," he teased, and the smile that lifted the corners of my mouth was genuine.

SHALLOW: The barking dog was making my stomach clench.

DEEP POV: My stomach clenched. When was that barking dog going to shut up?

SHALLOW: That condescending tone always made my teeth grind.

DEEP POV: Whenever he used that condescending tone, I gritted my teeth.

SHALLOW: Just the sight of him made my heart leap.

DEEP POV: My heart leaped at the sight him.

SHALLOW: When I dropped my ice cream cone, it made her cackle.

DEEP POV: The ice cream cone slipped from my fingers and hit the pavement. My friend took one look and cackled like a witch.

SHALLOW: A shiver rips up my spine causing every little body hair to stand up.

DEEP POV: A shiver zips up my spine, and every fine body hair stands on end.

SHALLOW: The close contact had caused a heat to rise deep inside her.

DEEP POV: He stood too close to her and heat rose deep inside her.

SHALLOW: The weight of disappointment caused Claire's shoulders to sag.

DEEP POV: Claire's shoulders sagged. Losing the football game meant no after party. And no hooking up with the cute quarterback.

SHALLOW: He grips my hips harder, causing my joints to ache.

DEEP POV: His grip tightens on my hips and my joints ache at his rough touch.

SHALLOW: He glared at her with hatred, causing her heart to stutter.

DEEP POV: He glared at her as if at any second he would breathe fire out of his nostrils. Her heart stuttered and she took a step back.

Please study these longer examples…

SHALLOW: The bumpy bus ride caused her to drop her purse and the contents spilled out.

DEEP POV: The bus rumbled down the street, hitting every pothole. She was jostled from her seat, and the purse sitting in her lap tumbled to the dirty floor. *Just great.* The contents spilled everywhere, rolling and sliding in the aisle.

***

Just remind yourself as you revise that "telling" with filter words is shallow writing that removes the reader from the experience that the character is going through or feeling. Anything that describes the narrator's thought or mode of perception is considered *telling* the reader about whatever the characters are experiencing. If you can revise any filtering sentences, the point of view will feel deeper.

To be clear, I'm not saying that "telling" or filter words should be completely eliminated from your manuscript. That would be impossible and make some of your prose become particularly awkward.

SHALLOW: DECIDED

Quote: "Cut out Filter Words. Filter words are a mark of authorship. When you write that a character *thought* or *wondered* or *saw* something, you are taking your reader out of the Deep POV experience. A character doesn't think these filter words while living out their life, so you shouldn't include them in your writing." —*Kristen Kieffer, writer and blogger of She's Novel*

Overusing filter words can have a negative effect on the writing. Filtering puts a distance between the character and the reader, and instead of describing the experience, the filter word *tells* the reader what the character is sensing rather than letting the reader sense it directly.

In Deep POV, writers don't usually need to include filter words such as *he/she decided* or *he/she considered*. These types of phrases can be murder to Deep POV, because they smack of author intrusion. Readers are now distanced from the character, and they are not in their head where they belong.

Examples on how to revise shallow writing:

SHALLOW: I decided to walk home instead of taking the bus.

DEEP POV: Walking home would give me some much needed exercise, *and* I'd avoid sitting next to Loud Mouth Simon on the bus.

SHALLOW: If he had decided on which girl to take the prom sooner, he wouldn't be dateless now.

DEEP POV: If he hadn't waited until the last minute to ask two different girls, he'd be having a blast at the prom right now.

SHALLOW: Maryann heard about the quiz in Trig and she decided to ditch class.

DEEP POV: From the classroom door, grunts and groans echoed off the walls. Maryann backed up into the hall. *Pop quiz?* No thanks.

SHALLOW: Lucas stared at the menu and decided on the turkey sandwich.

DEEP POV: Lucas's stomach rumbled while he scanned the menu. Hmmm, a turkey sandwich sure would quiet those hunger pangs.

SHALLOW: Lori considered dressing as a ghost for Halloween.

DEEP POV: Lori grabbed a white sheet from the closet. This would make an easy costume for the Halloween party. All it needed was two eyeholes.

SHALLOW: Amy decided that wearing pink made her look too pale.

DEEP POV: Glancing into the bathroom mirror, Amy grimaced. Pink was so *not* her color.

SHALLOW: I wanted to go to the movies with Jack, but then decided I was too tired to go.

DEEP POV: I already said I'd go the movies with Jack, but I couldn't stop yawning. Maybe he'd take a rain check.

SHALLOW: The second he touched me I decided I wasn't scared of him anymore.

DEEP POV: The instant he softly touched my arm, my fear dissolved.

SHALLOW: "Beneath all the dirt, he's not half bad looking," the woman decided.

DEEP POV: The woman eyed him closely. "You know, beneath all the dirt, he's not half bad looking."

SHALLOW: DECIDED

***

Those examples should give you a clear idea how the word *decided* can weigh down your writing and distance your readers. Here is one more that should help. The first example lacks "voice" and it is weighed down with author intrusion by using filter words.

Please study and compare these examples…

SHALLOW:

Callie decided to raise her hand up to the spot where she'd felt the offending prickle against her flesh and touched it, her fingers feeling chilled against the warmer spot on her skin. Something must have bitten her, she decided.

Great. Now I'll die of a spider bite, she thought. But even at her attempt to humor herself, she almost felt tears stinging her eyes.

DEEP POV:

Callie lifted her hand to gently touch the wound where the offending prickle against her skin ached and rubbed it lightly. Her fingertips were ice cold against the warmer spot. Odd. Something must've bitten her.

"Great. Now I'll die of a spider bite," she mumbled.

But even with her attempt at humor, tears stung behind her eyes.

***

Hope these examples help you to revise your own stories into amazing reads!

SHALLOW: WONDERED

Quote: "Choose a chapter or page of your current project and dissect it line by line specifically looking for sentences that can be made more active. Do you have any passive sentences that would be more interesting if made active? Do you have any filter words that are bogging down your paragraphs? Eliminate them!" —*poet and blogger, Carol Despeaux*

Writers should always strive to remove any filter words to deepen the reader's experience. The problem is that a scene that should be active and close-and-personal becomes shallow when a filter word is inserted.

However, if a writer has a few filter words sprinkled throughout the narrative, then they most likely aren't weakening the story.

But are the filters improving it? Probably not. So learn to be ruthless when you can.

And if the reader is already inside a character's head, then the writer doesn't need to state that *he/she wondered / wonder / pondering / ponder* when we could proceed directly to whatever it was that the character is wondering about by using Deep POV.

Examples on how to revise shallow writing:

SHALLOW: I wonder if it will rain this afternoon, he pondered.

DEEP POV: Uh-oh. Those clouds were coming in fast. He put on his raincoat just in case.

SHALLOW: I pondered life's meaning after losing my husband.

DEEP POV: Sitting alone in my room with our wedding album resting on my lap, I sobbed openly. *How could I go on without him?*

SHALLOW: She pondered last night's strange events.

DEEP POV: Too many freaky things happened last night for her to ignore.

SHALLOW: Cassie wondered if Drake was single.

DEEP POV: Cassie flirtatiously winked at Drake. *Hmmm, no ring on his left hand.* Must be her lucky day!

SHALLOW: She wondered if they'd serve chocolate cake at the wedding.

DEEP POV: She walked over to the towering wedding cake. Yum. Hopefully, it was chocolate—her favorite!

SHALLOW: I eyed Marcus and wondered if he had finished his essay on time.

DEEP POV: I sighed heavily. Marcus was going to flunk if he didn't finish that essay on time.

SHALLOW: Sam gazed at the new car in the showroom and wondered if he could afford it.

DEEP POV: The brand new car sparkled in the morning light. If Sam cut back on his other expenses, he could afford to drive that baby out of the showroom within two months.

SHALLOW: I wondered where Stacy was.

DEEP POV: Where the heck was Stacy? Third time she'd been late for work this week.

SHALLOW: Kami wondered why she was always picked last at P.E.

DEEP POV: When the second to last kid was chosen for the soccer team, Kami inwardly groaned. It sucked always being picked last.

SHALLOW: I wondered for a second if he was going to stab Paul with his fork.

DEEP POV: For a second, it seemed like he was going to skewer smart aleck Paul with his fork.

SHALLOW: Lynn wondered frantically which element would be the best to summon if she needed to fight.

DEEP POV: Lynn scratched her chin. Which element would be the best to summon if I need to fight?

***

The following two examples demonstrate first what your sentences might look like with that annoying, visible narrator "telling" the story, and then what they might look like with the narrator eliminated. Please study and compare these examples…

SHALLOW:

Jennifer wondered if there would ever be a time when she could stop being careful. If there would ever be a time when she could use all of her powers. She missed it. It felt like part of her had been numbed.

She pondered if Susie and Michael cared about losing them. They acted as if it didn't bother them, but Jennifer wondered if it did. Living without using her powers was like having a pair of huge wings—but not being able to fly.

There's no point in thinking about it, she told herself. But Jennifer wondered if she used her powers openly, if it might be dangerous like the warlocks warned.

DEEP POV:

Jennifer drummed her manicured fingernails on the table.

When could she stop being so careful? Use her other powers?

Her heart lurched. Without using her magical powers, her body felt numb like it had been injected with Novocain. Almost dead.

Maybe Susie and Michael didn't care about things like that. But Jennifer sure did. It sucked not being able to use her powers anymore. It was like having big, beautiful wings—but never being able to soar above the clouds.

Jennifer sighed and hung her head. No need to keep stressing it. The warlocks repeatedly warned about using their powers in public. They could all end up dead. Period.

***

As you revise, keep in mind that Deep Point of View is only one of many techniques that writers can utilize to craft a story that takes their writing skills to the next level.

In upcoming chapters, I will explain and illustrate even more ways to rewrite any shallow writing, in addition to offering the tools necessary to perform these revisions.

SHALLOW: NOTICED

Quote: "Of course, you want your reader to live the characters' experiences, but filter words won't help you. They're some of the weakest words you can write, in fact, because instead of putting your reader in the character's shoes, you're putting another layer between them." —*Leah Wohl-Pollack, Lead Editor, Invisible Ink Editing*

"Noticed" is a shallow type of telling that can appear in early drafts of any manuscript. I encourage writers to avoid the overuse of the word *notice / noticed* within the narrative. It is considered a filter word, and one that can be easily removed.

By revising the filter word(s), the story becomes much more immediate and intriguing. The outcome is worth the extra effort to remain in Deep POV. Although, some shallower words tend to weaken the narrative, it doesn't mean that the filter word or phrase cannot be used. There are generally exceptions to every rule.

If you find a filter word like "noticed," then also look for variants, such as *noticing, perceiving, detecting, become aware of,* or *notice,* etc.

Examples on how to revise shallow writing:

SHALLOW: I noticed for the first time that her hair was no longer crimson. Instead, her blond locks were streaked with dark purple.

DEEP POV: Her crimson highlights were now dyed a deep purple hue.

SHALLOW: I noticed Diego making his way toward the lobby.

SHALLOW: NOTICED

DEEP POV: Diego marched toward the lobby.

SHALLOW: I noticed that there was something tucked inside the book.

DEEP POV: A piece of paper stuck out of the book, and I opened it to read the note.

SHALLOW: I was about to take my usual seat when I noticed that the schedule on the desk wasn't mine.

DEEP POV: Just as I was about to plop down on my seat, I squinted. That schedule on the desk wasn't mine.

SHALLOW: He noticed that the wrinkle between her eyebrows appeared whenever she was worried.

DEEP POV: That slight wrinkle formed between her eyebrows. She must be worried about something.

SHALLOW: She found herself looking at his mouth, and noticed that scar on his chin.

DEEP POV: She stared at his mouth, before her gaze lowered to a scar on his chin.

SHALLOW: Emily noticed Travis stayed right beside her.

DEEP POV: Travis stayed close to Emily's side.

SHALLOW: Hazel noticed my expression and smiled.

DEEP POV: Hazel glanced over and smiled at my expression.

SHALLOW: Halley noticed Isabel smirking at the mascot.

DEEP POV: Halley titled her head and caught Isabel smirking at the mascot.

***

Revising shallow writing and filter words should be one of the last things a writer does on their final draft, but once you become more aware of these filter words, then the easier it will become to avoid them in the first place. There are times when leaving the word *notice* in a sentence is needed, but most of the time it can be removed and the sentence rewritten into Deeper POV.

This next longer scene should give you a stronger understanding of *show vs. tell*. Please study and compare these examples…

SHALLOW:

"Hi. I'm Anna Woodburn," my cousin said, and I noticed her long brown hair tumbled over her one shoulder.

"David Allen," the guy replied.

I noticed that David was wearing a dark wool coat although it was summer.

"And that's my friend, Kristen," David said, lifting his hand toward the pretty girl, who I noticed wore a thin white dress with a long, delicate gold necklace.

"Hey," she said.

"I'm Beth," I said, and looked downward, noticing that I needed a pedicure.

Looking up, I noticed that Kristen's gaze trailed over me as if analyzing my outfit. I noticed a swanky confidence about her, which wasn't all that surprising considering how lovely she was.

"I like your haircut," she mused, touching a red curl.

"Thanks." I felt myself squirm under her touch.

DEEP POV:

"Hi. I'm Anna Woodburn," my cousin said, her long brown hair tumbling over her one bare shoulder.

"David Allen," the guy replied.

I lifted an eyebrow. David was wearing a dark wool coat although it was a hot summer day. Really, really weird.

"And that's my friend, Kristen." David lifted his hand toward the pretty girl, who wore a white dress with a long, delicate gold necklace.

"Hey," she said.

"I'm, um, Beth," I mumbled, and looked downward at my sandals. The polish on my toes was chipped and the skin dry. *Yuk!* I was in serious need of a pedicure.

Looking up, I caught Kristen's gaze trailing over me as if she were a fashion designer analyzing her work. She had a classy confidence about her, which wasn't surprising considering how lovely she was.

"I adore your haircut," she mused, touching a red curl.

I squirmed under her touch. "Oh, thanks."

***

Deeper POV allows a reader to actively participate in the scene and ignites the reader's imagination, as well as helps them to forget that they're *just* reading a story. And a reader who feels like they're vividly experiencing the narrative is a reader who won't be able to put your story down.

SHALLOW: WISHED

Quote: "Filtering is when you "filter" the novel through the character's senses, creating an extra layer of distance between the reader and the story. Unfortunately, filtering is something widely known among industry professionals (it can be a red flag that work is amateur), but it's much less known to aspiring authors." —*freelance editor, Ellen Brock*

Every author's main the job (and goal!) should be to keep the reader "close-and-personal" within the narrative.

If an author can generate a visceral reaction or emotion, and make the reader care about what happens to the characters, then they've succeeded in a Deeper POV. Now the reader will be deeply emerged within the fictional world that a writer has worked so hard to create.

So, I recommend ditching these commonly overused filter words *wish / wished / hope / hoped* that can make your writing become shallow.

Examples on how to revise shallow writing:

SHALLOW: I wished that I could confide in him.

DEEP POV: Staring at Drake, I chewed on a strand of my hair. No way could I tell him the truth.

SHALLOW: Cam wishes he had bought that newer TV.

DEEP POV: Watching the football game on Carl's new flat-screen only drove home the fact that Cam should've bought one for himself.

SHALLOW: He <u>wished</u> he could help.

DEEP POV: He yearned to help the others, but he was forbidden.

SHALLOW: Claire <u>wished</u> things could have been different.

DEEP POV: If only things could've been different.

SHALLOW: She <u>wished</u> that she had a fairy godmother to tell her what to do.

DEEP POV: What she needed was a fairy godmother to tell her what to do.

SHALLOW: Cindy <u>wished</u> that she could go back in time.

DEEP POV: Going back in time would be the only way to fix this mess.

Whenever possible revise this filter word: HOPED

SHALLOW: She <u>hoped</u> Ryan would forgive her before the weekend.

DEEP POV: Ryan just had to forgive her before the weekend started.

SHALLOW: I just <u>hoped</u> I wasn't deluding myself with optimism.

DEEP POV: Now was not the time to delude myself with optimism.

SHALLOW: She <u>hoped</u> he couldn't hear the tightness in her throat.

DEEP POV: Maybe he hadn't sensed the tightness in her throat.

SHALLOW: Grabbing the ax, I hoped it would slow down any zombies who decided to pursue us.

DEEP POV: I grabbed the ax. Now this baby would slow down any zombies who were stupid enough to pursue us.

SHALLOW: She <u>hoped</u> he would get home first.

DEEP POV: If she slowed her steps, he might get home first.

***

This next example is longer and filled with those dreaded filter words that make the writing shallow and create narrative distance. Please study and compare these examples…

SHALLOW:

Dallas watched her emerge from the kitchen and saw her crossing in front of the windows, a bottle of beer in one hand. He thought it was something dark and bitter. Dallas knew she didn't like light beer. He wished now that he'd brought a six-pack with him on the stakeout.

His shoulders felt tight and he shrugged. He felt sweat wetting his shirt as he watched her switch on her stereo. She tipped her head back, closed her eyes, and her body moved to the music. Dallas wished he knew what she was listening to. He had no clue.

I bet it's a soft classical piece, he thought.

DEEP POV:

She emerged from the kitchen, crossing in front of the windows with a beer in one hand. Something dark and bitter. She didn't go for cheap light beer.

Dallas shrugged his tense shoulders, sweat dampening the back of his shirt. Stakeouts were brutal. He shifted in the driver's seat, trying to get more comfortable.

Through the binoculars, his gaze tracked her every movement as she switched on the stereo. Her head lolled backward, her eyes closing, her body seductively swaying to the tempo.

What was she listening to? Jazz, rock, country, or some popular pop song?

He had no idea. Dallas bet it was a smooth classical piece. Light, timeless, elegant.

SHALLOW: WISHED

***

Just to be clear again, filter words or *naming the emotion* isn't always the wrong way to write a sentence or convey an emotion. It doesn't lead to weaker, shallow writing. *Showing vs. telling* is all about finding a good balance.

SHALLOW: REALIZED

Quote: "As a fiction writer you will often be working through 'some observing consciousness.' Yet when you ask readers to step back and observe the observer—to look at [the character] rather than through the character's senses—you start to tell-not-show and rip us briefly out of the scene." —*Janet Burroway, from Writing Fiction*

The primary goal of fiction is to entertain and offer escapism. For a few hours each day while we're reading a good book, we get to be someone else, visit exotic lands, and experience new things. So, to really experience these things, a writer should apply the Deep POV technique. But if your story is riddled with filter words, then the reader will be distanced and unable to experience anything.

Sometimes it can be extremely difficult to avoid filter words when writing in first-person or in close third-person point-of-view. Problems occur when a writer inserts the filter word into a sentence because then the extra words distance the reader from the emotion or action, and they're forced to view events from afar, instead of up close-and-personal.

The two unwritten rules of fiction writing, or should I say, the two most important guidelines to be aware of and avoid are: filtering and an overuse of adverbs.

Even if we think that we understand the difference between *showing* vs *telling*, shallow writing can sneak into our stories. A few red flags that writers can easily search for in their current WIP (work-in-progress) are use of the filter words, such as: *realize / realized / realization*.

SHALLOW: REALIZED

Examples on how to revise shallow writing:

SHALLOW: I should have <u>realized</u> that right then was a good time to run.

DEEP POV: This might be a good time to run!

SHALLOW: I suddenly <u>realized</u> I didn't want to be left alone.

DEEP POV: The house was too lonely and quiet, and I had the sudden urge to escape.

SHALLOW: I <u>realized</u> that I'd totally spaced out on what she'd been saying.

DEEP POV: I blinked out of my daze and said, "Um, do you mind repeating that?"

SHALLOW: Alone in her room, she <u>realized</u> that on some level, Mark was right.

DEEP POV: Alone in her room, she sat down on the bed and sighed. Mark had been right about everything.

SHALLOW: They were at the beach, he <u>realized</u>.

DEEP POV: Damn, they must be at the beach already.

SHALLOW: Chandra finally <u>realized</u> the gravity of her faux pas.

DEEP POV: Chandra groaned at her obvious social blunder.

SHALLOW: He isn't coming home, she <u>realized</u>.

DEEP POV: As the sun rose in the east, she sighed. He wasn't coming home.

SHALLOW: Then with a start of <u>fear</u>, <u>realization</u> hit him. It had been his sister stealing the car parts.

DEEP POV: Clutching at collar of his shirt, he groaned. If the mobsters found out it that it was his sister stealing the car parts, they were both doomed.

SHALLOW: I had a startling realization (Cliché) that he wasn't human.

DEEP POV: Stumbling backward, I leaned on the wall. He wasn't human!

SHALLOW: A dizzy feeling swept over me with the realization that I could cast spells.

DEEP POV: Dizziness assaulted me. I could actually cast spells!

These next two examples are a bit longer, and they will give you a clear-cut idea on how to revise shallow writing and remove filter words to turn your stories into riveting prose.

As you revise, keep in mind that especially in first-person POV, there are much better ways for the protagonist to convey to the reader that they're aware of their actions than simply stating it by using words like *realize / realized*.

This next excerpt was taken from my novel, SHATTERED SILENCE (book two) and has a "before" revisions and an "after" example.

Please study and compare these examples…

SHALLOW:

At the Jeep, I fell forward, and felt myself panting and saw dirt rising around me, as I looked back at the clearing.

My breath was ragged and my chest felt like it was ready to explode. For only a moment, I rested against the bumper. Relief gradually hit me when I realized that the howling sounds in the woods hadn't followed me.

What a big coward I was turning out to be, I realized. I knew Evans would be ashamed.

SHALLOW: REALIZED

Opening the door to the Jeep, I sat on the seat and locked myself inside. I <u>felt</u> my hands shaking and I <u>realized</u> that it took me five tries to get the engine started. The Jeep made a loud <u>sound</u>, and I <u>felt</u> a breath push itself past my lips.

"Just get home."

I <u>realized</u> that I had said the words repeatedly as I drove home. I wouldn't think about what had just happened.

I was only sixteen, I <u>thought</u>, but at that moment, I suddenly <u>wished</u> I had my dad right then. He gave good hugs.

I <u>knew</u> this was bad. Real bad.

And I <u>knew</u> that I was fooling myself if I thought I was ready to take on paranormals. And I <u>realized</u> that my magick had been infected by Esael's blood.

I <u>realized</u> that Evans was right about my demon brand.

DEEP POV:

At the Jeep, I fell forward onto my knees, panting for breath—dirt rising around me—and stared back at the clearing.

My breath was ragged and my chest heaved like it was ready to explode. For only a moment, I rested against the bumper. My body somewhat relaxed. Thankfully, the howling *thing* in the woods hadn't followed me.

What a big coward I was turning out to be. Some demon hunter. Evans would be so ashamed.

Opening the creaky door to the Jeep, I hopped onto the seat and locked myself inside. My hands were shaking so hard that it took me five tries to get the engine started. The Jeep rumbled to life, and a breath pushed itself past my lips.

"Just get home." I said the words repeatedly as I drove. I wouldn't think about what had just happened. Couldn't think about what had just happened.

Ah, hell! I was only sixteen, but at that moment I suddenly wanted nothing as much as I wanted my dad right then. He gave the best hugs in the world. Hugs that made everything awful seem so much better. Not so terrible.

Because this was bad. Real bad.

And I was fooling myself if I thought I was ready to take on paranormals. Or that my white magick hadn't been infected by Esael's evil blood.

Evans was right about one thing. I had been branded by a freakin' demon.

***

In a first draft, the words can flow out of us in creative mode, but when it's time to edit and streamline our prose, writers should step back with deliberate wisdom and skill and rewrite shallow scenes into Deeper POV whenever we can.

SHALLOW: CONFUSION

Quote: "There are different types of confusion. We can actually understand the emotion better if we read how the character expresses it. Readers are also drawn into the scene more if they can visualize what's happening. And, since your narrator usually isn't a mind reader, it makes more sense to describe it." —*aspiring novelist and blogger, Teralyn Rose Pilgrim*

This chapter will offer some helpful examples on how to rewrite your sentences from "telling" into showing by eliminating this filter word: *confusion*.

While confusion is not an emotion, it *is* a mental state. Cognition and emotions are closely entwined. Just stating that a character felt confused or was bewildered seems like weak writing in my opinion.

And if a writer continues to state an expression or feeling or mode of thought, then it is *telling* and the narrative can become static and uninteresting. Compelling plots need some conflict or tension within the storyline, and one way to do that is to use a Deeper POV, or a reader might put down the book and never pick it up again.

A character could be confused by the directions to a friend's new house while driving there and become lost, or the character could feel confused about the mixed signals she/he is getting from the love interest.

To convey a sense of confusion, a writer could apply short, choppy sentences, or insert a rhetorical question, but don't overuse the latter. When feeling confused, a character's nose scrunches up, eyebrows knit together, and they frown.

One way to stay in close-and-personal (and there are many!) is to try to reduce as many filtering references as you can from your writing, such as *confused / confusion / doubt*, etc.

Some physical signs of confusion or doubt might be:

Nose scrunched up

Eyebrows knitted together

Staring sightlessly

Unsettling feeling

Hesitate to respond

Briskly shaking head

Licking lips

Tip head to the side

Ask someone to repeat information

Frown deeply

Scrunched up expression

Wrinkled forehead

Scratching head

Blank look on face

Twitching lips

Examples on how to revise shallow writing:

SHALLOW: She was so confused by Hunter's story.

SHALLOW: CONFUSION

DEEP POV: She scrunched her eyebrows and tilted her head to the side. "Huh? I don't understand."

SHALLOW: He <u>felt</u> utterly <u>confused</u> by the group's announcement.

DEEP POV: He looked from one person to another, with a blank expression on his face. *He didn't get the job?*

SHALLOW: She was <u>perplexed</u> and <u>bewildered</u> by this turn of events.

DEEP POV: Her eyes grew wide. She opened and closed her mouth, but no words leaked from her twitching lips.

SHALLOW: She <u>looked</u> <u>confused</u> and <u>upset</u> by the news.

DEEP POV: She shook her head and wet her lips. "Are you serious?"

SHALLOW: I stare at him in <u>confusion</u>.

DEEP POV: My stomach pitches. I'm unable to digest the words. *Is he really breaking up with me?*

SHALLOW: Feeling <u>puzzled</u>, I gaped at Jessie in <u>confusion</u>.

DEEP POV: I tugged hard on my earlobe and swallowed several times before I could speak again. "Are you sure it was my mom, Jessie?"

SHALLOW: I blinked in <u>confusion</u>. (Cliché)

DEEP POV: I blinked rapidly. My nerves jangled. *Was he for real?*

SHALLOW: Cole's harsh tone left me even more <u>confused</u>.

DEEP POV: Slumping onto a seat, I tried to figure out why Cole was upset.

SHALLOW: I was <u>perplexed</u> by the cat's hissing.

DEEP POV: I shook my head. What the heck was that cat hissing at now?

SHALLOW: My brows furrowed in <u>confusion</u>. (Cliché)

DEEP POV: Blowing out a breath, I stared at him.

***

It is okay to use the word *confused/confusion* at times in a scene; however, you can use it more effectively in dialogue instead of stating it in the narrative. Or if the main character is noticing the emotion in another character. But it is always so much more powerful to be *shown*.

Here is a longer example to illustrate how effective Deep POV can be if you use this method to describe the emotion instead of just stating it.

This excerpt is taken from my novel, BEAUTIFULLY BROKEN. The first version is crammed with shallow writing and filter words. However, the second is a good example of how to describe *confusion* without *naming the emotion*, and it blends "voice" with emotion, dialogue, and action.

Please study and compare these examples…

SHALLOW:

"Really?" I asked in confusion. "Because he didn't seem too interested when Brittany was stalking him at church on Sunday."

Brittany didn't respond, but gave me a hard look. I heard Heather and Elesha snicker. I thought that Heather wasn't as tall as Elesha.

Then I noticed that Elesha had flawless dark brown skin and an athletic body. With her chestnut hair and a thick fringe of bangs framing her angular face, tight-fitting plaid skirt, and blazer, Heather looked overdressed.

"What do you know, freak?" Heather stepped closer and seized my upper arm. I felt her nails in my flesh. I felt her mouth near my ear, her words very cold sounding. "Let me clue you in: guys like Trent Donovan only date girls like *us*." She let go of my arm.

"Oh, yeah? Well, what if I told you he was smiling at me on Sunday?" I lied. Feeling uneasy, I wanted to take the words back.

"I'd say he was just being polite," Brittany said rudely. "Because I've got a date with him tonight."

I felt nervous. My face scrunched into confused lines.

A spark of jealousy boiled my insides. My skin bristled with hate. A strange energy—magickal power—stirred within me. I felt it heat my flesh and flow into my fingers, blending with my anger. It awakened something within me. Then I noticed a dark force gnawing to get out.

DEEP POV:

"Really?" My whole body tensed, muscles quivering. "Because he didn't seem too interested when Brittany was stalking him at church on Sunday."

Brittany stayed quiet, but gave me the stink eye. Heather and Elesha snickered. Heather wasn't as tall as Elesha, who had flawless dark brown skin and an athletic body. With her chestnut hair and a thick fringe of bangs framing her angular face, her gold hoop earrings, tight-fitting plaid skirt, and blazer, Heather looked ultra-preppy and runway ready.

I tried not to roll my eyes. She was attending public school, not a fashion show.

"What do you know, freak?" Heather took two steps and seized my upper arm. Her nails dug into my flesh. Her mouth was next to my ear, her words cold and clear as ice water. "Let me clue you in: guys like Trent Donovan only date girls like *us*. Girls who know how to show a guy a good time. We're *it* at this school. What would he see in a loser like you?" She let go of my arm.

"Oh, yeah? Well, what if I told you he was crazy smiling at me on Sunday? Huh?" I lied.

The words flew out of my mouth before I could think. Maybe I was growing a backbone after all.

"I'd say he was just being polite," Brittany replied. "Because I've got a date with him tonight."

My stomach flipped over hard. What? My forehead scrunched up as I stared at her. Trent and Brittany? *No effing way.*

My insides boiled. My skin bristled. A strange energy—magickal power—stirred within me like a dangerous live wire. It heated my flesh and flowed into my fingers, blending with my anger. It awakened something within me. A dark force gnawing to get out.

***

It is usually better when writing a conflicted main character to *show* the internal struggle through action, dialogue, internal-thoughts, and emotion like I did in my second example. By using Deep POV, the character will naturally convey their true feelings to the reader.

Well, I sincerely hope these examples help you to revise, revise, revise!

SHALLOW: ANTAGONISM

Q uote: "Instead of stating a situation flat out, you want to let the reader discover what you're trying to say by watching a character in action and by listening to his/her dialogue. *Showing* brings your characters to life."
—*bestselling author, Janet Evanovich*

This chapter will demonstrate how writers can *show* opposition or hostility toward another character through the expressions and body language of a villain or another opposing character. It is also a great way to reveal insight into your antagonist or even the mighty hero. These tips and tools should also help you revise any fight scenes. The examples will "show" how to convey the aggression through the Deep POV method to strengthen your writing.

Let's start with expressive body movements and animated gestures that are commonly used to signal aggression toward another character. Outward aggression can be shown in the facial expression, from judgmental frowns and puckered lips to snickers and full-on growls. The character's eyes can be used to convey a threat through a bold stare, and body temperature can increase as well to show heated cheeks and a sweaty brow.

When someone is about to attack another character, they usually give a visible signal such as clenching their fists, or spreading their feet apart for stability, or they might get red in the face. A character might pace with restlessness, or invade the personal space of the hero in a display of aggression by the villain.

Some physical signs of aggression might be:

Clenched teeth and jaws

Pointing or jabbing with a finger

Shaking body

Clenched fists

Rapid breathing/sharp drawing in breath

Rigid posture

Restlessness, fidgeting

Flushed face or extreme paleness of face

Verbal threats

Examples on how to revise shallow writing:

SHALLOW: I was so angry at Leo that I wanted to punch him.

DEEP POV: My body shook and my fingers curled into tight fists.

SHALLOW: Major looked furious and he lifted his chin in angry defiance. (cliché)

DEEP POV: The tip of Major's ears reddened, and he lifted his chin a notch to stare down at me like a bug he wanted to smash under the heel of his sneaker.

SHALLOW: I was very angry and I wanted to kick Charles in the face.

DEEP POV: I raised both hands, my fists clenched as if ready to strike, and took a boxer's stance.

SHALLOW: Carl looked extremely aggressive and moved his arms in an angry way.

DEEP POV: Carl's chest puffed out and he wildly waved his hands around as he spoke.

SHALLOW: ANTAGONISM

Please study and compare these longer examples…

SHALLOW: Miguel marched in outraged strides in front of me and then he moved closer to me.

DEEP POV: Miguel stomped back and forth like a jumpy tiger, until he unexpectedly spun on his booted heel and stepped right up to me.

Please study this longer example of aggression…

SHALLOW: I angrily went into the building, and flung open the door. Then I heatedly marched to his desk and used my arm to slide everything off the desk.

DEEP POV: I burst into the building, the door swinging open and banging into the wall. Huffing, I stomped over to my boss's desk and with one brutal sweep of my arm, slid everything off the surface and onto the floor.

***

Try not to clutter your prose with too many filter words that will convey obvious information like aggression. The fact that the character or villain was antagonistic should be understood by the reader without being bluntly told. Use all of these illustrations to spark your own creative muse!

SHALLOW: INDIFFERENCE

Quote: "Truly emotionless characters are tricky to pull off because outside of programming, brainwashing, and curses, you can't really have motivation or conflict without emotion. Even a truly evil villain, hellbent on destruction, is probably motivated by hate, fear, greed, or disgust. That said, indifference will be easier to work with, because the emotion can be there and just muted or very well hidden..." —*anonymous, Writing Questions Answered blog*

Indifference is an emotion or a forced reaction that a character might use to hide their true feelings. It can mean a lack of concern, boredom, disinterest, apathy, or nonchalance in any given situation. To add an extra layer of depth to the characterization, a writer could have one character who is compassionate and generous, and another who is indifferent and detached. This can add some great conflict and tension whenever these two diverse characters are on the same page together.

An indifferent character might actually be trying to disguise a deep hurt or emotional scar, so they pretend not to care and appear detached, flippant, and even sarcastic. This type of complex character might even be an outsider or recluse, who believes no one else will understand their pain or circumstances.

For instance, in a romance novel, a character that is cynical and indifferent (makes a good character growth ARC) might be protecting themselves by keeping the love interest at arm's length or closing off their heart to avoid getting hurt.

SHALLOW: INDIFFERENCE

Some shallow words for indifference or boredom can be *glazed, tortured, listless, detached, remote, etc.* but these weak visualizes should be revised whenever possible with Deeper POV.

Signs of indifference might be:

Yawning loudly

Half-open eyelids

Rolling eyes

Shrugging shoulders

Sighing heavily

Limp posture / relaxed muscles

Head down or held in hands

Slouching in a seat or slumping in chair

Waving hand in the air dismissively

Glance up at the ceiling

Examples on how to revise shallow writing:

SHALLOW: I was bored listening to his stories at summer camp. They were so monotonous that I didn't listen.

DEEP POV: With my lips compressed, I slouched lower in my seat and ignored him.

SHALLOW: She felt detached from the lecture her mother gave and said, "I don't care."

DEEP POV: Her eyes rolled up. "Whatever."

SHALLOW: His expression looked bored.

DEEP POV: He yawned and closed his eyes.

SHALLOW: Tara was bored of answering questions.

DEEP POV: With a loud yawn, Tara said, "Well, I don't know."

SHALLOW: I didn't have time for a lecture on driving too fast.

DEEP POV: I crossed my legs and folded my arms. "Get to the point."

SHALLOW: Erin felt detached from the conversation and said in a dull voice, "I do not want to hear anymore."

DEEP POV: Erin sagged in his seat and sighed heavily. "I've heard enough."

SHALLOW: Lisa talked about her new boyfriend and I found it boring to listen to.

DEEP POV: I blinked, trying to keep my eyes open and not fall asleep while Lisa droned on about her new boyfriend.

SHALLOW: He thought the movie was dreary and mind-numbing. "I'm bored to tears," he said in an uninterested voice.

DEEP POV: His head fell back against the seat and he stared at the theater ceiling. "If I have to watch any more of this nonsense, I'm going to shoot myself."

SHALLOW: Billy looked at the wall while I was talking and I thought it was rude.

DEEP POV: Billy seemed to be spacing out, so I grabbed his arm and gave it a shake. "Don't tune me out again."

***

The following two examples demonstrate first what your sentences might look like with an annoying, visible narrator *telling* the story, and then what the writing might look like without the narrator.

SHALLOW: INDIFFERENCE

Please closely examine these two scenes…

SHALLOW:

The long car ride to Aunt Jenny's house was uninteresting. There was nothing to do, but look out the window at the trees and houses and other cars. I was so bored that I thought about taking a nap. But then my dad tried to talk to me about school, but that was a dull subject.

I tried changing the radio station to hear some better music yet I couldn't find anything to fight the boredom, so got out my phone and texted my friend.

DEEP POV:

This had to be the longest car ride *ever*. Not much to do, but gaze out the window at the passing cars, and count the number of houses and trees whizzing by. When that become mind-numbing, I sighed and closed my eyes.

"How's that advanced math class you're taking this semester?" my dad asked.

"Fine," I said, opening my eyes. *There goes my nap.* "And the semester's over."

My dad glanced at me. "What about that art class—"

"Why don't we listen to some tunes," I suggested, changing the subject. I was seriously burned out on talking about school.

I switched radio stations until that proved futile. Only static or uninteresting talk shows, which equaled *yawn-fest*. I whipped out my cell phone and texted my best friend. She always had amusing stories that would help the time go by faster.

***

As you start to revise your own stories, remember that it is easy to inadvertently violate the *show, don't tell* principle when you're writing early drafts.

SHALLOW: COLDNESS

Quote: "Personality plays a large role in how a characters sounds. Their voice will reflect that personality and color every line of dialog and internal thought." —*author and blogger, Janice Hardy*

If a writer tells the reader that a character is cold or it was a cold day, it is considered shallower writing. Writers should find innovative ways to *show* through Deeper POV instead.

Everything a writer needs to set the scene and vividly describe a location or feeling for the reader can be accomplished by using sensory details. As a writer revises a scene, it is effective to imagine themselves in the actual location, then think about the details. *What is the character seeing, smelling, hearing, and touching?* Using the five senses is mandatory when a writer wants to put a clear, descriptive visual into the reader's mind.

Coldness in a character usually indicates a decrease in body temperature, or fear, or even an illness. And it can be used to describe the weather or how an object feels to the touch, but writers should illustrate it in a vibrant way that a reader will easily be able to imagine.

To revise any shallower writing, I would look for phrases such as, *he felt cold* or *I could feel the cold* or *it was a cold day*.

Some physical signs of coldness might be:

Trembling legs

Hugging one's body

SHALLOW: COLDNESS

Quivering lips

Blue skin

Teeth chattering

Chills shake body

Runny nose

Numb fingers or toes

Shivering body

Stuttering dialogue

Examples of cold weather for settings:

Frost on the windows

Howling winds

Birds flying south

Heavy fog

Overcast skies

Spiders spinning larger than usual webs

Ice on the ground

Icicles hanging from roof

Slick roads

Harsh rains

Bare trees

Somber clouds

Examples on how to revise shallow writing:

SHALLOW: When I went outside, I felt very cold today. I put on a jacket against the wind.

DEEP POV: The second I stepped out of the house, an icy wind slapped my bare skin. Shivering, I yanked on my wool coat and stuffed my hands into warm gloves.

SHALLOW: Liam was freezing while he worked outside. His hands felt cold as he shoveled the snow out of driveway. He wished he had put on mittens.

DEEP POV: Liam's fingers felt numb and his nose ran. He shoveled another heap of snow from the driveway and cursed at himself for forgetting to wear mittens.

SHALLOW: It was cold in the classroom and the heater was broken.

DEEP POV: Thick frost clung to the windows of the classroom, and my legs trembled. If the teacher didn't get that heater fixed soon, I was coming to school in skiing gear!

SHALLOW: Even though Emma wore a jacket, the weather felt really cold.

DEEP POV: Huddling inside her warm jacket, Emma's breath made little white puffs in the frosty air.

SHALLOW: The weather in October is extremely cold and it makes me shiver.

DEEP POV: My teeth are chattering, and I shove my hands deep into my pockets against the chilly October weather.

SHALLOW: Mason opened the door of the spaceship and some very frosty air came out. He felt cold and shivered.

DEEP POV: An arctic gust escaped the pod when Mason opened the door of the spaceship. He shivered and pulled up the collar of his coat, and then rubbed his hands together to get warmer.

SHALLOW: COLDNESS

SHALLOW: It was a cold, overcast day at the campsite.

DEEP POV: The wintry morning sent a glacial coldness around the camp.

Here are a few longer scenes on how to use Deep POV to describe the cold. (In the shallow example, I did not underline the shallower writing, but see if you can clearly identify it now that you're more aware of *showing* vs. *telling*.)

Please study and compare these examples…

SHALLOW: It had heavily snowed last night, and I need to walk with slow steps on the sidewalk so I don't fall down. I feel really cold. I notice the cars, houses, and street have lots of new snow on them.

DEEP POV: Outside everything is white. The world resembles a frozen wasteland with a fresh blanket of snow covering the street from last night's blizzard. I move slowly along the icy sidewalks, wrapping my arms around my torso to stay warm. Even the snow-bound cars seem abandoned today.

Please study and compare these examples…

SHALLOW: I built a snowman and then put a hat on its head. It started snowing and the cold made my lips feel numb.

DEEP POV: When I'd finished building my awesome snowman, I put a black hat on his white round head and smiled. A fresh swirl of powdery snowflakes danced in the intermittent gusts, and I caught sight of my quivering, blue lips in the window.

Please study and compare these examples…

SHALLOW: The air-conditioner was set to high and Olivia did not know how to turn it off. She felt cold and shaky. Her hands were the coldest part of her body.

DEEP POV: Olivia licked her dry, cracked lips and blew into her cupped hands for warmth. The air-conditioner was blasting in her office and she wasn't sure how to turn the dang thing off!

***

Here is a longer, more detailed scene showing that a character feels cold and it also describes the setting. Please closely examine this scene to get a clear indication on how to describe the cold weather and the feeling of being cold.

DEEP POV:

The burning sensation spreading on the bare skin of his arms and legs, along with his face and neck had started to get worse. Despite its angelic appearance, the icy sleet felt as though Ethan was being stabbed with thousands of sharp needles.

"I *never* should've told Amy that I wanted to see other people on her birthday," he mumbled.

It was shortly after that ill-timed statement that his girlfriend had jumped into the car and sped off. She'd left him outside of town without a jacket (he'd given it to her to wear), gloves, or a cell phone, when they'd stopped to make a snowman.

Yeah, she was 100% pissed off, and now because of his big mouth, he was going to freeze to death.

He sighed. He *had* to make it home before nightfall.

Ethan stomped in sodden boots through the knee-deep drifts, hugging himself against the subzero winds. The snow was falling incessantly and blurred the hills and rooftops in the valley below. He flexed his hands and swiped at his runny nose with stiff fingers.

The fluffy snowflakes drifting downward would make a pretty Christmas card, but the cold seemed to penetrate his flesh and pierce the very marrow of his bones.

Ethan shivered uncontrollably and his body was shaken with a wheezing cough. He searched the surrounding area with teary eyes for some trace of shelter to stay the night. But there wasn't a building in sight.

SHALLOW: COLDNESS

Just great. I'll look like a snowman myself by morning.

With each lumbering step, his toes tingled with pain, and the soft crunch of snow beneath his boots echoed in the dying light. The roads were icy and his feet slipped on the slick surface. Ethan stumbled down the hill toward the city lights blinking like a rescue beacon in the distance.

After drudging for miles, he fell to his knees in exhaustion. The snow steadily enveloped him in a powdery white blanket that would surely cover his frozen corpse.

***

These examples should spark your creative muse. And if you use the Deep POV technique to describe the cold, then I can guarantee your readers will notice an amazing difference in your stories.

SHALLOW: FATIGUED

Quote: "Description, *your* description, paints in the story-world just as a reader is walking through it. For the reader, the story-world doesn't exist before the moment he/she encounters it..." —*fiction editor, Beth Hill of "A Novel Edit"* (I had the honor to work with Beth on my adult PNR novel, IMMORTAL ECLIPSE, and she's an amazing editor.)

When your character is tired or fatigued, I would *show* the character's mental and physical exhaustion through Deeper POV. I realize that it is much simpler to just state that a character is drowsy or that a character looks exhausted, but I think it is much more fun to *show* the reader instead—*don't you?*

Exhaustion can come from many different things, such as an illness or depression. It can cause a character to use poor judgment or be a side effect of prescription drugs, and in some cases, dehydration may even be to blame. Stress and insomnia can also be major factors of extreme fatigue.

In this chapter, I have put together some examples to further explain what I mean. Please use them as a reference and inspiration for your own stories.

Some physical signs of exhaustion might be:

Loud yawning

Heavy eyelids

SHALLOW: FATIGUED

Droopy eyelids

Weakness in limbs

Cannot concentrate

Bloodshot eyes

Dark circles under the eyes

A disheveled appearance

Clumsiness

Slurred speech

Examples on how to revise shallow writing:

SHALLOW: I feel so exhausted from running the marathon.

DEEP POV: My legs wobble and a bout of dizziness strikes my senses when I finish running the marathon.

SHALLOW: When Clary saw Noah still wearing last night's clothes, she realized that he hadn't slept at all.

DEEP POV: Noah lumbered into the house like a zombie. His shirt and pants were wrinkled, and his face unshaven. He must've been up all night studying.

SHALLOW: I yawned, and then I went into the bathroom to put cold water on my face because I was so sleepy. My eyes looked tired in the mirror.

DEEP POV: Yawning loudly, I stumbled into the bathroom and splashed cold water on my face. My reflection in the mirror revealed bags under my bloodshot eyes.

SHALLOW: I felt sleepy and worn-out.

DEEP POV: My movements were heavy and sluggish like I was trudging through snow.

SHALLOW: Sophia felt so drowsy that she tried to not fall asleep during the lecture.

DEEP POV: Sophia rubbed at her eyes with tiny fists and fought to stay awake during the longwinded lecture.

SHALLOW: I wanted to go back to bed because I was so weary from being up with the baby.

DEEP POV: My body swayed and I dragged my feet into the dark bedroom. As I fell over into the softness of the comforter and pillow, my drooping eyelids instantly closed.

SHALLOW: Dan looked sleepy and he fell asleep in class. He started snoring loudly. The teacher got mad and woke him up.

DEEP POV: Dan's breathing slowed and his eyelids grew heavy. He rested his head on the desk and his eyes closed. He must've been snoring, because the teacher shook him awake.

SHALLOW (*cannot yawn dialogue*): "No, I'm awake," I yawned.

DEEP POV: "No, I'm awake," I muttered, yawning and stretching my weary limbs.

SHALLOW: She felt lethargic, but worry prevented her from falling asleep.

DEEP POV: She sagged onto a chair with a glazed look in her eyes. Sleep would be impossible now.

SHALLOW: I was exhausted and sat on the sofa. I could probably sleep standing up. (Cliché.) I closed my eyes and went to sleep.

DEEP POV: Collapsing onto the sofa, my eyes drifted shut. My whole body sagged into the cushions and sleep came quickly.

SHALLOW: FATIGUED

***

Here are two longer examples of showing an exhausted character. (In the shallow example, I did not underline the shallower writing, but see if you can clearly identify it now that you're more aware of *showing* vs. *telling*.)

Please closely examine these two scenes…

SHALLOW (info-dump):

Aaron felt very tired. He wanted to go to sleep, but he had to wait up until his little brother got home from the birthday party. He tried to stay awake by turning up the sound on the TV, but it did not help him stay awake.

Aaron went into the kitchen and he made some coffee. He hoped that the caffeine would keep him from falling asleep. His mom counted on him to look after his younger brother while she worked nights, but he was too young at seventeen to be like a parent to his brother. When the coffee was ready, he drank a lot of cups, and then he felt more awake.

He heard the front door open as Aaron entered the living room. Now his brother was finally home, and he could to sleep.

DEEP POV:

Aaron yawned and sank lower on the couch. His lids, heavy with fatigue, gradually began to close and his body seemed to liquefy into the softness of the sofa. He had the urge to go upstairs and climb into bed, but he had to wait until his little brother, Gabe, got home from the birthday party.

"Wake up," he said aloud to the empty room. "Do *not* fall asleep, Aaron."

His mom would kill him if he did.

He sat up and grabbed the TV remote. Aaron cranked the volume on the western he'd been watching, but within seconds, his head fell back onto the headrest.

No, no, no. Stay awake!

The seventeen-year-old stood and stretched, then shuffled into the kitchen. He made a pot of strong coffee and leaned against the counter, the floor cold beneath his bare feet.

Aaron glanced at the clock on the wall. Only eleven. His mom wouldn't be home for hours from the hospital. Since she'd started working the graveyard shift, she counted on him to look after Gabe.

"This sucks," he grumbled. "I'm too young to act like Gabe's damn parent. It isn't fair."

When the coffee finished brewing, he poured himself a steaming mug. Aaron gulped down three cups until the caffeine buzz jolted his system.

The front door clicked open as Aaron walked into the living room. Finally, Gabe was home and Aaron could hit the sack.

***

The tools in this chapter should help writers rework any shallower writing that appears in early drafts. And I would study the work of other authors in your genre to get ideas on phrasing and sentence structure, and also inspiration for characterization.

SHALLOW: PAIN

Quote: "Creating character emotions remains one of my toughest challenges as a budding novelist. To truly show these characters and put them forth on the screen [or in a book] as though they were living and breathing, without making it seem cardboard is in one word: a challenge." — *writer and blogger, Casey Herringshaw*

For many writers, trying to describe pain or discomfort can be difficult. Even though pain is not an emotion, but more of a *feeling*, it should be described through a Deeper POV.

When trying to describe a character's pain to readers, writers should try to "show" the feeling by being descriptive enough to let the reader visualize what the character is experiencing while also respecting their intelligence, which means *showing* and not *telling*.

In order to make the reader empathetic to the character's pain, a writer should use metaphors or some specific language. To really convey the character's suffering (severe, throbbing, tender or sore, abrupt or intensifying), a writer can describe pain through the actions and reactions of the character.

For instance, if you're writing an intense fight scene, describing the pain of a kick or a punch to the face, should be short and to the point to keep the action moving forward. Or to deepen characterization, a tough and apathetic type character might get shot, but only display pain by gritting their teeth. Alternatively, a wimpy or fearful character with any type of injury might whimper and cry over just stubbing their toe.

Some of the best advice I can give writers is to keep the reader "hooked" by *showing* the character's actions as opposed to stating them. If a character is injured, a writer can *show* the character grimacing when he moves and rubbing his back, so the reader can just conclude that the character has back pain.

Some physical signs of pain might be:

Elevated blood pressure

Dilated pupil size

Perspire heavily

Hands and/or feet can be cold

Clenching or grinding the teeth

Covering, rubbing, or grabbing the pained area

Wincing when touched

Eyes that water or excess crying

Writhing or constant shifting in position

Moaning or groaning

Below, I've put together some examples of shallow writing compared to Deeper POV to show a character in pain rather than state it for the reader. None of my examples are terribly original, but they should give writers ideas on how to revise their own stories.

Now to be clear, I think it's perfectly fine to use the word "pain" in your writing if needed; however, anytime you can revise with Deeper POV, you should.

Examples on how to revise shallow writing:

SHALLOW: I felt tense with pain in my upper body.

SHALLOW: PAIN

DEEP POV: The tightness across my shoulders increased.

SHALLOW: He closed his eyes against the pain.

DEEP POV: A flicker of agony passed behind his closed lids.

SHALLOW: My head hurt with a bad headache.

DEEP POV: My brain felt like the hot mash of decaying potatoes.

SHALLOW: He thought the pain was bad.

DEEP POV: His pulse beat a tattoo at the base of his throat.

SHALLOW: I moved slowly to get to safety, but my body felt sore.

DEEP POV: I crawled to safety, a sensation of coldness lapped around my heart.

SHALLOW: He couldn't see very well when the pain increased.

DEEP POV: His vision went white with discomfort.

SHALLOW: The gunshot hurt and caused a lot of pain. She felt dizzy as the paramedic leaned over her body.

DEEP POV: The throbbing from the gunshot wound pulsed. Everything funneled, so she only glimpsed the paramedic's face above her.

SHALLOW: I wanted to cry from the pain of the hot poker as it hit my shoulder.

DEEP POV: My insides writhed when the hot poker struck my shoulder.

SHALLOW: The older man's expression looked distressed.

DEEP POV: The old man's face grimaced and he moaned.

SHALLOW: Jane felt a pain in her head.

DEEP POV: Jane rested her head in her hands and began to rub her temples.

SHALLOW: He laughed and felt a pain in his stomach.

DEEP POV: When he laughed, the ache in his belly flashed hard and quick.

SHALLOW: She had a bad pain in her side.

DEEP POV: If only her hips would stop aching.

Please study and compare these next two examples…

SHALLOW: I realized that I had a hard time concentrating on the test because I knew that I had a pain in my forehead. I thought if I took some pain medication it would help my headache.

DEEP POV: I clenched my teeth and rubbed my temple. The sharp throbbing spread across my forehead, blooming into a full-blown headache. I needed aspirin and *quick* if I hoped to pass the test.

***

I have included two longer scenes that provide an illustration on how to *show* pain. (In the shallow example, I did not underline the obvious areas of shallower writing, but see if you can easily spot it.)

Please carefully compare these examples…

SHALLOW:

I felt the knife stab into my skin and then the man plunged it deeper into my stomach. The pain was intense and the knife felt like it was sinking into my organs, and then there was a horrible, excruciating feeling of pain. I felt my eyes roll into the back of my head as the knife was suddenly pulled out of my flesh. Then I panicked as I put my hands over my wound, because I felt desperate to slow the blood that was rushing out. The blood went straight through my fingers and I saw it hit the ground.

Bland paragraphs like the one above reveal a practice that's very common with new writers, where they not only tend to overwrite, but state facts in a bland way. Please closely examine this scene rewritten…

DEEP POV:

The knife speared my stomach, and I stumbled backward as the searing force seemed to strike every nerve in my body. A taste of bile rose in my throat. The man advanced and thrust the blade in deeper, striking my organs. I hissed out a breath and fell to my knees. My vision blurred when the knife was jerked from my flesh.

Instinctively, I placed my hands over the wound, but the flow of blood seeped through my fingers and hit the ground like a thick, scarlet stream of death.

***

This chapter should give writers some clever ideas on how to rewrite any shallower scenes. And please take all of these suggestions to heart, and *only* make the changes that you feel will best suit your writing style and story.

SHALLOW: WARMTH

Quote: "You might be an amateur if you rely too heavily on clichés. This item is obligatory for any writing handbook. Beware the automatic phrase, such as "white as snow" and "quiet as a mouse." If your heroic character roars like a lion, she'd better be a lioness."—*author, James V. Smith, Jr.*

It is bland and cliché to state that it was a hot day or that the character felt warm. Body temperature can fluctuate depending on the circumstances and the setting, so writers should use Deep POV to describe the sensation or the warmer climate.

Whether a writer is describing the weather, or how something feels to the touch, or if a character feels warm, the more detailed the descriptions are, the better your storytelling skills will become. A number of different things can cause a person to become warm such as, anxiety, nervousness, weather, embarrassment, and illness.

Certain types of genres require varied levels of detail when establishing the setting and world-building. For example, a high-fantasy, historical adventure, or a science fiction novel will have an observant readership that expects not only graphic details and powerful imaginary regarding the setting, but facts and accuracy, too. One way to convey the weather or depict the setting is to have a character describe the background in his/her own "voice" through the five senses, rather than using an omniscient POV.

And I urge writers not to describe the setting with a cliché such as, "It was a dark and stormy night…" because settings can establish a distinct mood and atmosphere, like in a gothic novel with a mysterious castle, or a spaceship in a galaxy far, far away. Consider the setting not just as a factual location, but as a crucial part of a story's ambiance and emotional impact.

Some physical signs of warmth might be:

Heavy sweating

A flushed or red appearance to the skin

Panting, gasping, or wheeziness

Slick-sweat hair

Feeling lethargic or drowsy

Heavy-eyed

Dizziness

Nausea or Vomiting

Thirsty

Examples of warm weather for settings:

Wilting flowers

Brown, dead grass

Cloudless sky

Bright, hot sun

Dry winds

Sizzling asphalt

Air-conditioned house

Condensation on glasses

Sunburned faces / bodies

Muggy heat

Examples on how to revise shallow writing:

SHALLOW: When I left the house and the sun felt hot.

DEEP POV: Outside, the sun warmed my skin.

SHALLOW: He felt hot under the desert sun.

DEEP POV: The blazing desert sun beat down on him like the fires of hell.

SHALLOW: My skin was too hot and it looked red like a sunburn.

DEEP POV: My skin turned a splotchy red and felt fiery to the touch

SHALLOW: She felt too warm, so she decided to go swimming in the pool.

DEEP POV: Her feverish skin cooled when she jumped into the swimming pool.

SHALLOW: The day was hot and sunny.

DEEP POV: The sun flared in the sky like a fiery ball.

SHALLOW: The summer weather was humid and hot.

DEEP POV: It was another torrid day. The brown lawns appeared shriveled and dry and the flowers wilted like sleepy children.

SHALLOW: The day was too hot and the sky looked very blue.

DEEP POV: The sun hotly glares down from a cloudless cobalt sky.

SHALLOW: I felt sweaty and thirsty.

DEEP POV: Sweat poured down my face and a deep thirst plagued my senses.

SHALLOW: She walked slowly in the heat to a fan.

DEEP POV: She moved sluggishly through the stifling air to the fan.

SHALLOW: The street looked really warm.

DEEP POV: Steam rose in blurry waves from the black-tarred streets.

SHALLOW: I looked up at the hot sun that was shining on the homes.

DEEP POV: I squinted at the blazing sun that violently shown down upon the houses.

SHALLOW: The dog looked hot and he was panting.

DEEP POV: The dog panted, its tongue hung down in an effort to stay cool.

SHALLOW: The sunny day felt scorching.

DEEP POV: The sun flared like a furnace with no gentle winds to relieve its fiery wrath.

SHALLOW: I heard the sound of insects buzzing in the heat.

DEEP POV: The buzz of the cicadas emanated their somber drone of summer's blistering oppression.

Here are two more examples of shallow writing and revising with a Deeper POV. (In the shallow example, I did not underline the shallower writing, but see if you can clearly identify it now that you're more aware of *showing* vs. *telling*.)

Please closely examine these two short scenes…

SHALLOW:

It was a very hot day in August. Everyone felt warm and looked miserable. I noticed that no one moved or wanted to go outside. It was too hot to do much of anything. Even the animals did not like the heat.

I stood at the front window and looked outside as I placed my face against the window. The glass felt cold to touch because my mom had the air-conditioner turned on. The street appeared hot outside, too.

DEEP POV:

Everything appeared to melt from the heat of the sweltering August sun, and even the sizzling asphalt resembled black liquid in the blaze of the afternoon glare. Heat waves were modulating off the pavement, just like I imagined the streets of Hell.

Nothing stirred. Not even the birds, squirrels, or dogs.

Sweat glistened on my skin and I pressed my warm face against the cool, perspiring glass of the living room window. Thank goodness, my mom had cranked up the air-conditioning.

***

Whenever possible, be specific in your descriptions. Use vivid metaphors and similes to create dazzling images. For example, offer vibrant, colorful details by describing the heat of the sun, and then how it affects the character's senses in a scene that features warmer weather.

SHALLOW: THOUGHTFUL

Quote: "Complexity is an indispensable ingredient of life, and so it ought to be with the characters we create in our stories. Paradoxes do not negate the consistencies, they simply add to them. Characters are more interesting if they are made up of mixed stuff, if they have warring elements." —*author, Stavros Halvatzis*

Just stating that a character looked thoughtful or was contemplative seems unoriginal and boring in my humble opinion. Books need some conflict or tension within the storyline, or a reader might put down the book and never pick it up again. If a writer states an expression or feeling or mode of thought, then it is *telling*—and too much telling is tedious to read.

A thoughtful character might be considered an intelligent person, who weighs the pros and cons before making any rash decisions. Or a tense character who likes to overanalyze events within the narrative could be depicted as brooding or pensive.

When someone looks thoughtful, the face is usually relatively neutral, although there can be a hint of a frown that tends to suggest concentration. The eyes are fixed on a wall, or staring off, and the lips are taut. If the person has a trace of a smile or he/she occasionally nods their head, this would indicate listening with interest.

One way to stay in close-and-personal (and there are many!) is to try to reduce as many filtering references as you can from your writing. Examples of shallow words are: *brooding, pensive, contemplative, reflective, introspective, wistful, deep in thought, comprehending, quizzical, curious, inquiring, puzzled, perplexed, confused,* etc.

Signs of thoughtfulness might be:

Unblinking eyes

Chewing lower lip

Staring into space

Quiet, not talking

Running hand through hair

Drumming fingers

Rubbing back of the neck

Tapping a foot

Furrowing brow

Eyebrows slanted or slightly raised

Examples on how to revise shallow writing:

SHALLOW: I was thoughtful as I contemplated with curiosity, then I asked what happened next.

DEEP POV: With my elbow on the table, I made a fist and rested my cheek on it. "Then what happened?"

SHALLOW: Lauren considered the situation thoughtfully. "So really?"

DEEP POV: Lauren tugged on her earlobes. "That really happened?"

SHALLOW: I was pensive while I reflected on my options.

DEEP POV: I stared down at my hands while trying to decide what to do next.

SHALLOW: THOUGHTFUL

SHALLOW: She comprehended the problem, and then she said thoughtfully, "That is interesting."

DEEP POV: She posed a finger under her chin. "Hmmm, interesting."

SHALLOW: I felt confused and I was struggling over the dilemma.

DEEP POV: I laced my fingers under my chin and frowned. *There had to be a solution!*

SHALLOW: Giles felt puzzled and confused. "I do not understand."

DEEP POV: Giles pinched the bridge of his nose. "I am quite flummoxed."

SHALLOW: I felt perplexed. "Are you sure it was a UFO?" I asked quizzically.

DEEP POV: I paced the room with my hands behind my back. "You *sure* it was a real UFO?"

SHALLOW: Thomas looked wistful. (cliché)

DEEP POV: Thomas fingered his jowl, and then said, "I've got it!"

SHALLOW: I was introspective about the movie.

DEEP POV: I scratched my head still unsure that I enjoyed the film.

SHALLOW: He looked deep in thought. (Cliché)

DEEP POV: He rubbed his baldhead. "You're not making this easy."

Next, I have provided two longer scenes of Deep POV vs. shallower writing. (I have underlined what I consider to be to be shallower writing in the first example.)

Please carefully examine these two examples…

SHALLOW:

There was three girls sitting in the high school cafeteria, and they were discussing the upcoming funeral and the party planned for afterwards.

The cafeteria looked really big and the girls heard lots of loud sounds. There were gross smells, too. The girls looked thoughtful while they considered what to do about the party. The three girls had heard that Nicki Button had been stabbed that morning and she would no longer be attending school, because she was no longer alive.

"We just need to pick out the invitations, thank you gifts, and alcohol for the party," Bonnie said thoughtfully. "But I don't know—do you two girls think an iPod, a black T-shirt, and Gloria Vanderbilt perfume is too boring?" she asked nervously.

"I think it is perfect," Charlotte said excitedly. "I mean, think how cool it is to have the newest technology, plus black clothing to wear, and a new fragrance?"

Bonnie nodded contemplatively. "Completely," she agreed seriously. "Plus, black doesn't show stains."

Which was good when there was a stain of blood on your clothes from killing someone, Bonnie thought.

"Hey, what about my idea?" Kathy inquired, looking upset. "I said we needed to have some chocolate, too!"

"That's too expensive to add now," Charlotte argued soberly.

"And too much work to do that." Bonnie sighed broodingly.

She did not really care about the party stuff. She knew she had a knife with blood on it to hide before her next class, she thought.

Kathy and Charlotte watched Bonnie lift her purse, open it up, and then take out a lipstick from her bag. She began to put it onto her lips.

"Where did you get that lipstick? Is that Nicki's?" Kathy asked with surprise.

Bonnie <u>appeared indifferent</u>. "I took it because she cannot use it now that she is dead," she said <u>thoughtfully</u>.

Did you see how bland and flat the writing was in the first scene?

It is boring for readers to be "told" what each character is thinking or feeling; and all those dialogue tags with emotional qualifiers are like red flags that the writing needs further revision.

Please study this revised version with "voice" and sensory details.

DEEP POV:

Three girls sat in the high school cafeteria, discussing the upcoming funeral after-party. The chatter around them seemed almost deafening. A fellow classmate Emily Emerson had been stabbed that morning, and the school was buzzing with murderous gossip. The stench of greasy food hung heavily in the air, making Bonnie wrinkle her nose.

She hated hamburger Thursdays.

"I can't believe Emily's dead!" Kathy was sniffling and dapping at her teary eyes with a napkin.

"Believe it," Bonnie said with a yawn. "Now onto more important topics. We need to finish picking out the invitations, gift bags, and champagne for the after-party." She tapped her chin with a sparkly blue finger. "I just don't know—do you guys think an iPod, a black T-shirt, and Gloria Vanderbilt perfume is too non-mourning?"

"I think it's perfect." Charlotte sat up straighter and smiled. "I mean, think how cool it is to have the newest technology, plus dark clothing for the funeral, and a new fragrance. It totally makes the whole dreary funeral less morbid."

Bonnie nodded. "I completely agree. Plus, black doesn't show stains."

Which was always a plus when there was blood on your clothes from your latest killing spree.

"Hey, what about my idea?" Kathy pouted, her bottom lip protruding "*I said we needed have chocolate, too. It's comfort food…*"

Charlotte shook her head. "That's way too expensive to add now."

"And too much work," Bonnie agreed.

As if she cared about the gift bags when she had a bloody knife to stash before her next class.

Charlotte gasped when Bonnie extracted a tube of Chanel lipstick from her Kate Spade bag and smeared the glossy texture over her lips.

Kathy's eyebrows shot up to her hairline. "Isn't that Emily's?"

Bonnie shrugged and tossed the lipstick back into her purse. "I stole it from her locker before lunch." When the two girls stared at her in silence, she rolled her blue eyes. "What's the big deal? It's not like she's going to need it anymore—*she's dead.*"

***

After reading the two examples, writers should be able to grasp how *naming the emotion*, too many "emotional qualifiers," and adverbs can make the prose stale and boring for readers.

SHALLOW: STUBBORN

Quote: "The "difficult" female character can—and will—do the shocking, the unexpected and, as a consequence, will give your story an immediate jolt of energy. She is the character who doesn't fit the mold."
—*bestselling author, Ruth Harris*

With any type of characterization, I think it is better to "show" a character's personality and flaws throughout the storyline rather than be told that a character is rude, or sad, or even stubborn.

For example, in a lot of popular romance novels, the alpha male character and their leading lady will display the stubborn trait. Sometimes stubbornness is just a resistance to change in his/her life, which can work as a great "fatal flaw" if your character has to overcome a significant growth ARC.

Most stubborn people have trouble admitting when they are wrong, which can add a lot of tension within your storyline between characters. These types of personalities would rather argue and fight than suffer a blow to their ego.

However, just stating a character trait like, "Tom was a stubborn person," or whether the trait is a negative or positive one can cause narrative distance. And for me personally, I like getting to know the characters as the story progresses, and if it is directly stated, then it takes some of the enjoyment out of getting to know the characters.

Signs of stubbornness might be:

Thinned lips

A fixed stare

Clenched fists

Both arms crossed

Place hands on hips

Deep frowns

Refusing to listen or agree

Giving a sideways glance

A constant fear and sense of insecurity

Being afraid of change

Examples on how to revise shallow writing:

SHALLOW: He looked very angry and stubborn. "Damn it. There are no such things as ghosts!" he shouted loudly.

DEEP POV: He smacked his palm on the table with a force that rattled the dishes. When he spoke, Laura had to sit back, or she might've developed hearing loss. "*Damn it*. There are no such things as ghosts!"

SHALLOW: I was stalwart type of person and I did not like Demi bossing me around.

DEEP POV: I lifted my chin and looked her in the eye. "Stop bossing me around, Demi."

SHALLOW: Scott was a very tenacious person.

DEEP POV: Scott stood rigid with his wide shoulders back. "End of discussion."

SHALLOW: I refused to be bullied into going out tonight.

SHALLOW: STUBBORN

DEEP POV: I tossed hair over my shoulder. "Not gonna happen."

SHALLOW: Carol stubbornly declined to help Daryl bury the zombies.

DEEP POV: With both arms crossed, Carol shook her head. "It's *your* turn to bury the walkers, Daryl."

SHALLOW: Julie didn't understand why her sister was so obstinate.

DEEP POV: Julie stiffened at the challenge in her sister's eyes.

SHALLOW: I saw Alyson shake her head persistently.

DEEP POV: Alyson shook her head and backed away.

SHALLOW: He was determined to win the argument.

DEEP POV: His arms overlapped, resting against his broad muscular chest.

Here is an excerpt taken from my novel, SMASH INTO YOU, where the main character is faced with a hard choice, yet stubbornly refuses to submit to cruel hazing tactics that are being forced upon her by the sorority that she's trying to join.

Please carefully examine this scene…

DEEPER POV:

"There's no way I'm doing this," I said, backing away. "If I get caught, I'll get expelled."

"You already have so many infractions that your legacy status is the only thing keeping us from dropping you like a bad habit," Jade replied. "You're still on probation."

"You do realize what you're giving up if you don't do what we ask, right?" Brooklyn crossed her slim arms over her chest. "You'll *never* be one of us."

"You'll be alone," Claire said. "No sisters. No real social life. You might as well crawl back under the rock you clawed your way out of."

I stared hard at glassy-eyed Claire. "Did you grow your hair out just to cover up the three sixes on your scalp?"

Claire glared at me, but did not respond.

I wanted to be a Zeta Beta sister. I wanted Paris. But a girl had to draw the line somewhere. And this was the place. I was sick of them screwing with me.

"I'm not going to get a man fired," I said, finding the courage to look each one of them in the eye. "There are certain things I won't do to join a sorority."

"It's your funeral," Jade said. "We're having a chapter meeting next week to discuss some *issues* that have recently transpired with two pledges, and I expect you to attend."

Claire stepped forward. "And maybe you should consider de-pledging in front of the other girls that night. Everyone will want to know why we're renouncing your bid."

My legs quaked as I turned away from them. Turned away from the life I was so desperate to have. Turned my back on my Paris dreams. All because I stubbornly refused to participate in these humiliating traditions that the pledges were forced to do.

***

It is easy to "show" a stubborn character through their actions, reactions, and internal-monologue like shown in the excerpt above. Stubbornness is an interesting character flaw that can add a lot of tension to any storyline.

SHALLOW: DOUBT

Quote: "These emotions—fear, pain, doubt—are part of the human condition. If your hero is impervious to them, it is harder to understand them and harder to imagine ourselves as them." —*author, Tristan Gregory*

If you write mysteries, thrillers, or suspense, then this chapter should help you strengthen your storyline with a Deeper POV. Having a suspicious character(s) is a useful trope in almost any drama, even if that shady character turns out to be innocent.

Suspicion or doubt can take on many forms, like the unreliable narrator, and these traits can be another way to add a deeper layer of characterization to any fiction novel.

In order to realistically explain any suspicious characters, I would use a traumatic event from the characters' past, or something that happens plot-wise to arouse your character's suspicion. (But be careful of it *not* becoming a sense of paranoia.)

Suspicion and doubt can also make a great "fatal flaw" for your character to overcome by the end of the story.

Doubt is closely tied with suspicion, but it can also be used to create unanswered questions about secondary characters or mysterious events throughout the storyline. It can also be used subtly throughout a narrative to build-up suspense.

Signs of doubt or suspicion might be:

Narrowed eyes

Brows drawing together

One eyebrow lifted

Squinty eyes

Long, hard stare

Throat clearing

Puckered lips

Nodding head

Folding arms

Stiff posture

Examples on how to revise shallow writing:

SHALLOW: I was doubtful that Shawn was telling me the truth.

DEEP POV: With narrowed eyes, I stared at Shawn. "Is that true?" I demanded.

SHALLOW: He felt doubtful about going on the vacation.

DEEP POV: He checked his bank statement, but the small number meant he probably couldn't go on the vacation.

SHALLOW: I did not believe Alex because he was a two-faced liar.

DEEP POV: My brows drew together and I sighed. "How can I trust anything you say?"

SHALLOW: I did not trust him and he was acting suspicious.

DEEP POV: I squinted at him and tilted my head to the side. "You're *not* fooling me."

SHALLOW: Maggie listened to Glenn's story with a shadow of doubt. (cliché)

DEEP POV: Maggie nodded her head while Glenn talked, but her gut instinct told her to be wary.

SHALLOW: I saw a strange, suspicious man outside.

DEEP POV: My posture stiffened when I glimpsed a strange man lurking outside.

SHALLOW: As a cop, Malcom didn't believe one word the suspect said.

DEEP POV: Malcom rolled his eyes heavenward and fingered the silver badge fastened to his belt.

***

Here is a condensed scene taken from my paranormal romance novel, LOST IN STARLIGHT, which depicts the feelings of doubt and suspicion in the main character. She is being blackmailed and everyone seems like a suspect.

Please carefully examine this scene…

DEEP POV:

When I stop at my locker before third period, Tanisha Jackson, one of my good friends and fellow lovers of dark-side apparel, rushes up to me in the corridor.

"Hey! I'm glad I caught you," she says breathlessly.

"What's up?" I ask, opening the locker.

Lowering my sunglasses, I check my teeth for lipstick stains in the mirror, rubbing one finger over a red smudge on my front tooth. As I lean back, a black envelope flutters out of the locker, and I barely manage to catch it before it hits the ground.

"Can I borrow your notes for trig tomorrow?" Tanisha briefly touches my shoulder, and I glance at her. "I'm leaving early for a dentist appointment."

"Um, yeah, I guess…" I say distractedly.

"I don't even want to go because the last time I had an appointment," she says, "it was *so* annoying when the dental assistant asked me to remove my tongue ring…"

While Tanisha is talking, I rip open the envelope and pull out a white slip of paper with the typed words:

I KNOW YOUR SECRETS. TELL ANYONE ABOUT THIS NOTE, AND THEY BECOME PUBLIC KNOWLEDGE!

My hands shake as I scan the note, and then I reread it because I can't quite believe what I'm seeing. My chest tightens painfully. I just learned the truth about my parents and I'm still dealing with the big reveal of my heritage, along with the breakup, and now someone is blackmailing me.

I am *so* screwed. This is like a bad slasher movie. Some twisted version of I-Know-What-You-Did-Last-Summer. I clutch the warning message to my chest so Tanisha won't see it. Not that she's even paying attention because she is still rambling about going to the dentist.

"…then when I do it," Tanisha continues, flipping her dreadlocks over one shoulder. "The dentist claims he lost the barbell during my teeth cleaning. But I think my mom put him up to it. So can I borrow them tomorrow?"

Images flash through my mind like an erratic slideshow, displaying everything bad that'll happen if my secrets are revealed, like Sector Thirteen soldiers storming my house, and next comes the painful ice pick lobotomy, followed by my dad being sent to prison. My family will be ripped apart…

"Sloane?" Tanisha touches my shoulder. "Are you okay? You look like you're gonna spew chunks."

"Huh? Yeah, I'm good." I thrust the note into a pocket of my backpack and zip it tight.

Tanisha stares at me. "So can I or not?"

For the life of me, I can't remember what she wanted.

Oh, right—math class. And something about notes.

If someone at school knows my dark secret, taking notes in trig will be the least of my worries.

But I can't very well lose my mind in the hallway, so I force a stiff-lipped smile. "Uh-huh. I'll give you the notes tomorrow."

"Thanks! I gotta take off now. See you later."

Once Tanisha walks away, I inspect the corridor. My mouth goes dry. Whoever left me this warning might be skulking nearby, watching my reaction. My squinty gaze flits over each student lingering in the corridor, searching their expressions for any signs of guilt.

Emma Fowler and Kaitlyn Carter are gossiping at their lockers, and when they catch me staring, my frenemies glare. The culprit could be Emma. My friend Raymond McGregor walks by with a classic chin jerk to say hello, but he doesn't stop. A pack of giggling freshmen amble by, giving me a weird look. Hayden's younger brother, Zach Lancaster, stands at the other end of the hall, talking with one of his basketball teammates with his back to me.

Yet it suddenly seems as if the entire population of Haven High knows the truth….

***

Deep POV can make the story more interactive and intimate. Showing allows readers to experience differing emotions or visit exotic places. And a reader who feels like they're connected and really experiencing the story, is a reader who won't be able to put the book down.

SHALLOW: CURIOSITY

Quote: "If, however, you want to write a character from the ground up, a character who is as *real* as any person living, yet wholly your own creation, then there are three aspects you need to know in depth: the physical, sociological and psychological."—*Moody Writing blog, mooderino*

A curious character is one that might be super nosey or just naturally inquisitive. This type of character can constantly question other character's motives and inquire about certain situations. But it could also lead to them sticking their nose where it doesn't belong and causing wonderfully delicious conflict within the storyline. It is this overwhelming desire to investigate and explore that can motivate a character to solve a crime or uncover a mystery.

Having your character wonder about things is a great way to explore their thoughts and feelings within the storyline.

Curiosity can be a positive character trait or a negative one, depending on the storyline. An inquisitive character might be more adventurous and unafraid to venture into dangerous situations. For instance, a detective who's instinctively curious will catch the bad-guy, and an inquisitive teenage girl will figure out who stole the school mascot. And possibly, one of the most recognized character tropes is the nosy neighbor, which I think can be a fun personality to include in any type of genre.

Curiosity can also be associated with *wondering, speculating, questioning, snooping,* or *prying*.

Signs of curiosity might be:

Head tilting to the side

Raised eyebrows

Eyes big and round

Slowly nodding

Gesturing with hand for someone to continue speaking

Eyebrows creasing

Staring intently

Eavesdropping

Increased awareness of sensory information

Fidgeting or restless

Examples on how to revise shallow writing:

SHALLOW: I was curious what Ed and Mary were discussing in the next room.

DEEP POV: I crept closer to wall and pressed my ear against the wood. I *had* to know if Ed and Mary were talking about me.

SHALLOW: Tom was an inquisitive person.

DEEP POV: When I caught Tom rifling through my trash can to see what type of wine I drank, I knew it was time to move.

SHALLOW: Mandy was an odd and nosey person.

DEEP POV: Mandy asked a million questions while peeking into my dresser drawers.

SHALLOW: His constant prying had become annoying.

SHALLOW: CURIOSITY

DEEP POV: Whenever anyone stopped by my house, my nosey neighbor would show up and casually ask me who had just left.

SHALLOW: He was curious about the monkey

DEEP POV: His gaze tracked the monkey swinging from the trees, waiting to see what he would do next.

SHALLOW: Her curiosity was an intricate part of her exasperating personality.

DEEP POV: Even as a child, Alice was always peeking into closets and rummaging through boxes in the attic.

SHALLOW: She was curious what he was thinking about.

DEEP POV: His stoic expression left no hint as to what he was thinking.

SHALLOW: I was curious about Melvin's whereabouts.

DEEP POV: I had no idea what Melvin was up to, but I was going to find out!

***

Here are two longer scenes illustrating how writers can avoid shallow writing and apply a Deeper POV. (In the first example, I underlined the shallower writing and any overwriting that is not needed.)

Please carefully examine these examples...

SHALLOW:

Harper did not know why her friend had suddenly returned.

"Do you know why Ella is back?" Aiden asked <u>Harper inquiringly.</u>

Why had my former best friend, Ella returned after inexplicably disappearing twelve months ago? Harper <u>wondered with curiosity</u>.

"Maybe was abducted by aliens," Aiden mused out loud.

Harper ignored her Aiden's absurd speculations. Ella was too pretty and amiable to ever join a cult or kill anyone, Harper thought. Harper even had to do all the dissecting in high school Biology because Ella couldn't bring herself to hurt the poor frog. But she was dying of curiosity (cliché), and it was fun to speculate.

"Harper, do you have any idea why Ella came back to town or not?" Aiden asked Harper again in a questioning tone. "Please tell me about your theories because I'm very curious."

Harper stared at him with a curious expression, and felt her face blushing hotly. The truth was, she hadn't spoken to Ella in over a year. Maybe Ella really had turned into a brainwashed cult leader or spent the last year in a penitentiary, Ella thought to herself.

"I have no idea," she said softly, and then added inquisitively, "But I'm curious to find out..."

The next version has been rewritten with more "voice," Deep POV, and more characterization.

DEEP POV:

"Hey, Harper, any idea why Ella suddenly came back to town?" Aiden wiggled his eyebrows. "Maybe she's been in jail for something like murder!"

She shook her head. Ella, her former best friend, had returned after mysteriously skipping town a year ago. Ella was too smart to ever join a cult or murder anyone. Harper smiled, remembering how she'd even done all the slicing and dicing in Biology because Ella couldn't bring herself to dissect the stupid frog.

Tilting her head, Harper tapped a finger on her chin. "I haven't got a damn clue."

"But it's weird, right?" Aiden scratched his curly head. "You must have a theory."

Harper blinked, and her oval face flushed hotly. For all she knew, Ella really had turned into a brainwashed cult leader or been locked up in some woman's insane asylum.

"Yeah, it *is* strange," she said, rubbing her chin. "But don't worry, I'll find out…"

***

By giving your characters realistic emotions and reactions, it gives them even more complexity. And being able to describe those emotions through Deeper POV adds mastery to your writing.

SHALLOW: RELAX

Quote: "One of the most common characterization mistakes writers make is granting their characters too much self-awareness. That sly pitfall puts tension at risk, limits believability, and inhibits the ability to *show* rather than *tell*." —*fiction coach, editor, and writer, MJ Bush*

To avoid stating the character's emotional state, like he/she relaxed, a writer can *show* a character taking a breather or loosening up in slower, reflective scenes.

Relaxing is a physical response to a lot of different emotions or events. For instance, if the character was almost caught stealing, but then managed to allude the cops, they would relax or calm down.

If the character had been tense or worrying about something, once it was resolved, they might visibly relax their posture or the stiffness in their shoulders.

Or if the character is feeling relieved after a strange turn of events within the storyline, and the writer wants to give the character a short reprieve before ramping up the action or tension again, they could show them unwinding.

Some physical signs of relaxing might be:

Breathing becomes slow and deep

Muscles become less tense

SHALLOW: RELAX

Yawning and stretching

Cracking the neck

Torso sags slightly to one side

Shoulders are not tensed up

Limbs hang loosely

Legs casually flung out

Putting hands behind head

Forehead lines un-creased

Examples on how to revise shallow writing:

SHALLOW: I saw my dad trying to relax before saying, "Okay. Tell me everything."

DEEP POV: My dad stretched out his arms, then let them drop. "Okay. Tell me *everything*."

SHALLOW: Tommy felt nervous, but then he relaxed. "It wasn't me. Honest," he said mildly.

DEEP POV: Tommy shook out his hands and kept his voice steady. "It wasn't me. Honest."

SHALLOW: I felt tense and I decided to try to relax.

DEEP POV: Tension stiffened my posture and made my jaw tight. I rolled my shoulders, trying to draw the stress away from my muscles.

SHALLOW: Trent wanted to relax, but it was difficult until he exhaled.

DEEP POV: Trent held in a breath, and then slowly released it.

SHALLOW: I felt determined to relax my body.

DEEP POV: I forced myself to unclench my fists.

SHALLOW: Lydia felt wound up and upset, but she needed to relax.

DEEP POV: Lydia pushed the air from her lungs, and the tension left her body.

SHALLOW: I wanted to ease the tension and calm down.

DEEP POV: I took a few deep breaths to steady myself.

SHALLOW: She forced herself to release the tension in her chest.

DEEP POV: She lowered eyelashes, and she let the breath swoosh from her lungs.

SHALLOW: I couldn't relax until I knew I was safe.

DEEP POV: Breath returned to me in a rush. I was finally safe.

SHALLOW: She decided to throw in the towel (cliché) as she said wearily, "Just bite my neck, Edward."

DEEP POV: Her shoulders sagged, her voice soft. "Just bite my neck, Edward."

Here are two longer scenes that illustrate how to avoid shallower writing and embrace a Deeper POV. (I have underlined what I consider to be shallower writing.)

Please closely analyze these two very different scenes...

SHALLOW:

"I need to find and kill that warlock," I said gravelly because I could not relax. "He might hurt my grandfather."

I saw my brother Peter visibly relax and I felt him wrap his arms around my shoulders. "I think you are ready to fight the warlock. Please try to be careful, sister," he whispered softly, then I saw him sped off down the hall.

SHALLOW: RELAX

I felt my body unwind as I watched him go into the kitchen. I turned to Ryan and breathed a sigh of relief. (cliché)

"Are you ready?" I asked Ryan honestly.

I saw him hold out his hand and I took it. I felt him squeeze it gently. "It'll be okay," he reassured calmly, but I didn't believe him.

I looked around at the room, at how empty the living room was and felt a little disappointed when I realized that my best friend hadn't shown up yet. I'd texted her the night before, but I realized she thought that there was no reason to say goodbye to someone who was going to risk her life to fight a warlock.

I looked into Ryan's blue eyes. "She didn't come to say farewell," I told him matter-of-factly.

"No, she didn't," he stated truthfully. "But I am here."

"I guess there is no need to wait. I will right back," I told him and headed toward my grandfather's office.

DEEP POV:

"I *need* to kill that warlock." My posture stiffened "Before he tries to hurt Grandpa."

"Yes, yes. I agree. You're ready to face your enemy." My brother Peter rolled his shoulders, then wrapped his arms around me in a quick hug. "Please try to be careful, Sis," he whispered, then sped off down the hall and into the kitchen.

I blew out a breath and the tension in my body lessened. I turned to Ryan and slightly smiled. "Ready to do this?"

He nodded, then took my hand, and squeezed it gently. "It'll be okay."

But I didn't believe him. Fighting a warlock to protect my family was high up on the crazy scale.

My gaze swept over the empty living room and my stomach dropped. My best friend hadn't shown up. I'd texted her the night before, but maybe saying goodbye to someone who was going to fight a warlock was too hard.

I gazed into Ryan's blue eyes, then pulled my hand free of his. "She didn't come to say goodbye," I said, lowering my head and kicking at the ground with my scuffed combat boot.

He shrugged. "No, she didn't…but *I'm* here."

"Guess there's no need to wait. I'll right back." I marched out the door with my head held high and entered my grandfather's office.

***

Just remember that anytime a writer can remove the sensory "tell" from a scene and clearly describe whatever it is the character *saw* or *felt* or *tasted* or *heard* or *smelled*, it will automatically enhance the reading experience for the audience.

DESCRIBE THE SENSES

Quote: "A common writing fault and often difficult to recognize, although once the principle is grasped, cutting away filters is an easy means to more vivid writing." —*Janet Burroway, Writing Fiction*

To write using the Deep POV technique, writers should involve all of the five senses in their emotional descriptions. Try to vividly describe every sensation, reaction, and emotion that your character(s) is experiencing.

Remember that "telling" a reader what a character is feeling or experiencing is *not* using Deep POV. The right way is to show by describing what is unfolding in every scene by the use of action, description, dialogue, and the five senses.

Powerful descriptive writing should always strive to involve the use of every human sense. It is also a great way of making your scenes three-dimensional. In order to do this, I think it's important to stay in Deep POV to construct a more realistic and engaging scene. Because if we don't, as writers, we are cheating our readers by limiting their use of the five senses in our scenes, or by not using them at all.

Please study and compare these examples…

SHALLOW (touch): I <u>touched</u> the dress to <u>feel</u> the fabric.

DEEP POV: My fingers caressed the silky fabric.

If you're going to describe how something tastes, sounds and looks, then you can leave out how it feels and smells. You never want to assault your reader's senses, or they will skip ahead to get back to the action.

There are many ways to achieve Deep POV, but here are a few sure-fire ways to enhance your prose.

THE MAIN FIVE SENSES ARE:

Sight: What your character sees. Describe images and the setting through their eyes.

Hear: Noises that surround your character(s) in every scene.

Smell: Make clear the scents, aromas, and odors.

Touch: Show the feel of icy snow or the luxurious feel of silk sheets.

Taste: Describe the tart flavor of a lime or the harsh burn and acrid taste of whiskey.

***

Below I have provided some examples of the wrong way to describe something and the correct way through use of Deep POV by including the five senses. The filter words are underlined. Please study and compare these examples…

SHALLOW (touch): I felt cold when I stepped outside the warm house.

DEEP POV: The chilly winds nipped at my cheeks and I shuddered.

SHALLOW (scent): Lori could smell the trees and pine scents in the air.

DEEP POV: Aromas drifted from the meadow—pine and cedar—as a strong gust blew across the rippling lake.

SHALLOW (sight): I could see Malcolm walking toward me.

DEEP POV: Malcolm strode toward me with a brisk gait.

SHALLOW (hear): I heard ghostly moans coming from within the haunted house.

DESCRIBE THE SENSES

DEEP POV: Ghostly moans came from within the haunted house.

SHALLOW (taste): The steak was burnt and tasted nasty.

DEEP POV: He bit into the blackened piece of meat, the steak had a charred flavor.

***

As writers, we want our readers to experience the story through the senses of our characters. And by engaging the five senses, plus describing the emotional reactions, it helps readers engage more closely with the character's experience. Shallow writing with filter words can and *will* have the opposite effect.

Please compare the next two examples...

SHALLOW:

When Scott heard the growling sound, he looked down and saw a large dog blocking the trail. He knew it would attack if he moved. Scott felt a sense of terror build in his heart.

DEEP POV:

Scott halted at the warning growl. Standing in front of him was a large dog, flashing its teeth. He stifled the girlish shriek that leaked from his lips with one hand. His heart jackhammered in his chest as he took a stumbling step backward.

***

Can you tell the difference?

In the second example, you can imagine much more vividly the dog and Scott's emotional response. It is always better to attempt to make your scene unique by inserting some of the five senses into the narrative.

Now try to use these examples as inspiration to revise your WIP by using some of the five senses in your own writing.

DESCRIBE THE EMOTIONS

Quote: "Use specific, concrete nouns instead of vague ones like *happiness, kindness, arrogance*, and *courage*. Instead, try to show characters being happy, kind, arrogant, and courageous. Also, use only the most vivid, active verbs, and avoid the passive or linking verbs. Limit modifiers." —*novelist, Maria V. Snyder*

This chapter will include even more great ways to "show" emotion through vivid description without *stating it* to the reader. Try to describe what the character is feeling or experiencing. All well-written novels share one thing in common—character emotion.

The best way to convey your character's thoughts, senses, emotions, and feelings is to *show* them though powerful description. To do this, try depicting the character's physical reactions along with the emotional ones.

Remember to always use the concept of the *show and don't tell* in your fiction writing. This tenet means describing what a character is feeling without actually "telling" the reader or using filter words. Showing takes a lot more creativity than "telling," but trust me, it will pay off by giving your readers a much more powerful and believable story.

Whenever possible revise filter words and *show* emotions instead.

Please study and compare these examples...

SHALLOW: "Go get it," he said <u>angrily</u>, slamming his fist on the table.

DEEP POV: He slapped his meaty fist on the table with a force that rattled the glasses. When he spoke, his voice held an ominous quality. "Get it *now*."

DESCRIBE THE EMOTIONS

***

Strive to *show* immediate reactions through active physical gestures, emotional responses, clever dialogue, and action descriptors. There aren't any hard or fast rules, but often a character's reaction to something usually follows this order:

physical (involuntary) reaction

emotional response

thought / deliberation

dialogue (internal or external)

purposeful action / decision

If you write a character's reactions in this simple order, it will usually give a stronger visual image in your reader's mind.

Try to keep in mind that *all* plot points, big events, or plot twists should have a visceral, emotional, or physical reaction. Readers need to see a character's emotional and physical responses to almost *every* event that happens in your storyline. If he/she has no reaction to pinch or plot points, or inciting incidents, or overall story problems, then it's as if those actions and revelations have no meaning. If they mean nothing to the character, then they mean nothing to the plot or to the reader.

In most cases, emotional description shouldn't be too specific. The reader should know without being told with shallow writing that the character is, for instance, frightened. It is always better to use stronger words like *shudder, startle, froze,* or *turned away* to show emotions and not use non-specific "telling words" like *surprise, afraid, joy, terror,* or *disappointment.*

I have included an example of intense emotions, effective dialogue tags, and realistic reactions that are written in Deep POV.

This excerpt was taken from my novel, MOONLIGHT MAYHEM. The heroine, Shiloh, has recently broken up with her boyfriend and this is the first time they've seen each other in weeks. Notice how her inner monologue flows naturally with the external conversation and action—all written in Deeper POV.

DEEP POV:

Then the swoon-worthy Trent Donovan sauntered into the restaurant. My ex with the smoldering eyes—*yeah, I'm a total girl*—and the wide shoulders. Trent with the charming, intimate habit of sweeping the hair from my face. Trent with the electrifying touch…

Dammit. I had to stop going all fangirl every time I saw him!

Still, the air whooshed from my lungs. I closed my eyes and took a deep breath. When I opened them, I swear my body froze. My heart stopped beating. A volatile, insistent thrill shot through my veins, and I shuddered.

Ariana jerked her chin at the counter. "Uh-oh. Ex-boyfriend at one o'clock."

Lifting my head, I groaned. "Maybe he won't spot us."

"Unless you know an invisibility spell, Trent's got natural radar when it comes to you."

My hands trembled in my lap. My stomach pitched and rolled. I had no place to hide. I was tempted to get up and run out the door before he noticed me…

***

Could you see, feel, and sense the character's emotions? Good.

Now open up your manuscript and start revising your own stories into Deep POV to create a gripping narrative that your readers will be unable to put down.

DESCRIBE THE EMOTIONS

By giving your characters *real* emotions and reactions, it gives them even more realism. Being able to describe those emotions through Deep POV adds mastery to your writing. Add your character's five senses to describe how he/she is feeling without *naming the emotion*, and watch your scenes come vividly to life.

Still not convinced?

By applying the Deep POV method, your writing will become more alive and intriguing. Try it and you'll notice an immediate difference. Your readers will be able to actively relate to whatever your characters are feeling or experiencing in that moment.

In the next several chapters, I will offer some great examples on how to rewrite the most commonly used emotional descriptors. Since this handbook would be thousands of pages long if I listed them all, I have narrowed down the biggest offenders to the most frequently used "telling" emotions that can make your writing become shallow.

EMOTION: EXCITEMENT

Quote: "Deep Point-Of-View describes how deeply into the POV character's experience the reader is drawn. Regular POV uses words that let the reader know somebody is telling her a story: *Jane thought, Jane decided, Jane felt*, etc. Deep POV just puts what Jane thought, decided, and felt on the page so that the wall between the reader and the character disappears and the reader becomes the character." —*bestselling author, Jennifer Crusie*

Excitement can be felt by a character that wins the lottery, makes the winning touchdown at a football game, or gets asked to the prom by their crush.

Excitement is a state of exhilaration and physical stimulation, which heartens a character and makes them feel a rush of adrenaline. It is an emotion that can add a layer of depth to your scenes if written in Deeper POV.

But within most of the early drafts that I edit for other writers, I notice an abundance of filter words like*: excited, excitement, exhilaration, exhilarated, anticipation, anticipate,* and *anticipated*, etc. As I've stated before, sometimes *naming the emotion* is perfectly acceptable, but only if it helps create easier readability.

Some physical signs of excitement might be:

Body vibrating with anticipation

EMOTION: EXCITEMENT

Hands trembling

Heart swelling

Jumping up and down

Laughing out loud

Hugging people

Bouncing on balls of feet

Rocking on heels

Unable to sit still

Talking quickly

Squealing and raising voice or screaming

Pumping fist into the air

Skin buzzing

Huge smile

Examples on how to revise shallow writing:

SHALLOW: I felt excited and alive for the first time in months.

DEEP POV: For the first time in months, I smiled at everyone I passed on the street.

SHALLOW: "This is gonna be awesome!" he said, his voice thrumming with excitement.

DEEP POV: He was practically jumping up and down as if he had ants in his pants. "This is gonna be awesome!" he exclaimed.

SHALLOW: My heart started pounding with excitement.

DEEP POV: My heartbeat sped up and I bounced on my toes.

SHALLOW: Excitement sang through her, and it was all she could do to stand still.

DEEP POV: Her body thrummed with energy as she rocked on her heels.

SHALLOW: A tremor of excitement crept up his spine.

DEEP POV: He shivered and let out a throaty laugh.

SHALLOW: "So Isaac's going to sit with us tomorrow, too?" she asked excitedly.

DEEP POV: Bouncing in her seat, she asked, "So Isaac's going to sit with us tomorrow, too?"

SHALLOW: Catarina's heart fluttered in excitement. (Cliché)

DEEP POV: Catarina's heart fluttered and her big blue eyes sparkled.

SHALLOW: I felt a rush of excitement. (Cliché)

DEEP POV: A tingle spread throughout my body and warmed my heart.

SHALLOW: His lopsided smile sent a sweet burst of excitement through her.

DEEP POV: At the sight of his lopsided smile, her skin prickled and a pleasant buzz flowed through her.

SHALLOW: She gasped, sending a tremor of excitement up his spine.

DEEP POV: When she gasped, a quivery tremor shot up his spine.

SHALLOW: "I don't believe it," he says with a spark of amusement in his eyes. (Cliché)

DEEP POV: "I don't believe it," he says, his eyes crinkling up into a smile.

EMOTION: EXCITEMENT

***

The following examples from my own novel RECKLESS REVENGE (book four) illustrates how to revise shallow scenes into Deeper POV by eliminating the weaker filter words from the sentences.

Please study and compare these examples...

SHALLOW:

"Tonight sad thoughts are not allowed," Trent said <u>enthusiastically</u>. "At least for three hours."

"How exactly do you intend to do that?" I asked <u>eagerly</u>.

"Maybe like..." He said and leaned over the console to kiss my mouth.

A warm rush of <u>excitement</u> hit me. I smiled at my boyfriend. "Good start."

"Just you wait." He shifted back and chuckled deep in his throat. That's the way a laugh should be, I <u>thought</u>.

Soft music seeped through the speakers and I <u>realized</u> that I was humming along.

"If you like this playlist, I can burn you a mix CD to load it into your iPod," Trent said.

"Sure," I said <u>excitedly</u>.

Trent wore a <u>happy</u> smile as he took my hand and I <u>felt</u> a jolt. His hand was warm and rough. I <u>knew</u> that my smile had widened. I <u>felt</u> my heart pounding so hard I couldn't do anything else.

As <u>excitement</u> bubbled up inside me, I <u>wondered</u> if tonight was going to be fun.

DEEP POV:

"Well, tonight deep thoughts are not allowed. Only fun," he said. "I consider it my duty to make you forget all about your troubles. At least for a few hours."

"Oh? And how exactly do you intend to do that?"

"Like this." He leaned over the console and kissed me hard on the mouth.

A rush of warmth hit my skin. I smiled at my hotheaded, crazy, yet loveable boyfriend. "That's a good start."

"There's more where that came from, sweetheart." He shifted back into his seat and chuckled, a throaty, uninhibited laugh. The way a laugh should be.

The almost hypnotic sounds of *Lifehouse*'s "You and Me" seeped through the speakers and I hummed along with the tune.

"If you like this playlist, I can burn you a mix CD to load onto your iPod," Trent offered.

My grin widened. "Yes, please!"

Trent's face broke into that killer smile as he took my hand and a jolt shot through me. His hand was warm and vaguely rough, his grip confident and steady. My heart was pounding so hard I couldn't do anything else. Tonight was sure to be loads of fun.

***

Did you compare the last two examples? Are you starting to grasp how shallow writing with annoying filter words pulls the reader out of the story? Good!

Naming the emotion is a bad habit that writers easily fall into, which focuses the storyline on "telling" rather than "showing."

EMOTION: FRUSTRATION

Quote: "…without frustration, there is no plot. Frustration means that someone is not getting what he/she wants, and that's what makes a story work. Motivation, values, and desires start the character on her/his fictional journey. Climaxes are often provided in scenes of love, battle, or death. But everything in between, the meat of your story, is driven by frustration." —*author at Writer's Digest, Rachel Scheller*

Most psychologists would state that frustration is a negative emotion that occurs in situations where a person is blocked from reaching a desired outcome (goal), or a common emotional response to opposition (opposing force). And frustration can often provoke feelings of insecurity, discouragement, or disappointment.

Ordinarily, whenever a character reaches a goal, they should feel content, but whenever the same character is thwarted from reaching a goal by the opposing force, they might feel irritable, exasperated and indignant.

So in my opinion, a character should be feeling frustrated throughout most of the storyline when their goals get sabotaged by the villain or opposing force.

There is usually no need to *name the emotion*. A reader will understand the emotional reactions, like frustration, without the writer telling them if it is shown. Trust me, readers will be grateful that you are respecting their intelligence.

These offending filter words like *frustrated, frustration, aggravated, irritated, annoyed, exasperated*, can be found in almost every published novel that you read, but should be revised whenever possible for Deeper POV.

Some physical signs of frustration might be:

Brain feels tied up in knots

Talking to inanimate objects

Constant pacing

Urge to throw something

Bunch hands into fists

Snap a pencil

Punch whatever is in front of character: wall, pillow, locker, tree, etc.

Slapping the antagonist

Heart beating more quickly

Breath speeds up

Body shaking

Tapping a pencil or pen

Jiggling keys

Biting lip

Drumming fingers on table or desk

Examples on how to revise shallow writing:

SHALLOW: A bout of frustration churns inside me.

DEEP POV: Pinching my lips together, I stomp my foot.

EMOTION: FRUSTRATION

SHALLOW: The vampire slayer rushed at me with a scream of frustration and buried the stake in my chest.

DEEP POV: The vampire slayer rushed forward with jerky movements and plunged the wooden stake into my heart.

SHALLOW: "No! It's not like that," I said, suddenly frustrated.

DEEP POV: Clenching my jaw, I blurted, "*No!* It's not like that."

SHALLOW: Frustration flicked across Jerrod's face. (Cliché)

DEEP POV: Jarrod snorted and threw his hands up in the air.

SHALLOW: Nikki groaned in frustration. (Cliché)

DEEP POV: Groaning, Nikki dropped her head in her hands.

SHALLOW: Frustration bubbled in my veins. "Accept it. Lisa has a new boyfriend."

DEEP POV: I just wanted to reach out and grab him. Slap him as hard as I could. Instead, I blurted, "Just accept it! Lisa has moved on, and so should *you*."

SHALLOW: She was angry and frustrated. (Cliché)

DEEP POV: Pulling at her hair, she grumbled, "Just stop it!"

SHALLOW: Jack looked frustrated.

DEEP POV: Jack jiggled the keys in his pocket, and a muscle ticked in his jaw.

SHALLOW: Edward made a frustrated noise in the back of his throat.

DEEP POV: Edward grunted low in his throat and shoved his hands under his arms.

***

These subsequent longer examples exemplify how to modify shallow sentences into Deeper POV by eradicating the filter words from any scene.

Please study and compare these examples…

SHALLOW:

At the start of class, I noticed Holly walk over to me with an irritated expression. "I don't know what the hell you think you're doing, harassing Elden like that," she hissed.

Although I was startled and frustrated by her badgering, I managed an innocent look. "I have no idea what you're talking about, Holly."

She frowned at me in anger for a moment, and then turned away with a toss of her messy hair. "I was just trying to save you some awkwardness, Luce," she said, in a frustrated voice. "He likes me now."

I felt my face turning red. Though I knew Holly was just being a jealous brat, I couldn't help worrying that she might be right.

Maybe Elden *was* just being nice to me because he felt sorry for me. I felt more and more depressed as the class dragged on.

I wondered when the bell would ring and I'd be able to escape.

DEEP POV:

As the warning bell rang, Holly entered the classroom and marched over to me with a nasty twinkle in her eye. "What the hell do you think you're doing? Stalking Elden?" she spat. "Do I need to remind you that he's my boyfriend now?"

My body tensed up and I flinched at her harsh tone. My eyes grew wide and I said in my sweetest voice, "I have no idea what you're babbling on about, Holly. You're not actually worried that Elden might still like me?"

She glared in silence, and I swear smoke was pouring out of her ears. Finally, she turned away with a toss of her windblown hair and sauntered over to her own desk. But she wanted to have the last word. So typical.

"Just trying to keep you from making an ass out of yourself, Luce," she said, in a high-pitched voice. "He likes me now. Got it?"

My face turned red and I slumped in my seat. Holly was just being her usual hateful self. But what if she was right?

Maybe Elden *was* just being nice because he felt sorry for me. I shouldn't let Holly get under my skin, but my shoulders sagged and I hung my head.

The clock ticked slowly and class dragged.

When was the damn bell gonna ring so I could escape?

***

Do a search to find the filter words in your own story if you want to revise into Deeper POV. But remember that there are times when *naming the emotion* or using a filter word will add to the rhythm of your sentences and it is simply necessary, so don't stress yourself out if you can't revise them all.

EMOTION: DISAPPOINTMENT

Quote: "If the reader is in the heroine's POV and she walks into a bar where she doesn't know a soul…she can't look at a man and think, "Wozza, Joe is cute." She has to look and think, "Wow. Who's the hot guy with the tats by the pool table?" She can't see herself blush a beet red. But she *can* feel the stinging heat climb into her face." —*bestselling author, Rebecca Zanetti*

A disappointed character might feel dissatisfaction that results from a failure of expectations, or goals, or core values.

Disappointment is considered a negative emotion that can cause a character to also feel sad and/or angry. The feeling can hover in the character's mind like a dark cloud and niggle at them as the story progresses, causing a dismal perspective. Disappointment is a part of everyone's life, and it can help a character grow and change through their growth ARC.

But writers create narrative distance and author intrusion when they unintentionally insert a shallower POV by stating the emotion. Writers should search and destroy words such as *disappointed / disappointment* and all variations.

The examples presented in this chapter should offer creative ways to avoid identifying this emotion, which only serves to distance the reader.

Some physical signs of disappointment might be:

Mouth turning downward

EMOTION: DISAPPOINTMENT

Tears burning eyes

Tipping chin down and frowning

Heavy sighing

Swaying on feet

Sluggishness

Puckering brow

Leaning on a wall

Dropping head into hands

Shaking head and crying

Stomach hurting

Crawling into bed and hiding under the covers

Weeping in the shower

Examples on how to revise shallow writing:

SHALLOW: He was disappointed that Rachel stood him up.

DEEP POV: Lowering his head, he shuffled into the movie alone. Rachel had stood him up for the last time.

SHALLOW: Bitter disappointment pricked Julianna's chest because she didn't get the lead in the school play.

DEEP POV: Shoulders drooping, Julianna blinked back tears. No way would she cry at school over not getting the lead role.

SHALLOW: Michele felt so disappointed that she'd failed her driving test again.

DEEP POV: Lips pressed tight, Michele dragged her feet all the way home. *Can't believe I failed that test. Again.*

SHALLOW: For the third year in a row, I was <u>disappointed</u> about not being picked for the swim team.

DEEP POV: Looking up with her hands raised skyward, she mumbled, "Why does this *always* happen to me?"

SHALLOW: A stab of <u>disappointment</u> punched Amanda in the gut.

DEEP POV: Covering her face with her hands, Amanda sighed loudly. "This majorly sucks," she muttered.

SHALLOW: How many more <u>disappointments</u> would Alex have to endure until he found another job?

DEEP POV: Tilting his chin downward and frowning, Alex sat heavily on the bed. He was *so* sick of being a jobless loser.

SHALLOW: My voice was low, severe and acrid <u>disappointment</u> tied knots in my gut.

DEEP POV: My voice sounded low, harsh—sour emotions tying a knot in my gut.

SHALLOW: <u>Disappointment</u> swelled so quickly in my chest it trampled the passionate desire.

DEEP POV: Not meeting his eyes, the heat intensified in my chest and squelched the passionate desire.

SHALLOW: A spasm of <u>disappointment</u> hit me hard in the chest.

DEEP POV: My skin flushed. The whole thing was about a hundred levels of awkward and a warehouse full of someone-please-kill-me-now.

***

EMOTION: DISAPPOINTMENT

Here is another example of how to avoid *naming the emotion,* and instead show the character's reaction through the Deep POV technique.

Please study and compare these examples…

SHALLOW:

I <u>looked around</u> me, at how empty the dining room was and <u>felt</u> a stab of <u>disappointment</u>. I <u>realized</u> that Andrea and the rest of my friends hadn't shown up yet to the party.

I <u>knew</u> I had texted everyone the night before with a reminder, but apparently no one was on time.

DEEP POV:

My heart squeezed. *This royally sucks.* Where is everyone?

I took in the empty dining room and breathed out through my mouth. Andrea and the rest of my friends should've been here by now. I'd texted everyone the night before with a reminder.

But damn if I was going to let their lateness ruin my birthday.

***

I hope these examples help you to rewrite scenes in your own manuscript or short story.

EMOTION: ANGER

Quote: "Anger is an interesting emotion because it fuels us with a particular type of energy that demands action, and it can affect characters in many different ways. For some, it clouds judgment and incites violence, for others it inspires an unquenchable motivation, and still for others it pushes them into deep, dark places. I like to make my characters angry for a couple reasons: It's a particularly strong and passionate emotion... ." —*YA author, Ava Jae*

Anger is often considered a "secondary emotion" because people often have a tendency to resort to feeling angry in order to defend themselves or conceal vulnerable feelings. But the initial feeling a person has, is actually what is immediately felt *before* the anger. For instance, a character might first feel afraid, offended, shocked, or pressured (bullied), and then angry. Because if any of these feelings are intense enough, it can trigger a feeling of anger.

And anger is one of those negative emotions that can be self-destructive and lead to various problems within a character's life if not resolved. Which makes anger, whether passive or aggressive, a wonderful fatal flaw in any genre. This emotion can be the result of many different factors, like a character's dark history. Letting go of a past hurt or anger at someone within the storyline can be an intriguing growth ARC for a character.

Anger can compel a character to confront someone (like the villain), which drives the plot forward. Or a character might use it as motivation to make a life-changing decision.

EMOTION: ANGER

Yet it's redundant to be told by a writer that the character is "angry." It is so much more interesting to *show* how the character reacts. In order to show these emotional reactions, try to omit filter words, such as: *anger, angry, fury, furious, rage, enraged, antagonism, wrath, annoyance, irritation, irritated, etc.* from your narrative.

Some physical signs of anger might be:

Face reddens or turns purple

Tension in body

Shouting or raising voice

Swearing / Crying

Punching something

Stomping or marching

Eyes flashing

Mouth quivering

Slamming door

Ears get hot / red

Flaring nostrils

Examples on how to revise shallow writing:

SHALLOW: He looks very angry.

DEEP POV: His mouth is set in a grim line, jaw tense.

SHALLOW: Anger was simmering through my veins.

DEEP POV: Heat licked my skin, and my limbs vibrated. *He was dead meat!*

SHALLOW: My anger returns in full force.

DEEP POV: My fingers clutch tightly at the armrests, my nails digging into the soft fabric.

SHALLOW: A sudden rush of anger surfaces.

DEEP POV: My eyes narrow and my hands shake as I take a menacing step closer to my enemy.

SHALLOW: A red cloud of rage swam across Michael's vision.

DEEP POV: Michael's vision clouded with swarms of dark red.

SHALLOW: I tried to quell my jealousy and rage.

DEEP POV: My body twitched as I stared holes into my friend's back while she flirted away with the boy I was crushing on.

SHALLOW: When he spun back around, his face was drawn with fury.

DEEP POV: When he whirled back around, his eyes bulged and his jaw clenched.

SHALLOW: His face erupted into a map of surprise and rage.

DEEP POV: A vein in his forehead throbbed and he shook a fist in the air.

SHALLOW: She felt an absolute rage boiling inside her.

DEEP POV: An infusion of adrenaline rocked her body.

SHALLOW: Her face screwed-up into a twisted mass of rage.

DEEP POV: With her eyes flashing, her mouth twisted into an ugly sneer.

***

EMOTION: ANGER

Here is a longer paragraph that indicates how you can revise the emotion *anger* into Deeper POV and engage your readers.

This excerpt is taken from my novel, LOST IN STARLIGHT, and shows both the before revision and the published draft. The heroine just discovered that the guy she's crushing on might be dating another girl.

The first example has too much "telling" and no "voice" and the narrative is weighed down with extra words; however, the published excerpt has riveting "voice" and it is written in Deep POV.

Please study and compare these examples…

SHALLOW:

I am angry with Hayden. "Let's just say last night was a mistake," I blurt, thinking I had better not waver.

Hayden takes my hand, and I feel my heart skip a beat. I look at his face, and think that his eyes are so amazing, but a burst of fresh anger still simmers in my gut.

"Please believe me, Sloane. It's over with Tama," he says. "And I *don't* want to pretend that last night never happened."

I pull my hand away and fury heats my chest. "Or maybe she's more your kind?"

Hayden appears uneasy. "Yes." He glances anxiously at my face. "Sloane, let me prove to you that I'm not a jerk. Have breakfast with me on the beach."

I do not want to be alone with him. I know I cannot trust myself.

I stare at him, and that rage resurfaces. He's such a liar, I think.

While he stays quiet, I try to think of a good excuse. Our relationship needs to be platonic. Because if I go with him, the whole time I'll just be thinking about kissing him.

"Well, Peaches?" he asks. "Can we talk?"

I have no plans today, and I can't even <u>think</u> up good lie. I <u>feel</u> very curious about Tama. But it might be a bad idea.

I <u>know</u> I shouldn't go with him or trust him, yet I <u>feel</u> my <u>rage</u> slipping away. I can't resist Hayden. I look into his eyes and all of the <u>anger</u> dissolves. I <u>know</u> that I will regret doing this.

"Fine." I say, <u>dejectedly</u>. "I'll go."

DEEP POV:

"Let's just say last night was a colossal mistake," I say firmly, resolved to stick to my guns.

Hayden takes my hand, causing my heart to skip an alarming number of beats. I hazard a glance at his face. Bad move. God, those remarkable eyes. A person could die happy just gazing into them. But. Not. Me. I will not be a weak, simpering ball of need.

"Please believe me, Sloane. It's over with Tama," he says in a soft voice. "And I *don't* want to pretend that last night never happened. We had a moment, right? You must've felt it, too."

"Was that the moment you had with me or with Tama?" I jerk my hand from his. "Or maybe she's more your kind? Is she a hybrid, too?"

Hayden kicks at the ground. "Yes." He glances anxiously at my face. "Just have breakfast with me, Sloane, so I can prove to you that I'm not a jerk."

Alone? With Hayden?

Don't do it. Do not do it.

I stare at him, imagining a giant neon sign above his head that reads: *WARNING! Lying-girlfriend-haver!*

EMOTION: ANGER

While he stays quiet, I try to come up with a quick excuse. I cannot go. I need to keep this relationship strictly platonic. Because the whole time I'll just be thinking about kissing that perfect mouth. His soft, warm lips—

"Well, Peaches?" he asks. "Can we go someplace and talk?"

I shouldn't go, but I can't resist that strange, irresistible *pull* of Hayden. Another look in those incredible eyes and I'm a goner. I am *so* gonna regret this.

"Fine." A sigh creeps past my lips. "I'll go."

***

Did you see how Deep POV brings the scene and emotions effortlessly alive for the reader? Awesome!

We're inside main character's head throughout the entire second passage and experiencing her anger and frustration, and even confusion, right along with her as the scene unfolds.

EMOTION: SADNESS

Quote: "Emotions are an essential part of the human being. To a degree, we live to feel, and we spend most of our lives chasing after emotions like happiness and love. Emotions are a beautiful part of what makes us human, the good ones and the bad. Sadness is no different. It's part of who we are. Sadness in our life makes the joys seem all the brighter..." —*YA adventure/fantasy writer, Nate Philbrick*

A sad or depressed character is one that would be hard to write, but it would give the story a darker edge to it that might establish a strong emotional connection, or reaction, with readers.

Many emotions are related to sadness such as a feeling of loss, despair, grief, hopelessness, and disappointment. For instance, if a character is sad over the death of another character, then try to find ways to *show* the emotional impact and how it affects their life.

As you revise in Deep POV, you don't want your character's thoughts, actions, or emotions to be *told* or *explained* to the reader because they want to experience the events unfolding inside the character's head as they take place.

So, try to omit filter words like, *sad, sadness, unhappy, miserable, depressed, gloomy, sorrow, wretched, dejected, forlorn, depression, sorrowful, woeful, cheerless* from your scenes.

Some physical signs of sadness might be:

EMOTION: SADNESS

Loss of appetite

Tiredness

Drooping eyelids

Glossy or glassed eyes

Lips pulled down at corners

Sluggish movements

Trembling lips

Clutching blanket, stuffed animal, or pillow

Blubbering loudly

Closing eyes and not speaking

Eyes bloodshot

Dark shadows under eyes

Examples on how to revise shallow writing:

SHALLOW: A sad feeling makes my heart hurt.

DEEP POV: A tight fist constricts around my heart.

SHALLOW: He sounds so sad.

DEEP POV: My heart clenches at his dejected tone.

SHALLOW: I feel sad and lonely now that Craig's dead.

DEEP POV: Sobbing into Craig's old T-shirt, my heart aches fiercely. *I miss him so much.*

SHALLOW: Feeling unhappy, I start to cry.

DEEP POV: Tears sting my eyes and I sniffle, wiping at my runny nose with my sleeve.

SHALLOW: Grief and misery make me feel like crying.

DEEP POV: My arms hang at my sides, my body slack. I clutch at my chest and sob uncontrollably.

SHALLOW: The grief and frustration welling up inside me needs an outlet.

DEEP POV: A surge of pain wells up inside me. Needing an outlet, I grab the stuffed bear and punch it.

SHALLOW: Sadness and loneliness washed over him.

DEEP POV: The constant ache in his chest was made worse whenever he visited Amy's grave.

SHALLOW: I noticed his eyes held a touch of sadness. (Cliché)

DEEP POV: As he looked away, I glimpsed the tears welling in his eyes.

SHALLOW: "Just go away," I said, feeling miserable.

DEEP POV: My face went slack and my voice dull, "Just go away."

SHALLOW: Lauren felt a pang of grief as she went to work.

DEEP POV: Drooping her shoulders, Lauren shuffled into work.

SHALLOW: Jaime just looked at her feet, miserable.

DEEP POV: Jaime stared down at her feet with glossy eyes.

***

The following excerpt is from my book, MOONLIGHT MAYHEM, where the heroine has just lost her father and she is overcome with grief. Although it is straight exposition, there are descriptive details, action, use of the five senses, and emotion laced throughout this scene.

Please study and compare these examples...

SHALLOW:

The sadness I felt made me waver on my feet. I didn't want to faint. When a huge wave of depression tugged at my heart, my thoughts turned back to the funeral.

The grief was overwhelming, as wind lifted the hair off my shoulders. My feet were beginning to hurt in my heels. My best friend was frozen beside me, a gloomy expression on her face.

Another shift in footing, and the sorrow blurred my vision. Wavering, I was sure I would fall over.

Suddenly, I felt two arms wrapped around my waist, pulling me backward against him. A nose touched just beneath my ear, and I could hear his deep breathing.

Trent was here. I wanted to turn and look at him, but only a huge sigh of misery shuddered through my body.

DEEP POV:

Tears choked my throat, burning as they threatened to bubble over and spill from my eyes. I wavered on my feet, sure I was going to faint like some attention seeking diva. With a cotton-filled head, my thoughts returned to the funeral unfolding before my disbelieving eyes. The body of my dad enclosed in a casket that was about to be lowered into the ground.

Sunlight bathed the graveyard in a warm blanket and a mild wind lifted the hair gently from my shoulders, like Dad's soft caress.

My feet were already hurting in my heels, but my best friend seemed rooted to the spot, an agonized expression fixed on her face. Ariana's fingers felt sweaty in my hand, but held mine steadfastly. Neither of us were willing to let each other go.

Another shift in footing, and my mind pulled down a protective screen of translucent gray silk across my line-of-sight. Wavering, I was sure I would find myself on the ground.

Suddenly, two strong arms wrapped around my waist, pulling me back into a solid wall of muscle. A nose buried in the crook beneath my ear, and his deep breathing ghosted along my skin.

Trent. He was here. Now. I wanted to turn and look at him, but slumped against him instead. A huge sigh shuddered through my body.

***

I hope these examples help you to revise your own stories.

EMOTION: WORRY

Quote: "Emotions show up on your body in a variety of hand movements, eye twitches, breathing patterns and more. There are so many ways to show what your characters are feeling without boring readers by saying, Anabelle felt angry. *Yuck!* Show me, don't tell me!" —*author, Jacqui Murray*

This chapter covers how to omit this common filter word from your writing: *concerned / worried / anxious*.

According to Wikipedia: Worry refers to the thoughts, images and emotions of a negative nature in which mental attempts are made to avoid anticipated potential threats.

Worry should be considered a negative emotional trait. This emotional reaction can involve many different fears, concerns, and anxieties that could affect sleep, appetite, or concentration. If a character is worrying about something, they can become counter-productive. Because most worry is based on fear, it can enable a character from solving a problem, or being brave enough to confront the villain. Or even facing their own inner-demons or fatal flaws. Or a character with irrational worries might hinder the hero from accomplishing a goal.

Also, writers should make sure that when they search for the words listed in this handbook that they look for variations. For instance, if the word is "worry" then also search for *worried, worrying, upsetting, upset, distressing, distressed, fretting, fret,* etc.

Some physical signs of worry might be:

Face slackened

Brow furrowed

Eyes darting about in concern

Expression is pinched

Foot tapping

Unable to sleep or eat

Lip twitches

Blink excessively

Clamp and unclamp teeth

Face pales

Expression taut, drawn

Stomach clenches

Examples on how to revise shallow writing:

SHALLOW: I was <u>worried</u> about Brandon being allergic to the new puppy.

DEEP POV: Biting my nails, I gazed into the puppy's cute little face. "If Brandon's allergic to you, I don't know what we'll do." The dog wagged his bushy tail in response.

SHALLOW: I <u>felt anxious</u> and <u>nervous</u> the night before my trip.

DEEP POV: Rubbing my sweaty hands on the thighs of my jeans, I double-checked that I had packed my passport and plane ticket for the hundredth time.

EMOTION: WORRY

SHALLOW: He was worried that the birthday card had gotten lost in the mail.

DEEP POV: He still hadn't heard from his granddaughter about the card he'd mailed weeks ago. Eyebrows drawn together, he grabbed the phone to call her.

SHALLOW: I often worry about a zombie apocalypse.

DEEP POV: I ran a jerky hand through my hair as I watched the horror movie. What if there really was a zombie apocalypse? Would I be ready?

SHALLOW: The vampire worried that he'd drank too much of her blood.

DEEP POV: The vampire stepped back and wrung his hands. The girl's complexion paled to a ghostly white. He must've drunk just a little too much this time.

SHALLOW: I felt apprehensive the night before my wedding.

DEEP POV: Unable to sit still, I paced the hotel corridor. What if the caterer is late? What if the groom doesn't show up? Or worse…what if after eating that second slice of peach cobbler, I can't zip up my wedding dress?

SHALLOW: He was concerned about the accident on the road up ahead.

DEEP POV: His brow furrowed when he caught a glimpse of the accident on the road up ahead.

SHALLOW: Rachel looked worried.

DEEP POV: Rachel twisted a long strand of hair around her finger, and one leg bounced up and down.

SHALLOW: Cheri sighed, her expression troubled.

DEEP POV: Rubbing at a tic above her left eyebrow, Cheri sighed for the fiftieth time.

***

Next, I have a longer example to give you a better context of how to write in Deeper POV and avoid shallow writing. Please study and compare these examples…

SHALLOW:

I noticed that the guy looked really cute. His eyes looked blue. I was just about to interrupt the conversation when the guy cackled at something the boy next to him said. He laughed long and hard. I moved away, worried that he might be losing his mind. It was the most appalling sound I'd ever heard.

When he finally stopped laughing and started walking away, I felt too nervous to speak to him. But as he passed me by, I got a good look at his orange complexion.

I looked at my friends, baffled.

"Do you think he was wearing makeup?" Jessica asked worriedly.

"Maybe one of those spray-on tans," I said. "How shallow can he be?"

"I know," Amber said, giggling.

DEEP POV:

Damn, that guy was cute. His eyes sparkled like aquamarines. I was just about to tap his shoulder and introduce myself when the hottie chuckled at something his buddy had said. Hooted, actually. His laughter exploding all over the place like a crazy hyena. He doubled over with both hands on his knees and sucked in air with panting gasps.

What was wrong with this guy?

I shuffled backward. Sheesh, he was going to have a seizure at any moment. His horrible sounding giggles were the goofiest and most immature noise on the planet.

He finally straightened and sauntered out of the room with his friend, still wheezing.

As he passed by me, I got a very up close-and-personal glimpse of his "tan" skin. The fake color was virtually orange.

I glanced at my friends with an "oh-my-god-did-you-see-that?" expression.

Jessica frowned. "Was he wearing makeup?"

"More like one of those spray-on tans you can get at the mall," I said, rolling my eyes. "How superficial can that guy be?"

Amber shook her head with a smile. "I know, right?"

***

I sincerely hope that all of my examples help you to revise your own work.

EMOTION: FEAR

Quote: "To elicit fear...Reveal the menace, whatever it may be, in a place where your character should feel safe, where nothing bad is ever supposed to happen. If your character has allies, you can have them exacerbate things without understanding they're doing exactly the wrong thing with the best of intentions." —*Pat Cadigan, author of Chalk*

According to Wikipedia: Fear is closely related to, but should be distinguished from, the emotion anxiety, which occurs as the result of threats that are perceived to be uncontrollable or unavoidable.

The negative emotion of fear is commonly related to a strong reaction to something that threatens the security or safety of a character. Fear can alert a character to the possibility that they might be in danger, which consecutively motivates them to protect themself. Consequently, the concept of *fight or flight* is a direct response to feeling afraid of someone or something. And I also think that fears can be irrational or even imagined, like phobias.

Most horror and thriller/suspense writers find unique ways to create the sensation of fear in both their characters, and in their readers. In Deep POV, these types of writers get straight to the point by describing the emotion instead of bluntly stating it.

As with most writing rules, exceptions do exist, but only if using the filter word or stating the emotion will cause the sentence structure to read more smoothly. However, in most cases, a quick rewrite can almost always fix shallower writing into Deeper POV.

EMOTION: FEAR

For example, try to omit filter words, such as *fear / afraid / terrified / terror/ dread / fright / trepidation / apprehension / scared* to describe a character's emotion.

Some physical signs of fear might be:

Skin becomes clammy

Voice sounds high and hysterical

Screaming

Sweat prickling scalp

Pulse speeds up

A rush of blood through his/her head

A weight seems to press on chest

Body pumps out adrenaline

Hands get sweaty

Trembling hands

Brows drew together

Examples on how to revise shallow writing:

SHALLOW: I feel a brief thrill of fear.

DEEP POV: Trembles travel from my legs and vibrate up my neck.

SHALLOW: She was paralyzed with fear. (Cliché)

DEEP POV: She couldn't move. Until that fight-or-flight response kicked in, begging her to run into the house and lock the door.

SHALLOW: Terror whooshed up and around him like waves.

DEEP POV: His heart was beating at a dizzying pace.

SHALLOW: Terror shot through me.

DEEP POV: My heart thudded louder and louder.

SHALLOW: He was afraid of the dark.

DEEP POV: Staring into the utter darkness, his palms grew damp.

SHALLOW: She was terrified of spiders.

DEEP POV: Her hair caught in a sticky web and she yelped. *Sheesh, I hate spiders!*

SHALLOW: She felt a growing sense of dread. (Cliché)

DEEP POV: A weight seemed to press on her chest, robbing her of breath.

SHALLOW: Katie was frightened by the loud screams.

DEEP POV: Loud screams split the night air. Katie's face turned ashen.

SHALLOW: A sliver of apprehension made her legs wobble.

DEEP POV: Walking stiffly toward the door, her knees locked and she wobbled.

SHALLOW: A sense of dread crept into her heart. (Cliché)

DEEP POV: All the blood drained from her face and her heart thudded hard.

SHALLOW: Terror welled up in his eyes. (Cliché)

DEEP POV: His eyes bulged from their sockets and he started to hyperventilate.

SHALLOW: Tendrils of terror curled into her stomach.

DEEP POV: Her stomach turned to ice and she steadied herself against the car.

EMOTION: FEAR

SHALLOW: Zack felt the fear clench like a tight first around his chest.

DEEP POV: Zach's chest tightened like a clenched first around his chest.

SHALLOW: The trepidation in her voice caused him to become apprehensive.

DEEP POV: Her tone sounded so ominous that cold sweat trickled down his sides.

***

This longer excerpt is taken from my adult paranormal romance novel **IMMORTAL ECLIPSE**, and it shows how to portray *fear* effectively in your writing.

Remember that *every* word choice is vital to characterization and to making your writing style unique, so pick strong verbs. For emphasis, I underlined the filter words below in the shallow scene.

Please study and compare these examples…

SHALLOW:

At the sound of the thump, I touch the gun under my pillow. A girl like me living alone in New York must be careful. My fingers feel clumsy as I slide the safety off. Sudden fear chokes my throat.

I sit up slowly, and feel my body tense up. An eerie sensation batters my senses. Beneath my ribs, I can feel an alien power. The feeling is strange, but makes me feel clearheaded. I try to swallow, but the lump of dread in my throat won't let me.

Then I hear a scraping sound.

I switch on the bedside lamp, and light illuminates the room. I get to my feet and look at the closed bedroom door in terror. The hardwood floor feels icy, and I can feel the spread of panic.

I can hear the scratching sound from under the door. With growing fear rising in my heart, I move toward the door. A board groans under my foot and I feel a fresh wave of terror.

The blinds are pulled up, making me feel defenseless. Beyond the street lamps, I can see lights glow in the skyscrapers and notice the winds bend the trees. I feel the brownstone shift on its foundation.

I hear that scraping sound again.

I think it might be an animal or neighbor making those scary sounds.

I feel air move through the room. It fills me with dread. That weird psychic feeling kicks up my anxiety a notch.

***

This next example shows more "voice," action, and emotion by using the Deep POV method. And effectively illustrates how to convey *fear* in your character without *naming the emotion*.

DEEP POV:

I grab the handle of the baseball bat under the bed. A girl living alone must be careful, even on the Upper East Side.

Scrape, scrape, scrape.

An odd scratching noise resonates from the other side of the apartment. The red digital numbers of the alarm clock flash midnight.

I sit up slowly, listening hard. An eerie sensation batters my senses, like a sixth sense awakening, blooming, and soaking through my bones. As it intensifies, the sense of urgency clears any traces of drowsiness.

Scrape, scrape, scrape.

EMOTION: FEAR

The sound unnervingly echoes like fingernails grating down a chalkboard. I fumble to switch on the bedside lamp, and soft white light illuminates the room.

Staggering to my feet, I stare at the closed bedroom door. The hardwood floor is icy, and gooseflesh rises stiff and fast on my arms. My fingers are clumsy and moist as I hold the bat, the wood heavy in my hand. Whoever's trying to break into my apartment had better think twice.

As I tiptoe toward the door, a board groans sharply under my weight. So much for being quiet. I glance behind me. The room appears empty, but the blinds are open, making me feel vulnerable, naked. Beyond the street lamps, lights blaze from towering skyscrapers and a sharp gust bends the trees. The brownstone grunts and whines against the biting winds of approaching winter.

Scrape, scrape, scrape.

It could just be an animal making those noises, or a neighbor.

The building croons under a harsh blanket of wind. A cold draft moves through the room, reminiscent of sticky breath laden with foul odors, close and oppressive. It feels as though I've locked myself in a dark closet with a hundred vipers.

I force myself to move and hold the bat over my shoulder. My bare feet shuffle closer to the door, then I freeze.

***

Could you tell the huge difference between the two examples?

The first one is cluttered with filter words that caused narrative distance and *named* the emotions. However, the second example gets the reader in close-and-personal because it is written in Deeper POV, so that the reader can really experience the fear in the character as she moves through her apartment.

EMOTION: UNEASE

Quote: "Emotions are the lifeblood of characters and of stories. Without emotional characters, you are just writing events, but you're not drawing your audience into your story. To be a successful writer, you want to create emotional characters so your audience will become emotionally involved with them. It's important for readers and viewers to become completely engrossed in the emotional world of your characters." —*psychotherapist and author, Rachel Ballon*

Unease can be caused by many different things such as insecurity, anxiousness, worry, or feelings of apprehension.

An uneasy, nervous character might tend to be more aware of their surroundings and pay closer attention to the people around them. Maybe look for exits or fidget restlessly.

Or if the character experiences any doubts regarding certain events within the storyline, they might start feeling unsure, or even skeptical about a situation or about trusting another character. An uneasy feeling could also be a "gut reaction" to something or a niggling suspicion.

Most stories will become a page-turning read if writers revise any shallower writing, so strive to omit other filter words besides "unease," such as: *uneasy, uneasiness, panic, panicked, unnerved, rattled,* etc.

Some physical signs of unease can be:

Clutching at collar of shirt

EMOTION: UNEASE

Wringing shirt tightly

Lacing fingers taut until knuckles turn white

Loss of appetite

Heart feels like it drops into stomach

Nervous tics: fidgeting or rubbing forehead

Cannot relax

Mentally obsessing over a dilemma or predicament

Rubbing (wiping) sweaty hands down thigh repeatedly

Grinding teeth

Tense jaw

Examples on how to revise shallow writing:

SHALLOW: Her panic level shot sky-high.

DEEP POV: She stumbled backward, bumping into a chair.

SHALLOW: A feeling of unease skittered up my spine. (Cliché)

DEEP POV: A cold tremor shot down my back.

SHALLOW: The tiny seeds of her eyes showed unease.

DEEP POV: Grinding her teeth, she blinked rapidly. *No!*

SHALLOW: Panic made my stomach nauseous and I noticed my hands shook.

DEEP POV: My stomach was queasy and my hands wouldn't stop shaking.

SHALLOW: Anxiety overcame me when I checked my bank statement.

DEEP POV: Clutching tightly at the collar of my shirt, I stared at the zeros on my bank statement.

SHALLOW: Dan experienced a moment of body-numbing panic.

DEEP POV: Clenching his hands into tight fists, Dan's body went numb.

SHALLOW: I felt a huge bubble of panic build in my chest.

DEEP POV: Lacing my fingers taut until my knuckles turned white, I tried to remain calm.

SHALLOW: The whole idea of high school dances gave me anxiety.

DEEP POV: I shuddered. High school dances sucked.

SHALLOW: I look anxiously around the cabin.

DEEP POV: Mouth dry and heartbeat racing, I glance about the cabin.

SHALLOW: Maria shot Alexander a panicked look.

DEEP POV: Maria's body twitched and she faced Alexander with wide-open eyes.

***

This next excerpt (condensed) was taken from my new adult romance novel, SMASH INTO YOU, and gives another example on how to incorporate Deep POV by including "Voice," sensory details, description, and dialogue, without *naming the emotion*. In this scene the first-person narrator is pledging a sorority, but she's uneasy and nervous about joining and making a good first impression.

Please closely examine this example...

DEEP POV:

EMOTION: UNEASE

Two of the other girls standing with me in the foyer started squirming and sweating through Jade's rather longwinded speech. Raven chewed on her lip and the beauty queen twirled a strand of hair around her finger.

Jade continued in a soaring voice, "Pledges must obey our every command for the first eight weeks until initiation." She clasped both hands behind her back and stepped closer to the Zeta Beta sisters, who nodded in agreement to every point she made. "Our chapter expects potential members to acquire a certain amount of points to maintain status as an active member. These points can come from attending socials and mixers, participating in philanthropic activities, going to tailgates for football games, keeping a high GPA, or anything that we request you to do. And remember, what happens in-house, stays in-house. Now turn on the lights and let's get to know our legacy PNMs, ladies."

"What's a PNM?" I whispered in Raven's ear.

Raven rolled her eyes. "Potential New Member. Duh."

"Oh."

Interview time. I couldn't let *anything* screw it up. My body broke out in a light sweat, as if a stack of red-hot bowling balls had been surgically implanted in my stomach. I shifted my weight from foot to foot, my toes pinched in my new shoes. My hip bumped the table and the vase of purple tulips tittered dangerously.

The entire room fell silent. I quickly reached out with both hands and steadied the vase. Everyone stared. Raven folded her lips inward to suppress a smile.

A blaze of heat zinged across my cheeks. *Friggin' great.* Now I looked like a total spaz. I shuffled away from the table and demurely laced my hands in front of me.

The lights flickered to life and the Zeta Beta sisters removed their hoods. The members were all from diverse ethnic backgrounds and each wore a warm smile for us. Soft music erupted from speakers hung from the ceiling and a table of refreshments sat near one wall. The large room had sparkling hardwood floors and open stained-glass windows.

The girls mingled, chatting on topics ranging from Greek social events and party etiquette, to cool vacations they'd taken over the summer or unique hobbies. I overheard the pretty Asian girl retelling a story about her recent intoxicated shenanigans and boasting about her sexual escapades. The Zeta Beta sister she chatted with glanced around as if uncomfortable. Definitely TMI.

Raven let out a long sigh. She must be nervous, too. She leaned over and whispered, "The honeymoon period has begun. Better be on your best behavior, Serena."

***

Most scenes can be even more emotional, vivid, and visual if you try to go deeper with the five senses and include physical sensations. Consider revising your WIP by finding ways to make each scene more visceral and powerful through the Deep POV technique.

EMOTION: NERVOUSNESS

Quote: "It's often quoted as "Show, don't tell" because, on the whole, beginner writers do too much telling when they should be showing. But of course it's not nearly as simple as that. Both have their value; the key is to understand their respective strengths, and use each to your story's best advantage." —*author and mentor, Emma Darwin*

Nervousness might be considered a negative emotional trait if a character is timid or cowardly. Or it could just be a temporary reaction, like feeling nervous about starring in the school play, or a job interview, or going on a blind date.

Anxiety is an emotion that is closely related to feelings of nervousness, but anxiety would generally last longer. Nervousness is a stress emotion, and it can cause a strong physical reaction that affects the character's nervous system and musculature.

So if you have a character feeling nervous, try your best to show it to the reader. Because in order for readers to experience emotions right alongside the characters, they must feel what the character feels at any given moment within your fictional world. "Telling" the reader only achieves the opposite effect of Deeper POV.

I suggest that writers exclude filter words, such as *nervous, anxious, concerned, apprehensive, fretful, fearful, panicky,* or *uneasy* from their scenes.

Some physical signs of nervousness might be:

Facial tics or spasms

Sweaty underarms

Voice wavers / rises an octave

Shift nervously in chair

Hands intertwined with each other repeatedly

Constant fidgeting

Tapping of the foot

Limited eye contact

Talking fast

Trembling voice or stuttering

Sweat beading on forehead

Clenched fists to stop them from trembling

Examples on how to revise shallow writing:

SHALLOW: Piper felt nervous about the contest.

DEEP POV: Piper broke out in a cold sweat whenever she thought of the contest.

SHALLOW: A bout of nervousness struck Kent.

DEEP POV: Rubbing the back of his neck, Kent shifted his weight from one foot to the other.

SHALLOW: A nervous feeling stayed with Jamie all day.

DEEP POV: Jamie closed her eyes and took a calming breath, but it was no use.

SHALLOW: I felt nervous butterflies in my stomach. (Cliché)

EMOTION: NERVOUSNESS

DEEP POV: My hands trembled in my lap. My stomach pitched and rolled.

SHALLOW: Claire was too nervous to eat dinner.

DEEP POV: Claire pushed the food around on her plate without taking so much as a bite.

SHALLOW: I felt overly anxious that night.

DEEP POV: I was a bundle of raw nerves that night, my muscles twitchy.

SHALLOW: The closer we got to Grandma's house, the more nervous I became.

DEEP POV: As Grandma's house loomed ahead of us, my pulse quickened.

SHALLOW: Her stomach clenched with nervousness.

DEEP POV: Bile rose in her throat and her stomach clenched.

SHALLOW: Spencer looked visibly nervous.

DEEP POV: Her gaze darted around the room and she jumped at every sound.

SHALLOW: I shifted my weight nervously.

DEEP POV: I shifted my weight, my leg muscles quivering.

***

Sometimes it is okay to leave the filter word in a sentence, but I would advise for Deeper POV to at least try to weed any filter words from your narrative. If you read a ton of fiction like me, you'll notice filter words in almost every published novel, some more than others, but that doesn't mean *you* should do it in your own writing.

Here is another scene on how to avoid *naming the emotion*. Please study and compare these examples…

SHALLOW:

I stood in the doorway and my heart started to beat fast. I felt really nervous. I wondered if the students would notice my rising anxiety.

From the entrance, I saw seven grinning faces staring back at me. They fell quiet as soon as Hunter moved past me into the room. I gulped, my panicked nerves singing.

Hunter faced the kids. "Hey guys, this is the new teacher's aide, Mrs. Beckman—"

"It's only Miss Beckman," I said loudly. "I'm unmarried."

DEEP POV:

I dragged my size nine feet into the noisy classroom and my heart beat erratically. I wrung my hands on my already wrinkled polyester turtleneck. My body broke out in a light sweat as I glanced around the room.

Is it hot in here or is it just me?

I shuffled across the threshold and seven smiley faces turned toward the doorway. They fell quiet as soon as Hunter shouldered past me into the room. I gulped. Loudly.

Hunter faced the students. "Hey guys, this is the new teacher's aide, Mrs. Beckman—"

"It's *Miss* Beckman," I interrupted, my face flushing hot. "I'm not, um, married."

***

Hope all of these examples from my own stories spark your creative muse!

EMOTION: RELIEF

Quote: "I'm a huge believer that mastering point-of-view will solve 99% of common writing problems. If a writer understands POV, then *showing* comes naturally, description is easier to write, character goals are clear, the stakes are personal, and thus stories feel more organic. POV is all about being inside the character. To be inside a character you have to understand that character, and once you understand her, writing her becomes easier." —*author and blogger, Janice Hardy*

While relief is not actually considered an emotion, it *is* an intense feeling that can overwhelm the character. To avoid stating the character's emotional state, like "he/she felt relieved," a writer can *show* a character relaxing or taking the edge off in slower, reflective scenes.

Relief is an emotional response to a lot of different things. For instance, if the character was almost hit by a car, but managed to avoid a collision by jumping out of the way, then they would feel relieved. Or a character can feel relieved when a frustration or fear has been resolved, or they've managed to achieve a goal. Or it could be the feeling a character gets when an invisible weight has been lifted from their shoulders.

The filter word *relief/relieved* can weaken the prose, and I strongly urge writers not to rely too heavily on overused clichés like "he/she sighed with relief." Most clichés like this have been so stereotyped that now they sound weak and boring.

Some physical signs of relief might be:

Shoulders relax

Closing eyes and sighing

Mumbling a prayer of thanks

Sighing loudly

Tension in body diminishing

One hand over chest / heart

Body sags against wall

Throw head back

Wide smile

Clapping hands

Standing straighter

Muscles unwind

Breathing out / exhaling

Examples on how to revise shallow writing:

SHALLOW: Relief flooded her system. (Cliché)

DEEP POV: Shaking her head and closing her eyes, her body relaxed.

SHALLOW: Locating an empty seat on the bus, I plopped down with a rush of relief.

DEEP POV: Locating the last empty seat on the bus, I plopped down and smiled. *Ha!* Lucky me.

SHALLOW: I exhaled with a small measure of relief. (Cliché)

DEEP POV: Sagging against a wall, the tension in my shoulders dissolved.

EMOTION: RELIEF

SHALLOW: Tommy <u>felt</u> a little wave of <u>relief</u>.

DEEP POV: Tommy pressed his palm to his heart and the fast beating slowed.

SHALLOW: He sighed in <u>relief</u>.

DEEP POV: With tears brimming his eyes, he exhaled. *We were safe now.*

SHALLOW: <u>Relief</u> trickled through her veins.

DEEP POV: Softly thanking God, she closed her eyes and sighed.

SHALLOW: I breathed a sigh of <u>relief</u>. (Cliché)

DEEP POV: A sudden lightness struck my senses. Everything was going to be okay after all.

SHALLOW: Cat nearly sobbed with <u>relief</u>.

DEEP POV: Exhaling loudly, Cat swallowed the emotion.

SHALLOW: She'd been <u>relieved</u> that yesterday's fight hadn't ended in a horrible breakup.

DEEP POV: The tension left her body. Yesterday's fight wasn't that big of a deal and it hadn't resulted in a horrible breakup.

SHALLOW: At first, I'd <u>thought</u> he was completely undressed, but I was <u>relieved</u> to <u>see</u> the navy boxer shorts.

DEEP POV: At first glance, his bare torso gleamed in the dim light. *Holy smokes! He's naked.* Another peek revealed a pair of sexy navy boxer shorts. *Whew.*

***

Here are two longer examples, one is *telling* and the other is *showing*. The first one has too many filter words and overworked clichés.

Please compare these two examples…

SHALLOW:

Noel was so <u>relieved</u> that she'd passed the exam that she practically <u>jumped for joy</u>. She stepped outside the classroom and it <u>felt</u> like a <u>weight had been lifted off her chest</u>. As she hurried down the steps, <u>her heart felt lighter</u>.

***

The next example has been revised into Deep POV, and it *shows* the emotion without bluntly stating it for the reader.

DEEP POV:

A slow smile touches Noel's lips. *She'd done it!* Aced that exam.

She practically skipped out of the classroom, humming happily to herself. She hurried down the steps and hopped into her car. Her head fell back against the headrest and her grin widened. Time to celebrate.

***

These examples should give you some clear-cut ideas on how to revise your own manuscript into Deep POV.

EMOTION: SURPRISE

Quote: "Surprise is a gateway emotion. It doesn't stick around long, so it's almost instantly replaced with the *reaction emotion*, which is the more important emotion of the two. It is important to register the surprise of a character, but it may also be vital for the reader to know what that surprise becomes. For example, if a character is surprised, and then angry, that anger is probably more important to spend time describing than the surprise." —*WriteWorld blog*

While surprise is not actually considered an emotion, it *is* a reaction that can temporarily strike a character when they are startled or something unexpected happens. Alternatively, a feeling of shock would last much longer and have a much more dramatic effect on a character's senses.

Surprise can always be seen in the facial expression, such as raised eyebrows, flushed cheeks, and the jaw dropping open. And it can usually be heard by a loud gasp, squeal, yelp, or short scream.

This short-termed "feeling" can also be negative if the emotional reaction is caused by something like a malicious trick or a scandalous plot twist, where the emotions can range from a slight disappointment to profound shock. Showing the cause-effect connection is critical when expressing true emotions.

A lot of new writers and published authors often name this emotion and use these types of filter words to describe it, such as *shock, surprise, amazement, amazed, stunned, dazed*, etc. I've done it in my own novels, too. However, it is always better to *show* rather than *tell* as discussed in this handbook.

Some physical signs of surprise might be:

Gawk at someone

Mouth fall open

Eyes go wide

Hands flying to cover mouth

Eyebrows raised

Stare unblinking

Short harsh gasps

Nervous laughter

Facial muscles twitch

Cheeks blush

Stagger backward

Inhale sharply

Mouth moving wordlessly

Examples on how to revise shallow writing:

SHALLOW: He was shocked by her outburst. (Cliché)

DEEP POV: Squeezing his eyes shut, he rubbed his temples.

SHALLOW: Remy watched us, looking surprised.

DEEP POV: Remy stared at us with her mouth gaping open like a fish on a hook.

EMOTION: SURPRISE

SHALLOW: Ally was surprised by Haley's confession.

DEEP POV: Ally didn't know what to say as the blood drained out of her face.

SHALLOW: Dean wore a look of shock.

DEEP POV: Dean's face paled and he grabbed his brother's arm to steady himself.

SHALLOW: Missy turned red with astonishment.

DEEP POV: Missy gaped, a fluttery feeling striking her belly.

SHALLOW: He reacted with shocked concern.

DEEP POV: Spreading his fingers out in a fan against his breastbone, Jake swore under his breath.

SHALLOW: I looked at Luke with a little surprise.

DEEP POV: My breath hitched in my throat when I looked at Luke. No way could zombies be real.

SHALLOW: I jerked in surprise.

DEEP POV: My body jerked and I dug my fingers into my palms.

SHALLOW: I was shocked into silence by his confession.

DEEP POV: Both of my hands flew up to cover my mouth.

SHALLOW: She looked surprised when he touched her arm, as if she'd forgotten Bradly was there.

DEEP POV: Cheeks flaming, she took a startled step back. She'd forgotten Bradly was still there until he touched her elbow.

***

Here is another much longer example on how to revise your own work from shallow writing into vivid Deeper POV.

Please study and compare these examples...

SHALLOW:

I was shocked and surprised that Janet had actually come today. She didn't even dress for gym half the time.

Cheerleading tryouts had been ruthless, and as team captain, I knew that I had a tough choice to make. It was either my best friend, Bria, or the bigger girl, Janet.

Coach Malkin looked at me. "Who's it gonna be, Lacy? You have to pick either Janet or Bria."

"I'm not really sure," I said and bent down to tie the laces on my sneakers. "Do I have to decide right now?"

"Well, I can make the decision for you," Coach said with a look of concern.

"Okay," I said, brightening and hoping it would be my BFF.

Come on! I thought. *Pick Bria!*

"Bria Harvey," Coach announced.

"Yes!" I shouted loudly.

After a stunned silence, everyone broke out into quiet laughter.

Embarrassment flushed my face, but I couldn't stop the wide smile.

DEEP POV:

Cheerleading tryouts had been brutal, and as team captain, I had a tough choice to make.

Why had Big-Hipped-Janet even showed up today?

EMOTION: SURPRISE

Her chubby cheeks were red and sweat ran down her face. Janet leaned over, panting hard like a dog. She was uncoordinated and at least twenty pounds heavier than the other girls.

It was down to my *very* thin best friend, Bria, or overweight Janet, who was nice, but would be impossible to lift.

Coach Malkin glanced over at me with a raised brow. "Well, Lacy…who's it gonna be? Janet or Bria?"

"Um…yeah…well…I'm not really sure," I mumbled and bent down to retie the laces on my ultra white Skechers. "Do I have to decide today?"

"If you can't choose, it's all right. I can make the decision for you," Coach said softly and squeezed my shoulder.

"Okay," I said and a small smile lifted my lips.

Come on! Pick my BFF! Bria, Bria, Bria…

"Bria Harvey."

"Yay!" I jumped up out of my seat, clapping my hands.

The entire squad stared at me for a full minute of awkward silence, and then everyone laughed.

Oops. Guess that was a little bit melodramatic, even for me.

My face turned fire engine red, but I couldn't stop grinning like an idiot. Bria had made the team!

***

Now you should have even more insight and knowledge on how to revise your manuscript into page-turning prose.

EMOTION: HAPPINESS

Quote: "Happiness is like the color red. It is intuitively obvious but almost impossible to describe without referencing itself. Usually attempts to pin it down result in something pretty vague like, "Happiness means feeling good." —*writer and blogger, Scott H. Young*

This chapter will cover how to show *happiness / joy* without actually stating the emotion for the reader. The word "happy" can convey many differing emotions such as, excitement, enthusiasm, or animation.

Happiness could be considered a feeling *and* an emotion. Joy is a mental or emotional state of well-being distinguished by positive or pleasant feelings ranging from relaxed contentment to overwhelming exhilaration.

To be honest, characters that are happy are…well, boring. Now a writer *could* show a character feeling happy on the first page or two, but then something terrible or dire, like an inciting incident, better happen pretty quickly to quell this happy character's life in some big way. That's why conflict and tension make such page-turning reads. Characters generally shouldn't get their happy ending until the end of the story. And make them work for it…

Also, I'm not saying you cannot use the word "happy," if it is appropriate, but writers should try to revise any scenes without *naming the emotion*.

Some physical signs of happiness might be:

EMOTION: HAPPINESS

Eyes sparkling

Feeling of lightness

Bouncing on toes

Swinging arms

Explosion of endorphins

Laughing / giggling

Hugging him/herself

Skin glowing

Cheering and squealing

Hyper aware of surroundings

Singing or humming to him/herself

Voice high-pitched or shrieking

Examples on how to revise shallow writing:

SHALLOW: A flood of happiness poured through me. (Cliché)

DEEP POV: Swinging my arms while walking home, I couldn't stop grinning.

SHALLOW: She was so happy that she'd won the new car.

DEEP POV: Bouncing on her toes, she clutched the keys to her new car in one hand. "This is the best day of my life!" she exclaimed and hugged the stranger standing next to her.

SHALLOW: Elizabeth wanted to jump for joy. (Cliché)

DEEP POV: Holding both of her arms out wide as if she could hug the entire world, Elizabeth beamed at her husband. A second honeymoon sounded awesome.

SHALLOW: A sense of joy bubbled up in her heart.

DEEP POV: A sense of weightlessness struck her heart. She rubbed her cheeks, her face hurting from the wide grin that lifted her lips.

SHALLOW: "That's great news!" I cried happily.

DEEP POV: If my smile became any wider, I'd resemble the Joker. "Great news!"

SHALLOW: Sandy actually squealed in happiness.

DEEP POV: "Yay!" Sandy giggled uncontrollably and clapped her hands. "Let's party!"

SHALLOW: I felt happy when Sam told me the good news.

DEEP POV: A big goofy grin pulled at my mouth when Sam told me the good news.

SHALLOW: I'd never felt so happy to see the first rays of dawn in my life.

DEEP POV: As the first rays of dawn peeked through the blinds, I threw my arms wide.

SHALLOW: I sighed with true happiness.

DEEP POV: A sigh escaped and I beamed.

SHALLOW: I thought I might just die from happiness. (Cliché)

DEEP POV: Dancing around wildly, a bubbly sensation filled my heart.

***

EMOTION: HAPPINESS

This longer example illustrates how to revise "telling" sentences and filter words into *showing*. Again, it is fine to occasionally use the words *joy / happiness* in your writing, but if it's possible not to—then don't.

Please study and compare these examples…

SHALLOW:

Damon wrapped his arms around me, and then I felt him put his lips to mine. I felt a thrill of profound happiness as Damon stroked my back. I felt my heartbeat quicken.

But Damon wasn't a very good kisser. Maybe my friend Mindy could provide some instruction.

Damon pulled back. "I'll call you later, okay?"

I realized I had his slobber on my chin. "Sure." I stood there watching as the pickup drove away.

When the taillights had almost vanished into the darkness, I headed toward the porch. I felt my heart lift with joy, even though I knew the kiss had been awful.

***

I have included "voice," emotion, and dialogue in my next example to give you a better idea of how to redraft scenes in your own work.

DEEP POV:

Damon wrapped his arms around my waist and pulled me closer. My breath hitched in my throat. For a moment, a warm thrill shot through my body when his soft lips touched mine.

Yuk. Too sloppy.

But hopefully this kissing stuff would get better with lots and lots of practice. Maybe I could borrow Mindy's book on *Twenty-Five Ways to*

Be a Great Lover. That girl had to be a professional, the way she was always practicing her kissing techniques on her pillow.

Damon pulled back and smiled. "I gotta get going. Call you later, okay?"

Trying not to act grossed out that his slobber was wetting my chin, I said, "Yeah. Sure."

I grinned like a big doofus until the truck pulled away. When the taillights faded into the night, I skipped onto the porch, swirling the hem of my skirt back and forth like a little girl.

Wow. *My first real kiss.* What a disaster! But also all kinds of awesome.

***

Now I challenge you to rewrite a scene in your own novel or story where the characters experience true happiness and *show* it.

EMOTION: JEALOUSLY

Quote: "While I believe excessive jealousy falls into the category of emotional and mental abuse, I also think we have (most of us) felt jealous over something. Even if we're not talking about romantic relationships. For example, being jealous about your best friend talking very excitedly to someone else. Jealousy is a natural emotion just like love and anger. And it doesn't always have to be negative. It's how you react to the feeling of jealousy that shows whether it is a healthy or unhealthy reaction." — *Alex, Reference for Writers blog*

Everyone feels jealously at some point in their lives. Even I've felt envy over another writer's success, although sometimes it is hard not to feel that way.

Envy characteristically refers to the negative thoughts and feelings of other emotions such as self-doubt, apprehension, worry, and anxiety. It is a strong negative emotion that can affect friendships, family, and all other relationships.

A good storyline could include a character that starts off being jealous as a fatal flaw in some fictional world riddled with envy and greed, which are caused by a cutthroat, consumer-driven culture. This same character could overcome this feeling during his growth ARC and no longer feel jealous of others or circumstances. Or the character could be dealing with feelings of jealousy over a lover, and they need to conquer this insecure emotion within the storyline before the love interest decides to dump them.

In almost every scene, I think it's important to stay in Deep POV. As you revise, remember that there are a dozen different ways to describe a physical, internal, or emotional response. And by using the tips and tools in this book as a guide, you'll discover some interesting things about your characters.

Writer should eliminate the filter words: *jealousy, envy, envious, wariness, mistrustfulness, resentment, resentfulness, spite, begrudge* from your narrative.

Some physical signs of envy might be:

Breath harsh and shallow

Hands curling into fists at sides

Teeth clenched

Chest puffs out / heats up

Heart lurches

Burning sensation in chest

Wanting to cry

Crossing arms

Tight muscles

Quick toss of head

Voice low, snarky

Body tenses up

Examples on how to revise shallow writing:

SHALLOW: Darren was green with jealousy. (Cliché)

EMOTION: JEALOUSLY

DEEP POV: Shoving the hair from his eyes, Darren stomped inside the house. The nerve of Tom flashing his new lawnmower in front of all the neighbors. But damn, that machine was cool looking.

SHALLOW:

Tom <u>feels</u> a strong flare of <u>jealousy</u>.

DEEP POV:

Tom stares hard at his best friend and the girl he's crushing on. His hands curl into fists at his sides, itching to swing out and put a dent in the wall beside him. *She's my girl!*

SHALLOW: A spark of <u>jealousy</u> struck my heart.

DEEP POV: A pang struck my heart. How could Krystal buy the same dress I'd been drooling over for weeks? And the gown looked better on her than me.

SHALLOW: There was an edge of <u>jealousy</u> in my own voice.

DEEP POV: Clenching my teeth, I snapped, "I always *knew* you liked her better!"

SHALLOW: I tried very hard not to <u>envy</u> her.

DEEP POV: My best friend was beyond spoiled. New car. Expensive apartment. Trust fund. And she took it all for granted while I slaved away working double-shifts for minimum wage.

SHALLOW: Feeling a stab of <u>envy</u>, Christina glared at Yolanda.

DEEP POV: A burning sensation stabbed Christina in the chest. Yolanda thought she was *so* special with her new haircut and designer purse. Ha! That bag was a cheap knockoff and she'd prove it.

SHALLOW: I can't contain my <u>envy</u>.

DEEP POV: My eyes narrow. My breaths come out coarser as I stare down at the gifts under the lighted tree. *So unfair!* Jonathon always got ten times more Christmas presents than me.

SHALLOW: I felt jealousy growing inside me.

DEEP POV: Huffing, I tried to contain the green monster growling inside me, but failed. "Your book is on the bestseller's list *again?*" I spat. Mine hadn't even made *Amazon's Top 100*.

SHALLOW: Hot jealousy colored her dark tone.

DEEP POV: Her ugly tone luridly colored her accusation and I half-expected her breath to come out in little green puffs.

SHALLOW: Dean's jealous grip on me tightened. "Are you cheating on me?"

DEEP POV: Dean's grip tightened on my arm and his neck muscles bunched up. "Are you cheating on me?"

SHALLOW: Envy oozed from him in waves when he saw his ex with another man.

DEEP POV: His chest puffed out and his movements stiffened when he spotted his ex with that tall dude.

***

In this next illustration, I show how using deeper narration and vivid emotion allows you to effectively turn your shallow scene into a deeper reading experience for your readers.

Please study and compare these examples…

SHALLOW:

EMOTION: JEALOUSLY

I felt green with jealousy. There was something wrong with me. I had my own boyfriend, but I wanted to be with hers. I already knew Kyle was cute and sexy and nice. I wished that he'd seen me first.

"Wanna see another picture of Kyle at the beach?" Tamara asked sweetly.

"Sure," I said, jealousy tainting my voice.

She didn't notice as she scrolled to a photo of Kyle taken on her iPhone. I thought he looked very handsome in shorts and shirtless, his big smile, and his tousled dark hair.

My heart panged again with growing envy.

DEEP POV:

Pursing my lips into a flat, hard line, I tried to ignore the way my body flushed hot and cold. *What's wrong with me?*

My best friend was showing off pics of her hot new boyfriend, and instead of being happy for her, it made my own boyfriend seem like a boring nerd.

How selfish could I be?

"Wanna see another picture of Kyle at the beach?" Tamara asked with a smile.

No. I really, really *didn't* want to keep looking at photos of her perfect boyfriend.

Taking a step closer, fists clenched, I muttered, "Yeah…I guess."

Tamara smiled and handed me her iPhone. In the photo, Kyle looked insanely hot in board shorts with no shirt, his muscled chest sprinkled with salt water and his black hair tousled from the wind.

Damn, he was a hottie. And unfortunately, all *hers*.

***

A good thing to remember as you revise a scene into Deeper POV is that male and female characters should react, experience, communicate, and convey feelings differently. When writing a character of the opposite sex in Deep POV, try to get a second opinion by a beta reader or critique partner to ensure that the male and female character reactions, responses, and emotions are written realistically.

EMOTION: EMBARRASSMENT

Quote: "Counselors tell us that thoughts lead to emotions, and emotions lead to actions. As a writer, you can easily show your character's thoughts and actions. Readers are smart enough to deduce the emotions based on what the characters think and do. So often it seems writers are in a hurry. When you have a very emotional scene, slow it down. Let us hear your character's every thought. Highlight a few details. Show the actions." —*novelist and writing coach, C. S. Lakin*

This chapter provides a few examples on ways to show a character's embarrassing moments through a Deeper POV. For instance, when a character feels embarrassment the neck, ears, and face may appear flushed and the skin colors a reddish hue.

Embarrassment is considered a complex emotion and a universal feeling that everyone can easily relate to. It is a self-conscious reaction tied to other emotions such as insecurity (low self-esteem), self-judgment, and social discomfort, etc.

Humiliations are usually the direct result of unintentional behaviors that cause feelings of negativity about oneself—even when a person had no intent of breaking any number of so-called social standards.

For each scene, identify the emotion that your character needs to *show* and think of different ways you can reinforce the character's reactions through both verbal and nonverbal communication. One way is to omit filter words like *embarrassed, embarrassment, self-conscious, ashamed, mortified, humiliated, humiliation,* or *shame* from your writing.

Some physical signs of embarrassment might be:

Stomach roiling

Faintness

Feeling the urge to pee

Legs quivering

Swallowing hard

Voice squeaks

Glancing around at surroundings

Not making eye contact

Backing away or running away

Hiding face in hair

Leg bouncing

Tugging at eyebrow / earlobe

Examples on how to revise shallow writing:

SHALLOW: Feeling embarrassed, I jerked back.

DEEP POV: Jerking back, my neck turned red and I was breathing hard.

SHALLOW: I was actually embarrassed that he wanted to display that kind of affection in plain view of everyone.

DEEP POV: My cheeks flushed pink. *PDA in the cafeteria?* No. Thanks.

SHALLOW: I was so embarrassed that I wanted to run and hide. (Cliché)

DEEP POV: If the ground opened up and swallowed me right now, I'd be a happy camper.

EMOTION: EMBARRASSMENT

SHALLOW: "I'm not going!" she said, embarrassed to be treated like a child.

DEEP POV: "I'm not going!" she snapped, a bloom of heat staining her neck and ears. She was almost eighteen! Her parents couldn't keep treating her like a child.

SHALLOW: I tucked my hands under my butt, feeling embarrassed.

DEEP POV: I tucked my fidgety hands under my butt.

SHALLOW: I looked at the ground in embarrassment.

DEEP POV: Staring at my feet, I worked to steady my own breathing.

SHALLOW: I got that squirmy, embarrassed feeling that awkward conversations with parents can bring about.

DEEP POV: I got a squirmy feeling in my gut and shifted in my seat. This conversation with my parents was gonna be all kinds of awkward.

SHALLOW: An embarrassed blush stained my cheeks.

DEEP POV: A hot flush stained my cheeks.

SHALLOW: I took a deep breath and held it, squelching a humiliated giggle.

DEEP POV: Taking a deep breath, I held it in to stifle the unwelcome giggle.

SHALLOW: Embarrassed, I muttered, "Aren't you going to kiss me good night?"

DEEP POV: My heartbeat turned unruly and my voice became husky. "Aren't you going to kiss me good night?"

SHALLOW: She looked down, feeling embarrassed, but he pulled her chin up, turning her head so that she met his eyes.

DEEP POV: She turned away, her collarbone hot, but he pulled her chin up, turning her head so that she met his eyes.

***

These next scenes are written in both Shallow POV and Deep POV to exemplify how to revise sentences, paragraphs, and scenes in your own work.

This excerpt is taken from my novel, IMMORTAL ECLIPSE and the *shallow* example is an early draft before revision. In this excerpt, the heroine is meeting the love interest for the first time.

Please study and compare these examples…

SHALLOW:

As we stand there <u>looking</u> at each other, I <u>feel</u> a thrilling sensation and now I <u>feel confused</u>. I <u>look</u> at the dark-haired man in the doorway. He is a very good-looking man, I <u>tell myself</u>.

The tall man turns and I <u>watch</u> his eyes meet mine. I <u>notice</u> that he's dressed similar to the man in the portrait: a linen shirt under a black vest and he is wearing pants and boots. Although, he must be in his late twenties, I <u>think</u> he looks reserved and intimidating.

Matthew didn't mention a man like this living here, I <u>thought uneasily</u>.

The man shakes his head, and then he clears his throat.

"I'm Gerard Blackwell's niece," I say <u>nervously</u>.

Now I <u>feel embarrassed</u> for staring at him. My <u>nervous</u> voice made the <u>mortification</u> even worse. I <u>wish</u> I could start over and introduce myself properly, I <u>think to myself</u>.

The second example below is written in the Deep POV method and has lots of "voice,'" which makes it an up close-and-personal experience for the reader.

DEEP POV:

EMOTION: EMBARRASSMENT

As we stand there staring at each other, a thrilling electric current courses through my body and short-circuits my brain. I blink several times at the dark-haired man standing in the doorway, trying not to stare at his eyes, an intense shade of blue. Damn, he's better looking than most of the male fashion models I've photographed.

Mr. Tall, Dark, and Yummy tilts his head and his eyes lock on mine. Even from a distance, I can tell he'll tower over me, and I'm no midget. He's even dressed similar to the man in the portrait: a soft, white linen shirt—bulging biceps stretching the fabric—under a black vest paired with snug pants and boots. Although, he appears to be only in his late twenties, he looks reserved and intimidating.

Conclusion: no sense of style, but still smoking hot.

Matthew didn't mention anyone like *him* living on the property. Having eye candy like him around will be a nice distraction. The hottie regains his composure and clears his throat.

Stop acting like a drooling idiot and speak to him!

"Hello. I'm, uh, Gerard Blackwell's niece."

My face heats. That was brilliant. Great first impression. I could really, really use a do-over so I don't come across as an ogling idiot.

***

As you revise your own work, strive to look for the simplest clarification to remove the sensory filter words from your sentences and replace those offenders with Deep POV.

EMOTION: ANXIETY

Quote: "An author should know their character intimately, they should know their history, how they would react in any situation, they should know their look and mannerisms down to the smallest facial tick." — *author and blogger, Aaron Miles*

The easiest way to convey to a reader, without *stating the emotion*, whenever a character is feeling nervous or anxious, is to describe the character's body language. Since describing the body's movements and gestures can show readers what a character is feeling, it is often worthwhile to stay in Deeper POV.

For example, a character that is feeling anxious or worried might be described as defensive because they are subconsciously protecting themselves. Or a writer can *show* a character whose tense or apprehensive sitting on the edge of a seat, along with rapid foot tapping. Shifting weight from foot-to-foot or constant movement can describe a character that appears uncomfortable without stating it.

A nervous or anxious character might make bad decisions or cause tension for the hero. For this type of character, anxiety might not just be an isolated emotion, but rather a whole collection of real or imagined fears. The character might overreact because they perceive a threat, causing a fight-or-flight stress reaction.

Some physical signs of apprehension might be:

Men stand with their hands clutched in front of their genitals

EMOTION: ANXIETY

Women fold their arms across their chest

Increased heart rate

Inability to breathe deeply

Tugging at collar

Rigid muscles

Clenched jaw

Restless / unable to sit still

Sweaty Palms

Trembling hands

Examples on how to revise shallow writing:

SHALLOW: I felt nervous going to the party alone.

DEEP POV: My jaw clenched as I neared the door of the party. *Man, I hated going places alone.*

SHALLOW: He hated confrontations and he was anxious to face Adam.

DEEP POV: Rolling his neck and shoulders, he faced Adam.

SHALLOW: "Where is Becky?" I asked nervously.

DEEP POV: "W-where is *Bbb*ecky?" I stammered.

SHALLOW: She was agitated and angry that he came home so late.

DEEP POV: She stood with her arms crossed and her foot tapping. "Where the hell have you been?" she demanded.

SHALLOW: I was feeling anxious about the long drive home on the winding road.

DEEP POV: My fingers gripped the steering wheel tightly, my gaze glued to windy road.

SHALLOW: Manny was flustered while waiting for his wife to give birth.

DEEP POV: Manny was jiggling his keys and pacing the hospital waiting room.

SHALLOW: I felt apprehensive and fearful about giving the speech.

DEEP POV: Shaking out my hands and arms, I cleared my throat several times and said, "Hello, I'm Daisy Price…"

SHALLOW: Mercy was rattled and she looked agitated.

DEEP POV: Mercy clutched her handbag to her chest like a shield.

SHALLOW: I feel apprehensive.

DEEP POV: My mouth went dry and my hands were trembling.

SHALLOW: He felt very uneasy and restless today.

DEEP POV: With sweaty hands, he tugged at his collar.

I have included a few longer examples to further illustrate my point. The first is written in Shallow POV with too many "ly" adverbs tacked onto the dialogue tags, and the speech is lacking "voice." (I have underlined what I consider to be shallower writing in the first example.)

Please carefully examine these scenes…

SHALLOW (info-dump):

"Do you have any questions?" Lily asked, <u>feeling apprehensive.</u>

The place in the forest where they'd followed the werewolves <u>felt cold and damp.</u> She <u>noticed</u> an <u>intent look</u> on William's face.

EMOTION: ANXIETY

"There are really werewolves? And other supernatural creatures?" William asked nervously.

Lily nodded her head in agreement, although she felt anxious. "Yes, Except for some paranormal things," she said seriously.

"You should not have followed us," Jack said sternly, wearing an angry expression.

"Do you hunt werewolves?" William asked with eagerness.

"I only do when they attack innocent people," Jack answered honestly.

William looked thoughtful while contemplating how this news would change his world. This is weird, he thought. But so cool.

Lily was worried. She leaned forward anxiously, and touched William's hand. "Is this information upsetting you?"

"That is marvelous," he said with a glimmer of excitement in his eyes.

Jack looked startled. "Did you say marvelous?"

William nodded enthusiastically and it made the dark hair move on his forehead. He was delighted to know that paranormal creatures were real. "Yes, I did. It's like Supernatural, but *real*."

Jack felt nervous and anxious by William's response. "What are you talking about?"

"That is a TV show," Lily explained. She felt embarrassed. "On the TV show they mention a lot of paranormal occurrences."

Jack shook his head in disbelief.

William grinned with amusement. "You've never heard of Supernatural?"

"I have heard the word supernatural," Jack said thoughtfully. "And vampires, however, they have mostly died out."

William looked disappointed. "Vampires are extinct? That is too bad."

Wasn't that tedious and boring to read? Why, yes. Yes, it was!

Now this second example has been revised into Deeper POV. The scene includes a few of the five senses and "voice" both in the dialogue and internal-thoughts, along with descriptive details.

DEEP POV:

Lily chewed on her bottom lip. "Any questions?"

The cave in the forest where they'd tracked the werewolves had damp walls and an eerie coldness that seemed to penetrate her heavy jacket. She shivered and moved closer to Jack. At least the mutts had vacated their den for the night.

Jack sighed. "*He* shouldn't have followed us here."

"Why not?" William's eyes grew wide. "Are there *really* werewolves? Demons, witches, and other supernatural creatures?"

Lily scratched her head, then slowly nodded. "All true. Except for trolls and unicorns. Those are myths."

"So, you hunt werewolves?" William turned to Lily's new boyfriend Jack and a goofy smile spread his lips. "Like it's your job?"

Jack laced his fingers behind his head and leaned back on his heels. "Yes, but only when they attack innocents."

William grew quiet and stared down at his feet. A chilly wind swept through the space, stirring up the pine needles. A pair of fireflies danced at the mouth of the cave.

Lily leaned forward, and lightly touched William's hand. "Are you okay? I mean, are you freaking out?"

William lifted his head and a slow grin overtook his features. "No…this is *awesome*."

EMOTION: ANXIETY

The dark lashes gracing Jack's cheeks flew up. "Did you say awesome?"

Rubbing his hands together, William nodded, making the dark hair bounce on his forehead. "Yup. It's like Supernatural, but *real*."

The lines crisscrossing Jack's forehead deepened. "What are you talking about?"

"That's a TV show." Lily's face colored fiercely. "On the series, there are hunters and it has a lot of monsters, like vampires."

Jack just stared at William.

William grinned. "You've never heard of Supernatural?"

"I've heard of the word *supernatural*," Jack said in a serious tone. "And vampires. Even though, they've mostly died out."

William's smile drooped. "Vampires are extinct? That *sucks*. No pun intended…"

***

Just remind yourself that *showing* respects the reader's intelligence, and *telling* assumes that the reader is not clever enough to recognize the emotion or reaction unless the writer blatantly states it for them.

EMOTION: PANIC

Quote: "Basically, a panic attack is triggered by a thought. The thought itself could be originated by a variety of things, either it could come out of the blue, be a response to an outside stimuli or result from a long reflection..." —*Alex, Reference for Writers blog*

Panic is closely related to the emotion fear, and it also ties into worry or anxiousness. It is an emotion that brings upon a sudden sensation of terror or dread so strong that it can dominate or prevent rational thinking and cause overwhelming feelings of apprehension.

The important thing about writing any type of fiction is to always draw the reader deeply into the scene by relying on the POV character's senses and descriptions to paint a detailed picture, as though the reader is deeply experiencing everything right alongside the narrator.

If a character is having "panic attacks," it can add an extra layer of characterization to your story. When a character is experiencing a panic attack, it is common to feel their heart pounding, sweating, hyperventilating, chest pain, shortness of breath, nausea, tunnel vision, body shaking, etc. A character can become frozen and unable to move or react, or even defend themselves. Using short, choppy sentences to describe panic might work best.

Some physical signs of panic might be:

Tension in neck, back, shoulders

EMOTION: PANIC

Unable to sit still

Crossed arms

Breathing faster and shallower

Clearing Throat

Trembling hands

Sweating

Bug-eyed

Mouth freezes / unable to speak

Pupils are small and un-dilated

Examples on how to revise shallow writing:

SHALLOW: I felt panicked.

DEEP POV: My stomach felt queasy and my hands wouldn't stop shaking.

SHALLOW: He was unnerved by the baby crying.

DEEP POV: With quivering hands, he lifted the wailing baby from the crib.

SHALLOW: I felt really flustered this morning.

DEEP POV: My breath became fast and shallow.

SHALLOW: When he saw the huge phone bill, he panicked.

DEEP POV: The phone bill crinkled in his sweaty fist.

SHALLOW: I felt panicky when Tom asked me to lunch.

DEEP POV: Big knots formed in my stomach.

SHALLOW: I felt unnerved.

DEEP POV: My insides felt like jelly.

SHALLOW: I felt a bout of panic. How could I pay my bills this month?

DEEP POV: Clutching collar of my shirt, I stared at the zeros on my bank statement.

SHALLOW: I felt like a nervous wreck. (Cliché)

DEEP POV: My mouth went dry and I couldn't sit still.

SHALLOW: I was feeling overly anxious.

DEEP POV: I wanted to run out the nearest exit.

***

Here are two longer examples of *showing* panic instead of stating it for the reader taken from one of my short stories.

The first scene has too much shallow writing, and the scene is lacking any "voice" or sensory details. (I have underlined what I consider to be shallower writing.)

Please carefully examine these two examples…

SHALLOW:

When I opened my eyes, I noticed it was still dark in the room. Feeling half-asleep, I got out of bed and headed into the bathroom. It must be late, I thought to myself. We had been on the run from the mobsters for three days and I felt very exhausted.

Then I looked in the mirror. At first, I didn't recognize the face I saw reflected in it. I felt a headache come upon me. After washing my hands,

EMOTION: PANIC

I <u>looked</u> in the cabinet for aspirin, but I <u>realized</u> there wasn't any inside. So I left the bathroom, but then I stopped in the middle of the bedroom.

An unsettling <u>feeling of panic</u> welled inside me. I <u>realized</u> that something wrong, but I couldn't quite <u>decide</u> what it was. The atmosphere <u>felt really strange</u>. <u>Anxiety was building up within me.</u>

Suddenly, I <u>realized</u> what it was when I <u>looked</u> at the bed. I <u>realized</u> that my friend Elena was no longer in the room. I turned on the light and <u>looked around</u> the room. I <u>noticed</u> that her purse and shoes were gone.

I <u>felt terrified</u>. I <u>looked</u> at my watch and <u>saw</u> that it was almost midnight. *Where had she have gone at this hour? Why hadn't she told me that she was leaving? Why had she left me alone in a hotel room? When would she return? Should I call her cell phone?*

Now I <u>felt really alarmed and worried</u>. Hastily, I put on my jacket, then my shoes. I went out the door in a <u>blind panic</u>. (cliché) <u>I knew</u> I had to catch her before the mobsters did.

This second scene is the final draft that was revised to *show* the reader that the character starts to panic without stating it, and includes more detailed descriptions and a deeper character POV.

DEEP POV:

A soft *click* awoke me. I blinked into the dimness of the stuffy room, the faint glow of the bedside clock glowed eerily in the darkness. A sharp throbbing spread across my forehead, and I winced.

I fumbled with the scratchy blankets and stumbled into the bathroom, where I caught my reflection in the mirror. Being on the run from bloodthirsty mobsters hadn't done much for my complexion. Bloodshot eyes rimmed with dark circles and ashen skin made the face reflected back at me almost unrecognizable.

Opening the cabinet, I searched for aspirin, but only found a small bar of scented soap and a bottle of shampoo. I shuffled back into the bedroom and glanced at the bed. Even before my mind registered the emptiness, I knew she wasn't lying there.

Flipping on the overhead light, I scanned the room. My mouth dried. I couldn't swallow.

I spotted a leather wallet peeking out from under the jumbled pile of clothes. Sweat prickled my underarms and down my back. I hurried to the closet and checked inside. My garments were pushed to the far side, leaving a gap where her clothes should have been.

Spinning on my heel, I yanked on my jacket, shoved my bare feet into shoes, and bolted from the room.

***

If you're a beginner writer working on your first manuscript, or if you're reading this book to gain more knowledge and insight on the topic, I implore you to start using Deeper POV in all of your stories. You've heard the saying, "Practice makes perfect," right? After you finished at least five drafts of your current work-in-progress (WIP), it is time to go back and revise those shallower areas.

EMOTION: DISGUST

Quote: "*Changers* are characters who alter in significant ways as a result of the events of your story. They learn something or grow into better or worse people, but by the end of the story they are not the same personalities they were in the beginning. Their change, in its various stages, is called the story's emotional arc." —*author, Nancy Kress, "Write Great Fiction: Characters, Emotion & Viewpoint"*

One way to add conflict to a story and provide a growth ARC is to have a character that is seeking the approval of a boss or a parent, but only receives disgusted condemnation. Or a character who is repulsed by another character's actions or behavior in any given situation can add a level of depth to the scene if it is shown.

Disgust is a negative feeling of aversion or disapproval at someone or something. While feeling disgust, a character might notice an increase in heart rate, higher blood pressure, and a decrease in skin temperature. The saliva is overproduced, which could trigger the urge for a character to spit at the object or even at the person that they feel disgusted with.

Writers should avoid just stating that a character felt a sick feeling of revulsion (cliché), loathing, or nausea, and instead reveal that the character feels disgust by their facial expressions and reactions. And instead of using a cliché like, *Ron looked at his son's messy room and recoiled in disgust*, I would describe the room with sensory details so that the readers can witness the revulsion for themselves.

Some physical signs of disgust might be:

Curl of upper lips

An open mouth, the tongue pushing slightly forward

Wrinkled nose

Narrowing eyes

Lip corners are drawn down and back

Rolling of eyes

Making guttural sounds like "ewww" or "ugh"

Shaking one's head while muttering

Hands up, backing away with a fake shiver

Eyebrows pinched together

Recoiling away

Examples on how to revise shallow writing:

SHALLOW: I thought what he was doing was disgusting.

DEEP POV: Shaking my head, I muttered, "That's super gross."

SHALLOW: Nathan was repulsed by the dead body.

DEEP POV: Nathan recoiled and wrinkled his nose when he saw the cadaver.

SHALLOW: I was sickened by the sight of rotting food.

DEEP POV: I covered my mouth and nose when I got a whiff of the rotting food in the sink.

SHALLOW: She wore an expression of contempt. (cliché)

DEEP POV: She scrunched her brows and tilted her head to the side.

EMOTION: DISGUST

SHALLOW: Ben looked contemptuous.

DEEP POV: Ben's lips curled upward into a sneer.

SHALLOW: Lacy thought Jack was abhorrent.

DEEP POV: Lacy's steely gaze bore into his face.

SHALLOW: I was repulsed by his actions.

DEEP POV: My mouth puckered. "*Ewww!* Don't eat that worm."

SHALLOW: Cami thought he was a crude man.

DEEP POV: Cami leaned back and rolled her eyes.

SHALLOW: I saw Cordelia give me a disgusted look because I was wearing my gym clothes.

DEEP POV: Cordelia lifted her nose in the air as if the sight of me in my gym clothes offended her.

***

I have included two lengthier examples of how a writer might show "disgust" rather than bluntly state it. (I have underlined what I consider to be shallower writing.)

Please carefully compare these examples…

SHALLOW:

"Are you really not going to finish eating your food?" Amelia <u>looked at</u> Madison <u>with revulsion</u>. "You are going to make yourself sick."

Madison <u>looked down</u> at all the food that was on the table in front of her. <u>There was still a big amount</u> of fatty foods besides what she'd already consumed. "Can you put this food outside for me because I feel sick?" she asked.

Then Amelia <u>noticed</u> her stand up and <u>head</u> into the bathroom.

Amelia took the plates and deposited them into the trash can. She <u>could hear</u> Amelia being sick in the bathroom, the flush of the toilet, and then <u>the sound</u> of her rinsing out her mouth. She <u>felt disgusted</u> by her friend's bad habit of forcing herself to vomit after a heavy meal.

DEEP POV:

"Really?" Amelia shook her dark head and flashed Madison a tight smile. "You're going to *scarf and barf* again?"

Madison glanced at the pile of carbs still left on her plate. Her stomach pitched and bile rose in her throat. "Can you please dump this junk? I can't stand to look at it." Madison scooted back her chair, ran for the bathroom, and slammed the door behind her.

Amelia grabbed the plates and threw the leftovers in the trash. Through the bathroom door, violent retching, the slurping flush of the toilet, and then the gargling of mouthwash penetrated the wood.

***

Just keep in mind while you're revising your manuscript that great storytelling should be a mix of both showing *and* telling.

EMOTION: GUILT

Quote: "Usually, we combine internal and external conflicts for a richer story. That means we have to understand how our characters approach and resolve conflict." —*novelist and blogger, Jami Gold*

Guilt and shame can be great motivators for a character's actions and reactions. It can cause a lot of conflict within the storyline if guilt makes a character withdraw from their friends and family. Shame can even cause a character to lie about their past, or hide an ugly truth. These emotions can even cause a character to be in serious denial over a situation or about another character. Usually a character who feels ashamed will lower their head and look downward to avoid direct eye contact.

Remorse and shame are often obsessive emotional traits or reactions that can weigh heavily on a person's subconscious. While guilt might provoke a more positive response in a character, particularly when he/she is seeking to mend a broken relationship or correct a mistake, feelings of shame emphasizes what might be immoral or dishonest within themselves. Shame would have a much more inward focus for the character, and make them feel poorly about themselves, instead of just the actions they should've taken.

These emotions can become a character flaw that ties in with a theme, like redemption. For resolution, a character feeling guilty over something can overcome the fatal flaw through a heartfelt apology, or begging forgiveness, or by righting a wrong.

Some physical signs of guilt might be:

Avoid eye contact

Fidget when confronted

Flushed face

Angry outbursts / Defensive remarks

Rubbing the back of neck

Shoulders drawing up, elbows tucking into the sides

Becoming unnaturally quiet or still

A quivering chin

Hunched shoulders

Stuttering when talking

Examples on how to revise shallow writing:

SHALLOW: I felt very guilty.

DEEP POV: A sting of warmth stirred within my heart.

SHALLOW: He was overwhelmed with guilt. (Cliché)

DEEP POV: His chin quivered. He had to tell her the truth.

SHALLOW: I was too ashamed to face him. (Cliché)

DEEP POV: I couldn't look him in the eye.

SHALLOW: Elijah felt remorseful.

DEEP POV: Elijah's face flushed as he tried to explain.

SHALLOW: I felt so much shame.

DEEP POV: My scalp prickled with heat and I turned away.

SHALLOW: She was repentant for her actions.

EMOTION: GUILT

DEEP POV: She inwardly winced and wished she take those harsh words back.

SHALLOW: Shame engulfed me over what I'd done.

DEEP POV: Biting my lip, I hurried away with my head down.

SHALLOW: James felt regretful.

DEEP POV: He repeatedly swallowed, trying to find the right thing to say.

***

Here is an excerpt taken from my college romance novel, SMASH INTO YOU that depicts the emotion "shame" that makes the main character feel defensive and lie to hide her dark past. Please carefully examine this example…

DEEP POV:

"I just don't like you like *that*." I glanced away because this wasn't just one of my many lies. This was a lie that hurt the both of us. "I think you're a great guy, but you're just not my type and I need to focus on my studies."

"You're lying. Again."

My head snapped in his direction. "*What?* No, I'm not!"

"Please. Your eyes are darting all over the place and your words don't match what's coming out of your mouth."

Damn. He was too perceptive.

"You don't even know me, Cole. I meant what I said."

"You're just scared for some reason to explore whatever this is between us. Try being honest for once, Serena. I can tell you play a good game, but I can spot a liar from miles away, and you're clearly hiding something. They say the truth will set you free."

The truth. Who knew what that was anymore?

I wasn't sure if I could tell anyone the truth. Lying had become a vicious circle. Once a person started, it was hard to stop without spinning out of control. So I did the only other thing I was good at besides being a master manipulator—running away…

***

Try to stay away from using descriptive adjectives like angry or happy or sad or guilt that *tell* the reader the specific emotions of the character, and instead revise to stay in a Deeper POV.

EMOTION: RESENTMENT

Quote: "Even if you find the bad-guy generally repulsive, you need to be able to put yourself so thoroughly into his shoes while you're writing him that, just for those moments, you almost believe his slant [viewpoint] yourself." —*bestselling author, K. M. Weiland*

Resentment is typically a companion emotion to envy and jealousy, and also bitterness. Feelings of resentment can result in a combination of animosity, anger, or even hatred from a real or imagined wrong or insult. Resentment can be a great way to add an extra layer of tension to any scene, or it could be a character's fatal flaw.

Resentment is typically an indication of a weakness. The villain of your story could be harboring a deep resentment for your hero, or maybe it's your main character that has this fatal flaw to overcome. This emotion can have a very negative affect on your character and how he/she reacts to certain situations. As a fatal flaw, it can make envy churn through their veins. Bitterness taste like bile. And even stain their soul. Use this emotion to add another layer of depth to your character's personality or use it as a theme.

Some physical signs of resentment might be:

Speaking sarcastically

Eyes widening

Speaking in a demeaning way

Looking down or away

Furrowed brows

Bared teeth

Mouth slack

Posture stiff

Face reddens

Neck grows hot

Examples on how to revise shallow writing:

SHALLOW: "Not now!" he said cruelly and felt a deep resentment.

DEEP POV: His thin lips were pressed tight. His words slow and menacing, "I...said...not...now."

SHALLOW: Wendee sounded resentful when she asked for tea.

DEEP POV: Wendee picked lint off her sleeve. "What time is tea? You *did* remember to make tea didn't you, Willow?"

SHALLOW: He resented my promotion.

DEEP POV: His chin tilted defensively higher and he turned his head slightly away.

SHALLOW: She looked like she bore a grudge against me.

DEEP POV: Her cheeks puckered as if she'd tasted a sour lemon.

SHALLOW: I have hard feelings about losing the race.

DEEP POV: I forced a smile while I gritted my teeth.

SHALLOW: I could tell she felt bitter about the divorce.

DEEP POV: Whenever the topic came up about her divorce, she avoided my eyes.

EMOTION: RESENTMENT

***

Here are two scenes to further illustrate my point on the difference between *showing* vs. *telling* that should inspire your creative muse. (I have underlined what I consider to be shallower writing.)

Please carefully examine these examples…

SHALLOW:

I was supposed to get the lead role in the school play and not Avery Weinstein.

She walked onto the stage and I instantly resented her presence. I had no reason to hate her, but I did. I hated everything about the girl. I resented her curvy body and beautiful face, and because she was popular with the other boys at school.

My eyes turned green with envy as I stared at that girl who had stolen my part. I couldn't stand the sight of Avery.

"We're Romeo and Juliet," Avery said delicately. She was good, I thought resentfully. "And we'll love each other until we die."

It was time to rehearse the kissing scene. I saw Benjamin clumsily move toward her, but then I watched him trip and lose his balance.

"I love you, too, my Juliet," he said hoarsely as he fell forward into her body.

"I've got you." I heard Avery laugh, and then I saw her catch him before he fell.

Then I watched him kiss her mouth. It was a long kiss and I felt even more bitterness. I saw their arms go around each other and then I heard him groan into her mouth.

"Stop action," Sofia, the director, said loudly.

I had felt and seen the attraction between Benjamin and Avery and it made me feel sick with revulsion. I decided that they did not mind kissing in front of the cast. If there weren't so many people around, I would have told Avery how much I loathed her.

"What a fun time I am having," Avery said happily. "What did you think of my performance, London?" I saw her look right at me.

"You were great," I said bitterly.

Please study this revised version with "voice" and sensory details.

DEEP POV:

I was supposed to get the lead role in the school play—*not* stuck-up Avery Weinstein!

She strutted onto the stage like a queen with her commercial white smile.

I had no reason to hate Avery, but every fiber of my being felt strung tight. I hated her long, pale hair, her big brown eyes, and her flawless acting abilities. And the fact that she had more boys hanging on her than any other girl in school.

I stared at that disgustingly pretty girl who'd stolen my part, with an ugly sneer. I lifted a strand of my stringy black hair and then eyeballed her shiny blond waves. Yeah, I wanted her to break a leg. *For real.*

"We're Romeo and Juliet," Avery said in a light, whimsical voice. Damn, she was good. "And we'll love each other until we die."

Time to rehearse the kiss. Benjamin staggered toward her, tripping over the laces of his untied boots and losing his balance.

"I love you, too, my Juliet," he said, stumbling into her.

"Whoa there!" Avery giggled, catching him and he steadied himself.

Then he kissed her passionately. The seconds ticked by. Their arms wound around each other and he groaned softly.

EMOTION: RESENTMENT

Can anyone say, awkward?

"Cut!" Sofia, the director, shouted.

Not too soon either. The sizzling chemistry between Benjamin and Avery was totally nauseating, and they obviously had no qualms about making out in front of the cast. If there weren't so many people around, I would've pretended to gag.

"That was fun!" Avery smiled, then her gaze fell upon me. "What do you think, London? Was I great, or what?"

"Yeah, you were, um, great," I said, but my voice sounded tainted with sourness.

***

By giving your characters tangible emotions and physical reactions like in the revised scene above, it gives the people inhabiting your story-world even more realism.

EMOTION: PARANOID

Quote: "Developing a character with genuine depth requires a focus on not just desire, but how the character deals with frustration of her desires, as well as her vulnerabilities, her secrets, and especially her contradictions. This development needs to be forged in scenes, the better to employ your intuition rather than your intellect." —*author, David Corbett*

Giving a character an internal fatal flaw, such as paranoia when using the *man vs. himself* plot device to overcome might be an interesting growth ARC. A paranoid character will do reckless and rash things. He/she will be distrustful and fearful, or even unreasonable.

Recognizing the fatal flaw (character weakness) reveals what the character's internal journey will be. It becomes a big part of the plot in terms of a character's internal growth ARC, which will clarify the external conflict as well in your manuscript.

Flaws provide depth and tension, create empathy, and make a character more *human*. If a character has no flaws or seems too perfect, then all the conflict in the story is someone else's fault, and your main character is just drifting through scenes as an observer, and not actually connected or being affected by anything that occurs. The problem is, readers need to care about what happens to the main character(s), so including a fatal flaw is a great way to achieve this.

Some physical signs of paranoia might be:

EMOTION: PARANOID

Tight jaw

Grinding teeth

Darting eyes

Mouth twitches

Restlessness / Pacing

Hyper-Alert

Folding arms over chest and shaking head

Mumbling to themselves

A disheveled appearance

Racing heartbeat

Eyes big and wide

Examples on how to revise shallow writing:

SHALLOW: I felt very paranoid when I entered the cemetery.

DEEP POV: Dark imaginings filled my head, and I cast crazed looks around the graveyard.

SHALLOW: Aria's paranoia was getting worse and she didn't trust doctors.

DEEP POV: Shuddering uncontrollably, Aria pleads, "Please don't make me go in to the hospital."

SHALLOW: He spoke harshly and the tone made me feel even more paranoid.

DEEP POV: His voice didn't sharpen, but it had an undercurrent that made Julia's shoulders go up.

SHALLOW: I was paranoid and scared of the dark.

DEEP POV: I gritted my teeth and my gaze darted around the dark room.

SHALLOW: I felt paranoia every time I had to enter the police station.

DEEP POV: A creeping sensation inched its way across my arms as soon as I entered the building smarming with cops.

Here are two longer scenes to encourage writers to *dig deeper* with their descriptions and characterization. (In the shallow example, I did not underline the shallower writing, but please try to see if you can clearly identify it now that you're more aware of *showing* vs. *telling*.)

Please carefully examine these examples...

SHALLOW (reads like a boring info-dump):

Maybe I was just feeling paranoid, but I hated showering in public places like my college dorm. Everyone else in the bathroom seems to feel comfortable undressed in public except for me.

I saw an empty shower stall, I move quickly past the girls either partially dressed or naked and then I pull the curtain closed tight, and I get undressed, and then hang my clothes on the rack outside the stall by sticking out one arm from the curtain. I turn on the shower, feeling fearful. The water takes a very long to get hot, and while I'm standing in the stall, I'm feeling paranoid that someone will open the curtain and they will see my naked body.

The shower is small and I do not have enough room to move. When I turn my body as I wash my hair, my elbow touched the rack that my clothes are on, and the clothing falls to the wet bathroom floor.

"I cannot believe that I did that." I groan to myself, and shut the water off, and then wrap my towel around my body.

I grab my pile of wet clothes and then I leave the bathroom to walk down the corridor, and I hope no one sees me naked, but I feel paranoid that people are watching. I get to my room and open the door. As I push the door closed behind me, I see a tattooed, black haired young man sitting on my roommate's bed. This is very embarrassing for me and I feel myself blush.

Please study this next revised version with "voice" and sensory details.

DEEP POV:

Shuffling my feet, I trudge down the corridor toward the bathroom like an inmate on death row. Showering in my college dorm has always made my skin crawl. It's not about my body, but all the other bodies that were there before me. The need to let the water run blazing hot for ten minutes before I slid my flip-flops off and let my toes touch the floor is beyond OCD.

I hesitantly enter the humid space, clutching my toiletries firmly against my chest as my gaze scans the steamy room. Other girls are in differing arrays of dress, some half-naked while others walk around in just a thin towel. The combined odors of mildew and flowery shampoos assault my nose.

I spot an empty shower stall, and hurry into it, yanking the plastic curtain shut. With trembling fingers, I undress, and then lean out holding the curtain over my nakedness and hang my clothes on the rack. Quickly, I turn on the water, but it takes forever to get hot. The billowy steam helps to slightly ease my nerves.

Finally, in a cloud of steam, I'm able to speedily wash my hair. Just as I'm rinsing out the shampoo, my elbow pokes out of the curtain and hits the rack.

This. Cannot. Be. Happening. *It's like my worst fear come to life!*

Turning off the water, I dry off, and then peek out the curtain. My shirt, jeans, and underwear lay in a soggy heap on the wet floor.

"Dammit," I mutter.

I wrap the towel around my damp body. Leaning down, I snatch up my sodden clothes and make a mad dash back to my dorm room, holding the towel around me with one hand. I speed-walk like a racehorse galloping toward the finish line.

When I get to my room, I slam the door closed behind me, then slump against the wood and close my eyes. *Finally.*

Someone clears their throat. My eyes snap open, and a tattooed, black haired guy sitting on my roommate's bed waves hello.

I want to die. *Now.*

***

Did you compare the last two examples? Are you starting to grasp how shallow writing pulls the reader out of the story?

Naming the emotion is a bad habit that writers easily fall into, which focuses the story on *telling* rather than *showing*. But Deep POV can turn a dull scene into one that remains in a reader's thoughts long after the book has been read. So please don't just state how a character feels, but try to make the reader actually feel it, too.

CONCLUSION

Quote: "The bestselling writers who endured fifty, or even a hundred rejections, before finally achieving success would make for such a long list of names that I would develop carpal tunnel syndrome just typing them all. Perseverance is as important as talent and craftsmanship." — *bestselling author, Dean Koontz*

Now that you have a clearer idea on how to revise shallow scenes by using the Deep POV technique, search for *telling* scenes and revise them by applying this amazing tool, but please avoid using overworked clichés in your writing.

Although, most books will probably offer similar advice about the Deep POV method, you can still gain the balance of study, theory, and practice that you might need to fully grasp these wonderful skills through additional reading. If you'd like to discover even more ways to strength your prose, I suggest studying these amazing books by these talented writers.

Recommended nonfiction reading:

"Rivet Your Readers with Deep Point of View" by Jill Elizabeth Nelson

"Mastering Showing vs. Telling in Your Fiction" by Marcy Kennedy

"The Emotion Thesaurus" by Angela Ackerman and Becca Puglisi

"Writing With Stardust" by Liam O' Flynn

"The Art of Description: Bring Settings to Life" by Anne Marble

"How to Write Dazzling Dialogue" by James Scott Bell

"Take Your Pants Off" by Libbie Hawker

Well, that concludes my advice on self-editing filter words and how to revise your wonderful story into a Deeper POV that provides your readers with an amazing, unput-downable reading experience.

HUMBLE REQUEST

If you read this handbook and find the tools and tips helpful to improving your own storytelling abilities, please consider posting an honest review online.

Word of mouth is crucial for any author's success, and reviews help to spread the book love. So please consider leaving a short *(a sentence or two is fine!)* review wherever you purchased this copy and/or on Good-reads.

If I get enough reviews stating that this guide helped writers to hone their craft, then I'd love to include additional books in this Deep POV series with new topics, such as romance writing, creating suspense, and fictional world-building.

FICTION WRITING TOOLS

Bestselling author S. A. Soule shares her expertise with writers by providing surefire, simple methods of getting readers so emotionally invested in their stories that booklovers will be flipping the pages to find out what happens next.

Each of these helpful and inexpensive self-editing books in the *Fiction Writing Tools* series encompass many different topics such as, dialogue, exposition, internal-monologue, setting, and other editing techniques that will help you take your writing skills to the next level.

THE WRITER'S GUIDE TO VIVID SETTINGS AND CHARACTERS

Learn to Create a Realistic Setting with Atmospheric Detail and Lifelike Characters!

In this comprehensive writing fiction manual, you will learn how to create extraordinary worlds and deeply submerge your readers into the story. Constructing lifelike scenes isn't easy, unless you have the tools to write vibrant, authentic settings.

This manual also provides vital techniques on world-building with bonus examples on how to combine the five senses and use deep POV in all of your scenes. This valuable reference guide is useful in revealing a simplified way to create unique settings and vivid character descriptions flawlessly.

THE WRITER'S GUIDE TO AUTHENTIC DIALOGUE

A Powerful Reference Tool to Crafting Realistic Conversations in Fiction!

This manual is specifically for fiction writers who want to learn how to create riveting and compelling dialogue that propels the storyline and reveals character personality.

Writers will also learn how to weave emotion, description, and action into their dialogue heavy scenes. With a special section on how to instantly improve characterization through gripping conversations. All of these helpful writing tools will make your dialogue sparkle!

THE WRITER'S GUIDE TO PLOTTING A NOVEL

Awesome Tips on Crafting a Riveting "Hook" that instantly Grabs Your Reader

This manual offers amazing techniques for creating stronger beginnings and ways to write a page-turning "hook" for your fiction novel. Writers will learn how to make the first five pages so intriguing that the reader won't be able to put your book down, and reveal how you can successfully craft your first chapter.

Also, writers will get the tools needed to blend character goals with a riveting scene, and how basic plot structure can effectively and instantly strengthen the narrative. Plus, get bonus tips from other bestselling authors, advice on self-publishing a novel, and help with manuscript word counts. Whether you're writing an intense thriller or a sweeping romance, all novels follow the same basic outline described in detail within this book.

THE WRITER'S GUIDE TO BOOK BLURBS and QUERY LETTERS

An Awesome Book Description is One of the Most Important Tools a Writer Needs to Sell More Books, or to Gain the Attention of an Agent...

Whether you're self-publishing, or querying agents and publishers, this guidebook on book descriptions can help! Writing back jacket copy (blurb or marketing copy) can give most writers a major headache. In this in-depth reference manual, any writer can learn how to instantly create an appealing blurb with a captivating tagline, or write a perfect query letter.

In this valuable resource, there are numerous query letters templates and book blurbs examples for almost every fiction genre that will have an agent asking for more, and/or help a self-published author to write a compelling product description that will boost their book sales.

HOW TO INCREASE YOUR BOOK SALES IN 30 DAYS

Learn How To Sell More Books in a Month!

This in-depth marketing guide is perfect for writers publishing their first novel or indie authors trying to gain a wider readership. The manual includes valuable tips on networking, how to get more book reviews, and contains wonderful advice on how to best promote your work from established authors and popular book bloggers.

Whether you're a multi-published author looking to expand your audience or a self-published writer, this book will instantly give you the tools to market your fiction like a pro! Free bonus features include how successful authors use social media to connect with potential readers, reviewers, and how to sell more books.

ABOUT THE AUTHOR

S. A. Soule is a bestselling author and Creativity Coach, who has years of experience working with successful novelists. Many of her fiction and non-fiction books have spent time on the bestseller lists.

Her handbooks in the "Fiction Writing Tools" series are a great resource for writers at any stage in their career, and they each offer helpful advice on how to instantly take your writing skills to the next level and successfully promote your books.

Please feel free to browse her blog, which has some great tips on creative writing online at: *Fiction Writing Tools* and visit her *Creativity Coaching Services* site for help with writing book blurbs, fiction editing, and revising your stories with Deep POV.

Made in the USA
Las Vegas, NV
12 June 2021